ISLINGTON

Please return this item on or before the last date stamped below or you may be liable to overdue charges. To renew an item call the number below, or access the online catalogue at www.islington.gov.uk/libraries. You will need your library membership number and PIN number.

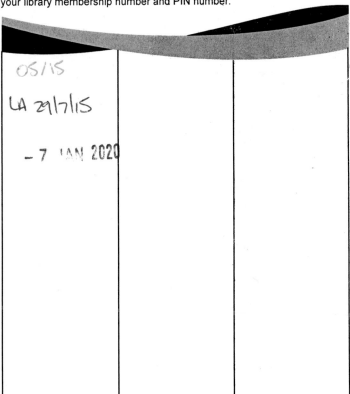

OS/15

LA 29/7/15

- 7 JAN 2020

Islington Libraries

D0239153

Contents

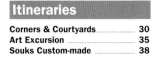

Don't Miss

Itineraries

Marrakech by Area

Essentials

Time Out Digital Ltd
4th Floor
125 Shaftesbury Avenue
London WC2H 8AD
Tel: + 44 (0)20 7813 3000
Email: guides@timeout.com
www.timeout.com

Published by Time Out Digital Ltd, a wholly owned subsidiary of Time Out Group Ltd.
Time Out and the Time Out logo are trademarks of Time Out Group Ltd.

© **Time Out Group Ltd 2015**
Previous edition 2008.

Editorial Director Sarah Guy
Group Finance Controller Margaret Wright

© **Time Out Group Ltd**
Chairman & Founder Tony Elliott
Chief Executive Officer Tim Arthur
Chief Financial Officer Matt White
Publisher Alex Batho

10 9 8 7 6 5 4 3 2 1

This edition first published in Great Britain in 2015 by Ebury Publishing
20 Vauxhall Bridge Road, London SW1V 2SA

Ebury Publishing is part of the Penguin Random House group of companies whose addresses
can be found at global.penguinrandomhouse.com

Distributed in the US and Latin America by Publishers Group West (1-510-809-3700)

For further distribution details, see www.timeout.com

ISBN: 978-1-90504-294-4

A CIP catalogue record for this book is available from the British Library.

Printed and bound in China by Leo Paper Products Ltd.

MIX
Paper from
responsible sources
FSC® C018179
FSC
www.fsc.org

Marrakech Shortlist

The **Time Out Marrakech Shortlist** is one of a series of guides that draws on Time Out's background as a magazine publisher to keep you current with everything that's going on in town. As well as Marrakech's key sights and the best of its eating, drinking and leisure options, it picks out the most exciting venues to have opened in the last year and gives a full calendar of annual events. It also includes features on the important news, trends and openings, compiled by locally based writers. Whether you're visiting for the first time in your life or the first time this year, you'll find the *Time Out Marrakech Shortlist* contains all you need to know, in a portable and easy-to-use format.

The guide divides Marrakech into four areas, each containing listings for Sights & Museums, Eating & Drinking, Shopping, Nightlife and Arts & Leisure, and maps pinpointing their locations; further chapters cover day trips from Marrakech, and Essaouira. At the front of the book are chapters rounding up these scenes city-wide, and giving a shortlist of our overall picks. We also include itineraries for days out, plus essentials such as transport information and hotels.

The area code for Marrakech is 0524. When calling from within Morocco you need to dial the area code even if you are calling from the same area. So to make a local call within Marrakech, you must still dial 0524. From outside Morocco dial your country's access code (00 from the UK, 011 from the US) or a plus symbol, followed by the Moroccan country code (212), then 524 for Marrakech (dropping the initial zero) and the number.

We have noted price categories by using one to four pound signs (**£-££££**), representing budget, moderate, expensive and luxury. Major credit cards are accepted unless otherwise stated, though cash is often preferred, especially in more modest establishments.

All our listings are double-checked, but places do sometimes close or change their hours or prices, so it's a good idea to call a venue before visiting. While every effort has been made to ensure accuracy, the publishers cannot accept responsibility for any errors that this guide may contain.

Venues are marked on the maps using symbols numbered according to their order within the chapter and colour-coded as follows:

❶ Sights & Museums
❶ Eating & Drinking
❶ Shopping
❶ Nightlife
❶ Arts & Leisure

Time Out **Marrakech** Shortlist

EDITORIAL
Editor Ros Sales, Claire Boobbyer
Proofreader Tamsin Shelton

DESIGN & PICTURE DESK
Senior Designer Kei Ishimaru
Designer Rob Baalham
Group Commercial Senior Designer
  Jason Tansley
Picture Editor Jael Marschner
Deputy Picture Editor Ben Rowe
Picture Researcher Lizzy Owen

ADVERTISING
Managing Director St John Betteridge

MARKETING
Senior Publishing Brand Manager
  Luthfa Begum
Head of Circulation Dan Collins

PRODUCTION
Production Controller
  Katie Mulhern-Bhudia

CONTRIBUTORS
This guide was researched and written by Claire Boobbyer, with extra contributions
by Tara Stevens, Rachel Blech and Mandy Sinclair.

PHOTOGRAPHY
Pages 2 (top left), 52 danm12/Shutterstock.com; 2 (bottom left), 34, 39, 40, 88 (top right),
113, 142 (top left and top right), 169 Olivia Rutherford; 3 (top left) Kamal Wadifi; 3 (top right)
Elena Moiseeva/Shutterstock; 3 (bottom left) Prometheus72/Shutterstock.com; 5, 61, 101
(top left), 139 (bottom) Christian Mueller/Shutterstock.com; 7 Abderrahmane Mokhtari; 8, 14,
42, 121, 133 (bottom) Karol Kozlowski/Shutterstock.com; 9 Anibal Trejo/Shutterstock.com; 11,
94 (top left) ppart/Shutterstock.com; 12 Rikard Stadler/Shutterstock.com; 13 John Copland/
Shutterstock.com; 18 bozulek/Shutterstock.com; 26 Elamine Sifeddine; 28 Pierre Antoine;
29 SUPACHART/Shutterstock; 30, 50, 66, 77, 93, 96, 114 Suzanne Porter; 38 nevenm/
Shutterstock.com; 41 Andrea Izzotti/Shutterstock.com; 44 Philip Lange/Shutterstock.com;
47 Nowak Lucasz/Shutterstock.com; 49, 58 (top and bottom left) astudio/Shutterstock.com;
58 (bottom right) Curioso/Shutterstock.com; 69 (right), 157 © Selman Gallery; 81 Freeshot/
Shutterstock.com; 88 (top left) alarico/Shutterstock.com; 88 (bottom), 94 (bottom), 101
(bottom), 139 (top left and middle right) The Visual Explorer/Shutterstock.com; 90 CHADIMI;
94 (top right) thomas bonnefoy1/Shutterstock.com; 101 (top right) zeber/Shutterstock.com; 130
ziggysofi/Shutterstock.com; 133 (top) N Mrtgh/Shutterstock.com; 135, 139 (top right) KMW
Photography/Shutterstock.com; 142 (bottom) Elan Fleisher; 146 Karim Tibari; 155 (top) posztos/
Shutterstock.com; 155 (bottom) Matej Kastelic/Shutterstock.com.

The following images were supplied by the featured establishments: pages 2 (top right and
bottom right), 3 (bottom right), 16, 17, 21, 23, 27, 31, 33, 35, 36, 37, 62, 69 (left), 71, 72, 78,
102, 106, 110, 122, 124, 127, 128, 151, 152, 158, 160, 163, 165, 166, 171, 172, 175, 176

Cover photography: Stephen Walford Photography/Getty Images

MAPS
JS Graphics (john@jsgraphics.co.uk).

About **Time Out**

Founded in 1968, Time Out has expanded from humble London beginnings into the leading
resource for those wanting to know what's happening in the world's greatest cities. As well as
our influential what's-on weeklies in London and New York, we publish nearly 30 other listings
magazines in cities as varied as Beijing and Mumbai. The magazines established Time Out's
trademark style: sharp writing, informed reviewing and bang up-to-date inside knowledge
of every scene.

Time Out made the natural leap into travel guides in the 1980s with the City Guide series,
which now extends to over 50 destinations around the world. Written and researched by expert
local writers and generously illustrated with original photography, the full-size guides cover a
larger area than our Shortlist guides and include many more venue reviews, along with additional
background features and a full set of maps.

Throughout this rapid growth, the company has remained proudly independent, still owned by
Tony Elliott four decades after he started Time Out London as a single fold-out sheet of A5 paper.
This independence extends to the editorial content of all our publications, this Shortlist included.
No establishment has been featured because it has advertised, and no payment has influenced
any of our reviews. And, for our critics, there's definitely no such thing as a free lunch: all
restaurants and bars are visited and reviewed anonymously, and Time Out always picks up the bill.
For more about the company, see www.timeout.com.

Don't Miss

Koubba El-Badiyin

Sights & Museums

Marrakech can be a bewildering place for the first-time visitor, and one of the confusing things is the lack of conventional 'sights'. There are scarcely a dozen must-see monuments and museums. Palaces have been left either ruined or bare by whoever came along to replace those who built them. Mosques and shrines can be seen from outside, but their interiors are off-limits to non-Muslims – a rule established by the French. There are no major museums and just a few galleries. On a tight schedule, you can scamper around all the principal sights in a few hours and still have time to spend more dirhams than you planned in the souk before dinner.

There wasn't a single paved road in the country when European capitals were opening national museums and erecting triumphal arches. But various waves of rulers still managed to leave their marks. The original Almoravid city, established in the 11th century, was more or less completely destroyed when the rival Almohad tribe conquered it after an 11-month seige in 1147. Only the city walls and the Koubba El-Badiyin (p60) remained as testament to its previous grandeur.

Having razed the city to the ground, the Almohads built the Koutoubia Mosque (p46) and the gate of Bab Agnaou (p81), and laid out the Agdal Gardens (p87). Several hundred years later the Saadians added the Badii Palace (p87) and the Saadian Tombs (p87). The French built a whole new city, the Ville Nouvelle (pp96-129), alongside the Medina. And the main contribution of the current monarch will perhaps turn out

to be the new *zone touristique* that is going up, piecemeal, to the south of the city, or the new four-year arts, culture and local services plan known as 'Marrakech City of Permanent Renewal'.

The paucity of essential sightseeing does have an upside. It's kind of relaxing. As there's little you might later regret having missed, there's a delicious lack of obligation to 'do' everything. Instead, you can feel extra free to lounge around on cushions at the riad, spend half the day people-watching from a café table, or wander aimlessly through the warrenous alleys of the Medina.

Wandering aimlessly is certainly the best way to get to know the place. It takes a while to get the hang of Marrakech, especially as the inward-looking orientation of the local architecture, where magnificence is typically concealed behind plain exteriors, means that much of what's interesting is not immediately obvious. But soon doors will start opening and interiors revealing themselves. You might not be

able to peer around the religious monuments, but it's worth eating in certain restaurants (such as Tobsil, p51; Dar Zellij, p76, or Dar Yacout, p75) as much for the showy surrounds as the expensive menus, and your boutique hotel, typically hidden behind an unmarked door in some dead-end alley, may turn out to be the architectural highlight of your trip. And meanwhile, every twist and turn of the Medina will reveal a new perspective, another mystery, one more doorway that could lead into anything from a poorhouse to a palace, sometimes in a fashion that is almost dreamlike.

The Medina

The Medina (it simply means 'city' in Arabic) is the area within the city walls, and this is where you'll spend most of your sightseeing time. The two principal landmarks of Marrakech stand at its heart. The minaret of the Koutoubia Mosque is the city's tallest structure, both an icon and point of orientation. Nearby is the vast open space that is the Jemaa El Fna (pp42-43), host to a unique and ever-changing carnival of street entertainment, and, in the evenings, the world's largest open-air eaterie. Now included on the UNESCO list of the Intangible Cultural Heritage of Humanity, it's often referred to simply as 'la place'.

The South Medina contains most of the other main sights. The melancholic Saadian Tombs, centring on the three pavilions built by Saadian Sultan Ahmed El-Mansour (1549-1603), are in the Kasbah quarter – the walled precinct of the off-limits Royal Palace. The Mellah (pp91-92), the old Jewish quarter, is over on the eastern side, with the atmospheric, ruined Badii Palace, also built by Sultan El-Mansour, in between. The palace is the temporary home of the new Marrakech Museum for Photography and Visual Arts. Just north-east of the Badii Palace, is the ornate and superlative 19th-century Bahia Palace (p92), erstwhile home of a powerful grand vizier.

To the immediate north of the Jemaa El Fna is the warren of the souks – a sight in themselves. To their north and east is a small cluster of monuments: the Musée

Jemaa El Fna

de Marrakech, the ancient Koubba El-Badiyn (p60), and the Ben Youssef Medersa (p59), a former Quranic school established in the 14th century and enlarged in 1564. Centred around a courtyard decorated with stucco and zelije tilework, it is one of the city's most beautiful buildings. Nearby is the absorbing Maison de la Photographie (p60), a fascinating collection of historic photographs of Morocco. To the west, near the Mouassine Mosque, is a hidden gem: the Douiria Mouassine (p66), a petite apartment, designed as a reception area for guests, restored to its original 17th-century glory.

The tannery quarter, where leather is still cured by medieval methods, is at the eastern edge of the Medina, and shrines to Marrakech's seven favoured saints are scattered around to the north.

The street layout can confound anyone's sense of direction, but it gets easier once you learn a few of the main arteries and ignore, for route-finding purposes, the hundreds of dead-end alleys that snake off them in all directions.

Small cars can get surprisingly far into this labyrinth, but most of the traffic is pedestrians and scooters (the latter an annoying and noisy presence but good for getting around narrow spaces), plus bicycles and donkey carts. The main through lanes bustle from early morning until around 11pm, and in the early-to mid-evening 'rush hour' some can get so busy there are people jams. The etiquette is to keep to the right, leaving passing room for two-wheelers and quadrupeds.

The ancient crenellated walls surrounding the Medina are another of Marrakech's landmark structures. Built of salmon-pink pisé, they make a ten-kilometre (six-mile) circuit, punctuated by 20 gates. Though they can look beautiful in the changing light, especially against an Atlas mountain backdrop, there's no place to get up on top of them. The traditional thing is to circumnavigate them in a calêche – horse and carriage – ideally at sunset. You can pick up a calêche at place Foucault, in between Koutoubia and the square (fixed prices are posted on the carriage). The circuit takes approximately an hour, but it's perhaps an overrated experience – lots of dust and traffic fumes, not actually that much to see.

Medina walls

Théâtre Royal

The new city

In the first decades of the Protectorate, the French built new cities that left the old Moroccan medinas intact, but relegated them to the status of 'native quarters'. Guéliz and the Hivernage were built in the 1920s and 1930s for the colonial administration and European community, and Marrakech's booming tourist economy is now underpinning a new wave of development.

Avenue Mohammed V, named for the king (grandfather of the current one) who led Morocco to independence in 1956, is both the main commercial thoroughfare and the principal connection between the old and new cities. You'll want to take a stroll along its central section – from place du Novembre 16 at the junction with avenue Hassan II, to place Abdel Moumen at the junction with boulevard Mohammed Zerktouni. The area is now a vibrant hub of modern Marrakchi life, criss-crossed by leafy streets like the rue de la Liberté and the rue des Vieux Marrakchis, which crackle with life spilling out of chic European-style cafés and bistros, smart designer boutiques and increasing numbers of art galleries.

The striking Majorelle Gardens (p100), towards the east of Guéliz, were created in the 1930s by French painter Jacques Majorelle and are today maintained by the Fondation Pierre Bergé-Yves Saint Laurent. With towering cacti, waterlily pools, flowering succulents and the famous Majorelle blue of the painter's modernist former studio juxtaposed with ochres and terracotta, they're a city highlight. The studio is now home to a Berber Museum, with some interesting artefacts.

Over on the west side of the new city, avenue Mohammed VI (named after the current king) is the city's formal civic boulevard, with landmarks such as Charles Boccara's still unfinished Théâtre Royal, the Palais des Congrès, and the big new train station.

Taxis are the easiest way to negotiate your way around the new city, and to shuttle between it and the Medina (pay a maximum of 20dh in the daytime, 30dh at night, for a ride between central Guéliz and the Koutoubia). As you drive or walk around the Ville Nouvelle streets, look out for some wonderful modernist villas and apartment blocks – all, just like the rest of the town, pretty in pink.

Guides

You don't really need a guide, but if you do feel one might be useful either for basic orientation or to explore a specialist interest, there are plenty of official guides, licensed by the local authorities. Your hotel will be able to arrange one for you, otherwise we've heard good things about these guides, all of whom speak English: Ahmed Tija (mobile 0661 08 45 57), Moulay Youssef (mobile 0661 16 35 64), Mustapha Chouquir (mobile 0662 10 40 99) and Mustapha Karroum (mobile 0661 34 07 78).

Eating & Drinking

The good news is that Morocco has its own distinct cuisine, quite different from that of the rest of North Africa and the Arab world. It can be sampled well at every price level – from the carnival of cheap eats in the Jemaa El Fna and the stalls in Essaouira grilling fish that's straight off the trawler, to upscale restaurants where dining becomes an extravagant oriental fantasia. And, Islamic country though this may be, you can often get a drink too.

The bad news is, well, couscous and tagine, tagine and couscous. Particularly in the middle price range, you're likely to find the same old dishes, prepared to an average standard and served in huge quantities, thanks to inflexible fixed-price menus. But, as Marrakech continues to boom, restaurants are growing in both quantity and quality.

The cuisine

Moroccan cuisine evolved from Persia via the Arabs, from Andalucia with the returning Moors and from the colonial French – but the overriding principle is to throw all the ingredients into a dish, spice it skilfully, and then leave it to cook slowly.

Prime exhibit is the national dish of tagine. Essentially a slow-cooked stew of meat (usually beef, lamb or chicken, but can be camel) and vegetables, with olives, preserved lemon, almonds or prunes adding complexity and sweetness, and warm spices like cinnamon, cumin and ginger adding depth. The name describes both the food and the pot it's cooked in – a shallow earthenware dish with a conical lid that traps the rising steam and stops the stew from drying out. In Essaouira you'll find seafood tagines. Running a close second for ubiquity is couscous – coarse, ground semolina flour, steamed and topped with another rich meat or vegetable stew.

The diffa

The fixed-price menu is a feature of most traditional restaurants of the pricier variety. Once customers are seated, the food simply arrives, banquet-style, in a parade of dishes known as a *diffa*. It always starts with a selection of small hot and cold *salades marocaines*, of carrots, peppers, aubergine, tomatoes and the like, each prepared differently, along with delicacies such as spiced, fried offal. *Briouats* – little envelopes of paper-thin *ouarka* (a bit like filo) pastry wrapped around ground meat, rice or cheese and deep-fried – might come next, or *b'stilla* (or *pastilla*), the same *ouarka* pastry filled with shredded pigeon or chicken, almonds, boiled egg and spices, baked until crisp and then dusted with cinnamon and powdered sugar. Next, a tagine of beef, lamb or chicken and, just in case you are still hungry, a great mound of couscous. Desserts consist of flaky pastry drizzled with honey or crème anglaise, and seasonal fruit platters piled high and served with limitless mint tea poured from huge silver teapots.

The entire *diffa* experience is set up to honour the guest with extreme generosity, and of course, to show off the talents of the kitchen. That a great portion of it is inevitably sent back to the kitchen almost untouched may sit uncomfortably, but culturally this is the norm. Uneaten food is eaten by staff, or in extreme cases distributed to the poor. Rest assured that nothing is wasted.

There are plenty of *diffa*-style dining experiences to be had around town, but if you want to escape the large tourist groups follow locals to

SHORTLIST

Best views
- Argana p45
- Café at Maison de la Photographie (p63)
- Kosybar (p89)
- Gastro MK (p48)
- Nomad (p63)

Modishly Moorish
- Gastro MK (p48)
- Palais Namaskar (p125)
- Le Salama (p45)

Fine Moroccan cuisine
- Dar Zellij (p76)
- Al Fassia (p105)
- La Grande Table Marocaine, Royal Mansour Hotel (p162)
- Maison Arabe (p79)
- Tobsil (p51)

Budget eating
- Association Amal (p103)
- Café Clock (p89)
- Café at Maison de la Photographie (p63)
- Jemaa El Fna (p49)
- Snack Al Bahriya (p108)
- Tiznit (p46)

Garden tables
- Le Bled (p129)
- Le Jardin (p70)
- Jnane Tamsna (p125)
- Rôtisserie de la Paix (p108)
- Trattoria de Giancarlo (p108)

Souk shopping break
- Café des Epices (p70)
- Le Jardin (p70)
- Nomad (p63)

Best cocktails
- Grand Café de la Poste (p105)
- Kechmara (p107)
- Maison Arabe (p79)
- O'Sky Bar (p107)

their favoured upmarket dining spots like Dar Zellij (p76), Tobsil (p51) and Dar Yacout (p75).

It is also possible to enjoy high-end cuisine without ordering a set meal at places including the legendary all women's co-operative Al Fassia (p105) and Maison Arabe (p79) with its summer poolside dining.

In addition, most riads have cooks, which is another way of sampling Moroccan specialities without having to order enough to feed a small army. Alternatively, there are cooking courses at Maison Arabe (p78) and Café Clock (p78), where you can learn the secrets of the Moroccan kitchen and then get to enjoy eating the fruits of your labour.

There are also a few rare places that are trying to bring modern twists to traditional Moroccan food. These include Gastro MK (p48) in the Medina, Palais Namaskar (p125) in the Palmeraie and – in Essaouira – Elizir (p143).

Also bringing touches of modernity in the style and substance of dishes and surroundings are the more casual café-eateries that have sprung up in the Medina in recent years, offering tea, coffee, plus light lunches and dinners. They include the likes of Nomad (p63), Le Jardin (p70) and Terrasse des Epices (p70).

Other cuisines

There are some decent French restaurants (Grand Café de la Poste, p105; Le Loft, p107; Le Verre Canaille, p108; Chez Joel, p104), as well as pretty good coffee and some fine pâtisseries (Amandine, p103). Italian food is also reasonably well represented (Portofino, p48; Catanzaro, p104; Trattoria de Giancarlo, p108) and now there is a scattering of places offering non-European cuisines such as Lebanese (Azar, p103; La Cuisine de Mona, p104), and Thai (Wok Bangkok, p109). Even Essaouira has an Italian restaurant (Vague Bleu, p144) and a Mexican café (La Cantina, p141).

Such establishments are somewhat constrained by the availability of ingredients, but this can make for ingenious and interesting solutions. They are also a godsend for vegetarians, who will tire more quickly than most of the limited Moroccan dishes available.

Cooking course at Maison Arabe

Gastro MK

And to drink?

You can certainly eat very cheaply in Marrakech, but forget about having a drink with your meal in budget places. However, most restaurants catering to tourists will serve alcohol. Wine lists all include the same small selection of Moroccan vintages, sometimes augmented by a few imported bottles. The local wines are getting better all the time, while the imports are overpriced.

There is an official fiction that Moroccan wines – and three locally brewed brands of beer – are produced only for consumption by visitors. In reality, many Moroccans do like a drink. Most of them do it discreetly, however, usually with friends at home. Only the wealthiest and most westernised, who frequent the same bars and clubs as visitors, or the desperate and disreputable, the denizens of dodgy dives where many tourists fear to tread, go out and drink in public.

Once theoretically a dry zone, there are now a good few places in the Medina for a drink, including the Café Arabe (p70), with its roof terrace, the colonial-style Piano-Jazz Bar (p79) at the Maison Arabe, and Nomad (p63), with its terrace overlooking the Rahba Kedima. Otherwise there is a sprinkling of more sophisticated places in Guéliz,

including Kechmara (p107), Jack is Back (p120), Djellabar (p120), O'Sky Bar (p107) and Grand Café de la Poste (p105).

Tea & coffee

The routine social lubricant is not alcohol, but mint tea. Served with great ceremony, sticky and sweet, it welcomes friends, facilitates discussion, cements deals, follows meals, or simply provides an excuse to sit in a café for a while. Moroccans credit mint tea with powers that, to the visitor, it simply does not seem to possess. 'Berber whisky', you sometimes hear it called. Nevertheless, it is refreshing enough, and goes wonderfully with Moroccan pastries.

French influence means coffee is also widely available and pretty decent quality. The main locus for cafés is around the Jemaa El Fna, where long-established places like Argana (p45) or Café de France (p45) offer a vantage over the daily proceedings. These have been joined by some more modern venues in the souks: the Café des Epices on Rahma Kedima, Dar Cherifa (p68) and Le Jardin (p70) offer caffeine relief in stylish surrounds. Other city standouts include Kaowa (p100) in the emerging Majorelle enclave and Café Clock (p89) in the Mellah.

Prices & tipping

For anywhere but the cheapest places, a reservation makes good sense. Your hotel will be happy to take care of it. Prices vary from the unbelievably cheap – Restaurant Tiznit (p46) or Café Clock – to the not insanely expensive (700dh per head at Dar Yacout). Cash is always best, as hefty surcharges mean credit cards are unpopular. Tipping is expected. Round the bill up or leave no less than ten per cent.

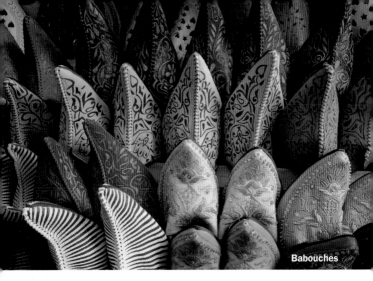

Babouches

WHAT'S BEST
Shopping

Marrakech is home to a lively artisanal culture that, while sometimes sticking to ancient methods, also does its best to produce items that might prise open the western wallet. Artisans will happily knock out whatever seems likely to sell and stay tuned to trends in interior decor. Good buys include fashion accessories, fabrics, spices, natural oils and pottery. But there's also fun to be had in considering a few less conventional purchases like magic supplies or old teapots.

For focused shopping, especially on a short visit, it might make sense to hire a personal shopper (Katie Lawrence UK +44 (0)771 348 6006, Morocco +212 (0)638 41 79 03; Maryam Montague, moroccan maryam@yahoo.com). Or dedicate time to one-stop shopping: Mustapha Blaoui (p80) is a handy one-stop for all sorts of Moroccan homewares; alluring Souk Cherifia (p74) sells *prix-fixe* homeware and fashions; 33 Rue Majorelle (p109) is a concept store showcasing the latest in cutting-edge products; the industrial zone of Sidi Ghanem (p114) is for serious buyers; and the conveniently located Ensemble Artisanal (p51) offers common items at fixed prices.

The hassle of haggling

It's a drag, but haggling is expected in the souk. There are no hard and fast rules, but when you've spotted something you want, it's smart to scout around and get a few quotes on similar items at other stores before making your play. Don't feel you need to go through the whole charade of offer and counter-offer like a B-movie dialogue; simply expressing interest then walking away on being told the price is usually enough to bring about some fairly radical discounting.

Souks vs Ville Nouvelle

The souks are commerce at its most colourful – a coalescence of different markets, each specialising in one kind of item. General handicraft shops are scattered everywhere, too, but particularly on the two main lanes: rue Mouassine and rue Semarine.

Shops in the Ville Nouvelle work like European ones. Most of the interesting ones are clustered on and around avenue Mohammed V, especially on rue de la Liberté and rue des Vieux Marrakchis.

Antiques

'Antique' is a manufactured style here – things may not be as old as they appear. Fraud is widespread too. Buy something because you like it, and if you discover it really is as old as claimed, then that's an added bonus.

Bric-a-brac shops offering old but less exalted items are scattered around the souk. On rue Sidi Ishak, the lane leading north from the east side of Rahba Kedima, there are several where it skirts around the mosque, and another as it passes through a short tunnel. There's another on the same road south of Rahba Kedima, a short walk down on the right, and one or two on rue Sidi El-Yamani, just east of the Mouassine fountain.

Babouches

Babouches (slippers) come in leather, nubuck, suede or sabra (which looks like silk but is actually a kind of viscose). The sole will be leather, plastic or rubber and can be sewn on (good) or glued (not good). Yellow is the traditional Moroccan favourite, but they come in all colours and degrees of embellishment. Expect

SHORTLIST

Moroccan-inspired fashion
- Art/C, Souk Cherifia (p74)
- Aya's (p92)
- Beldi (p64)
- Maktoub by Max & Jan (p74)
- Mysha & Nito (p112)
- Pop-up Shop – Norya ayroN (p74)
- Salima Abdel-Wahab, Sidi Ghanem (p114)

Traditional clothing
- Haj Ahmed Oueld Lafram (p65)
- La Maison du Kaftan Marocain (p73)

Jewellery
- Amazonite (p109)
- El Badii (p111)
- Mr Goodyear (p95)

Carpets
- L'Art de Goulimine (p63)
- Bazar du Sud (p64)
- Tapis Akhnif (p75)

Leather goods
- Founoun (p111)
- Galerie Birkemeyer (p111)
- Lalla, Souk Cherifia(p74)
- Place Vendôme (p116)

Moorish homewares
- Cherkaoui (p73)
- Moor (p63)
- Mustapha Blaoui (p80)
- Myriam Roland-Gosselin (p129)

Modern Moroccan design
- 33 Rue Majorelle (p109)
- Dinanderie (p92)
- Lup 31 (p89)
- Souk Cherifia (p74)
- Yahya Creation (p116)

Ceramics
- Caverne d'Ali Baba (p73)
- Chez Alaoui (p73)

to pay around 50dh for fake leather ones with glued soles, up to 150dh for the all-leather, stiched-sole variety. They're everywhere, but the obvious place to go is Souk des Babouches.

Carpets

There's one simple rule when it comes to carpets: buy it because you like it, not because you've been told it's worth money. Very few carpets are antique. And ignore claims that a carpet is made of cactus silk: genuine cactus silk carpets cost ten times as much as normal ones. Bear in mind that you're unlikely to find the double of a carpet you like in another shop, as most are unique.

Age, quality, fabric and type help to determine price. Popular carpets like Beni Ouarains can cost up to 7,000dh for an old piece, while a Bouchaourite rag rug costs between 200dh and 2,000dh.

The main places to buy carpets are along rue Mouassine (try Tapis Akhnif, p75) and rue Semarine, and in the Souk des Tapis off the Rahba Kedima, which is where you'll find L'Art de Goulimine (p63) and Bazar du Sud (p64). English-speaking guide Abdelhafid Serrakh (mobile 0661 55 37 36) is an understanding local with a wealth of carpet knowledge.

Ceramics

The local ceramic style is plain terracotta glazed in bright colours. Prices start at around 60dh for a soap dish rising up to 180dh for larger plates. Green Tamegroute pottery ranges from 20dh for a small bowl up to 600dh for a large platter. There are also tadelakt ceramics, smooth and satiny to the touch with more subdued tones. Ceramics are everywhere, but particularly in and around the Souk des Teinturiers and the lower part of rue Mouassine (notably Caverne d'Ali Baba, p73). The cheapest option is to

shop at the sprawling, open-air pottery market on the road just outside the south-eastern Medina gate of Bab Ghemat.

Lanterns

Styles range from traditional to art deco and avant garde – including tall, curly ones made of decorated goatskin. The cheapest are those made of tin, which is often rusted for colour. Brass and copper lanterns are pricier but generally better finished and harder-wearing. Prices range are around 30dh-300dh for tin, and 100dh-750dh or more for copper or brass. You can find lanterns in the Souk Haddadin (p59) and the Souk des Dinandiers.

Clothing & accessories

Marrakech is good for leather, but be careful: some of it is shoddy and you can end up with a bag that leaves its contents stinking or transfers its colour to your clothes (rub the bag with a wet tissue before buying). Vintage shoulder bags are popular and sell for between 200dh and 400dh, or you can get modern copies for around 300dh.

You'll find high-end contemporary leather in the northern end of the Souk El-Kebir (p53) or in the alleys of the Kissaria (p53) or, for something more modern and stylish, try Lalla and Art/C (for both, see Souk Cherifia, p74).

Beautiful vintage kaftans can be found at Amazonite (p109), while a huge and more modern selection is offered at La Maison du Kaftan Marocain (p73). Updated kaftans and innovative fashion and accessories with Moroccan twists can be found at colourful Pop-up Shop – Norya ayroN (p74), Intensité Nomade (p112), Mysha & Nito (p112), Aya's (p92), Art/C in Souk Cherifia, Maktoub by Max & Jan (p74) and KIS Boutique (p73).

Jad Mahal p22

Nightlife

Marrakech is a diverse city, where donkey carts vie with Mazeratis, and the designer shops of Guéliz take on the artisan crafts of the souks. It's a place of deep-rooted traditions and conservative religious values, but – at the same time – one where hedonism and consumerism are booming. And this mix has a soundtrack: Arabic pop in the supermarket, Berber folk music in the taxi, western jazz in city bars, and DJ sets in the clubs.

Nightclubs

The city's more upmarket nightlife is concentrated in Hivernage and in a strip of boulevard Mohammed VI in the Zone Hotelière de l'Aguedal on the outskirts of the city.

The opening of Pacha (p126) in the latter area went some way towards putting Marrakech on the international clubbing map. The mega-club draws international DJs and devotees of the brand for weekend parties and has inspired a host of others to set up shop along the same strip. One of these is the cavernous 555 (p126), which has gathered momentum targeting a home-grown audience as well as tourists with its crowd-pleasing mix of house, R&B and hip hop.

In Hivernage, Théâtro (p123) at the Es Saadi Hotel is now entering its second decade with a reputation as one of the hottest places in town. Each night an extravagant floorshow of costumed dancers, aerialists and fire-jugglers intermingle on the dancefloor. More sophisticated is the So Lounge (p123), annexed to the Sofitel, which attracts wealthy Moroccans, visitors

SHORTLIST

Local DJs
- Théâtro (p123)

International DJs
- Pacha (p126)
- Silver (p123)

Best for belly-dancing
- Comptoir Darna (p117)

Best bars with music
- Café Touco at the Fellah Hotel (p129)
- Comptoir Darna (p117)
- Kechmara (p107)
- Jad Mahal (p123)

Gnawa grooves
- Café Clock (p89)
- Essaouira Festival of Gnawa & World Music (p26)

and expats to its eating, chill-out and dancefloor complex. Then there's Silver (p123), an industrial-style space downstairs at the Jad Mahal, with techno and house and frequent guest DJs from Europe.

Aside from full-on nightclubs, some Hivernage bars have music and a club-like feel. La Casa (p117) has strobe lights and an Arab/Latin soundtrack, while Comptoir Darna (p117) is known for its nightly belly dancers.

Music & dinner cabarets

Aside from the full-on nightclubs, there is a growing trend towards inclusive dinner-cabaret venues, with live shows, musicians and DJs. The food is often expensive, and it is not always obligatory to dine – turn up after 10pm and buy an overpriced drink at the bar as a passport to your night's entertainment. The Lotus Club (p120) has a Vegas-style nightly cabaret revue and a live band. There's

more live jazz, blues and R&B at Le Blokk (p126), as well as acrobatic performances, before the DJs start and the dancefloor fills up. And there's a full-blown Brazilian carnival every night at Fuego Latino (p126) at the Hotel Palmeraie Palace, with a *churrascaria* barbecue, samba band and drummers, *capoeira* performers and exotic dancers.

Live music

Bars and restaurants with worthwhile live bands include the Jad Mahal (see Silver, p123) and the funky five-piece cover band the Kech Experience at the Epicurien Casino at Es Saadi Hotel (see Théâtro, p123). As mentioned above, the late-night cabarets listed also have live music components.

Outside the cabaret scene, it's pretty difficult to find good live music in Marrakech, with a near-total absence of concert venues. However, in certain corners of the city you can uncover sporadic performances, happenings and organised cultural events.

There has been a buzz of excitement around the 2014 opening of Café Clock (p89) in the Kasbah. Sunday evenings see Moroccan traditional acts and young Moroccan bands performing, jamming and fusing – *gnawa* groups, Berber musicians, *oud* players and so on. And, of course, you can hear clusters of musicians nightly at Jemaa El Fna, hustling for a few dirhams to play a tune. Have the coins ready in your hand, take a ringside view and beware of pickpockets. Be prepared, though, that most so-called *gnawa* musicians in the square aren't the real thing – for a better *gnawa* experience try to get to a session at the Clock or ask your riad to book a professional troupe. For more on *gnawa* and traditional music performances, see p24.

David Bloch Gallery

Arts & Leisure

Morocco is a poor country and Marrakech is a small city. Cinemas are few and far between, dedicated live music venues are non-existent, and the performers in the Jemaa El Fna are the closest you'll get to live theatre. But scratch the surface and you'll uncover a nascent arts and cultural scene. It's strongest in fine art, with a slew of new galleries and the Marrakech Biennale giving a much-needed boost to artists and creatives.

There's also a burgeoning sports and outdoors activities scene in and around Marrakech and, of course, after all that exertion, submitting to the hands of an expert hammam master and masseur is de rigueur.

Art & Galleries

The last few years have seen the scope of, and interest in, art in Marrakech go from strength to strength. Much of this is due to Vanessa Branson's Biennale, which celebrated its fifth edition in 2014. The Biennale is now a serious art event, and Marrakech artists are on a creative roll, broadening their scope by exploring street art, photography and video among other mediums. The city is becoming known for a unique local take on street art that embraces Arabic calligraphy and other traditional forms. For examples, see the works of Larbi Cherkaoui (www.larbicherkaoui. com) at the David Bloch Gallery (p111), and Hassan Hajjaj's striking films and pop-art-style photographs of Medina figures in funky renditions of traditional textiles that he makes himself. A good range of his work can be seen at Riad Yima (p60), his studio in the Medina.

Many of the interesting new studios and galleries are choosing the Medina over the Ville Nouvelle as their base, seeing it as being closer to the pulse of Marrakchi creativity. Dar Cherifa (p68), a beautiful exhibition space in a restored 16th-century Medina house, led the way and now hosts cultural events too. Laila Hida's new Le 18 project (https://fr-fr.facebook.com/dar dixhuit) has become a hub for young artists, photographers, dancers and filmmakers. Part venue for artists in residence, part budget hotel (p162), part artists' studio, part cultural centre, it hosts regular film screenings, contemporary dance workshops and readings, as well as art exhibitions and installations.

It's also worth heading out of town to the Dar al-Ma'mûn project at the Fellah Hotel (p175), which dedicates one of its riads to visiting artists in residence, has an extensive library and runs cultural events and local education programmes.

The Ville Nouvelle is still a magnet for high-end art galleries. In addition to the David Bloch Gallery, the Noir Sur Blanc Gallery (p116) showcases mainly contemporary Moroccan artists, while Galerie 127 (p112) exhibits international photographers.

Photography is booming here. Patrick Manac'h's lovely Maison de la Photographie (p60) features beautiful historic images of Morocco, and the Museum for Photography and Visual Arts (MMPVA) has rotating exhibitions at its temporary home inside the Badii Palace (p87). Fashionistas can also look forward to an Yves Saint Laurent Museum of Fashion.

Film

Morocco is a favourite location for filmmakers due to its wide range of scenery and urban landscapes, which can stand in for everywhere from Tibet to the Middle East, and the encouragement of the authorities. Moroccan filmgoers, on the other hand, have to content themselves with a few Hollywood blockbusters, Bollywood films, martial arts pictures and mainstream French releases. But a recent interest in supporting home-grown films has seen the local movie industry subsidised by six million euros a year.

The Cinéma le Colisée (p116) is the nicest picture house in town. In the new *zone touristique*, there is now also the nine-screen Megarama (avenue de 7eme Art, off route d'Ourika, www. megarama.info/marrakech). Movies are usually dubbed into French and shown with Arabic subtitles.

Only at the annual Marrakech International Film Festival, which takes place in December, is there ever very much to see. Its *raison d'être* is mainly to encourage filmmakers to shoot here, but screenings around town are open to all.

Music

Morocco has a rich musical heritage. Arabo-Andalusian music is sedate. *Grika* is Berber music – rootsy, rural stuff that is usually performed at harvest and religious festivals. But Morocco is perhaps best known for *gnawa*. The *gnawa* (the name for both the performers and the music) perform a kind of rhythmic, hypnotic music using iron castanets, *guimbri* (a long-necked lute) and chanting. Larger ensembles add drums, call and response vocals and dancing. At their most authentic, *gnawa* performances are part of all-night healing rituals involving trance and possession. Your chances of catching one of these is slim to none, and the dearth of performance venues means there's no obvious formal setting for *gnawa* either. However, there are informal sessions at Café Clock (p89). In addition, the

Dar Bellarj (p59), in the north of the Medina, hosts ad hoc traditional ensembles performing in the courtyard around the festivals of Ramadan and Ashura. And home-grown music, arts and entertainment can be sampled every July during the Marrakech Popular Arts Festival (p26). But for the best *gnawa*, head to Essaouira for the brilliant Festival of Gnawa & World Music (p26).

As one might imagine, Marrakech is not much of a destination for western classical music. The Institut Français (05 24 44 69 30, www.if-maroc.org/marrakech), just beyond Guéliz, next to the Lycée Victor Hugo, puts on occasional concerts of jazz, world and contemporary music. Classical music devotees in Marrakech have created Association des Amis de la Musique Marrakech (www.aammarrakech.com). It sponsors chamber music recitals by eminent artists in luxurious riads, usually involving a buffet dinner for around 500dh. Membership is obligatory, purchasable online 24 hours in advance, and costs 300dh for the year. And lastly, the Théâtre Royal hosts a hotch-potch of live music events plus occasional performances of the Orchestre Philharmonique de Maroc (www.opm.ma). It also serves as a venue for the Marrakech Popular Arts Festival.

Keep an eye, too, on the Mint Collective (www.mintcollectivemb5.com) and Le 18, which are creating sound-art, multi-media pieces.

Sport & leisure

There's no shortage of opportunities to enjoy the outdoors around Marrakech, with camel- and horse-riding, quad biking, ballooning, golf and more (see box p122).

At the other end of the leisure spectrum, spa culture has proved well suited to Marrakech, building on the traditional Moroccan

SHORTLIST

Best festivals
- Marrakech Biennale (p28)
- Marrakech International Film Festival (p27)
- Essaouira Festival of Gnawa and World Music (p26)
- Marrakech Popular Arts Festival (p26)

Best cinema
- Cinéma le Colisée (p116)

Best galleries
- Galerie Damgaard (p147)
- Riad Yima (p60)
- David Bloch Gallery (p111)

Best for photography
- MMPVA (p87)
- Galerie 127 (p112)
- Maison de la Photographie (p60)

Top activities
- Windsurfing, Essaouira (p152)
- Hot-air ballooning (p122)

Hottest hammams
- Hammam El-Bacha (p76)
- Les Bains de Marrakech (p91)

Sumptuous spas
- La Mamounia (p161)
- Royal Mansour (p162)
- Selman (p177)

hammam. Hammam El-Bacha (p76) is a popular traditional hammam, and the men and women who work here do a great scrub-down for a few dirhams. For a more boutique, visitor-oriented and soothing experience, there are Hammam de la Rose (p79) and Les Bains de Marrakech (p91). Or, at the top of the scale, you'll find sensational hammam spas and the last word in luxury at La Mamounia (p161) and the Selman (p177).

Calendar

Essaouira Festival of Gnawa & World Music

Morocco celebrates its unique musical heritage with a series of festivals. The most famous is the **Essaouira Festival of Gnawa & World Music**, while the **Marrakech Popular Arts Festival** includes the full spectrum of indigenous musical styles.

Marrakech's blossoming arts scene got a further boost with the establishment of the **Biennale** in 2005, encompassing film, literature and music as well as art, while the **International Film Festival** brings big names to the Red City.

We have also listed secular public holidays in this chapter. Dates of the major religious holidays vary from year to year, and are approximate as they depend on moon sightings. **Ramadan** begins on or around 18 June in 2015 and 7 June in 2016 and lasts for a month. **Eid Al-Fitr** is around 17 July in 2015 and 7 July in 2016, while **Eid Al-Adha** is around 23 September in 2015 and 13 September in 2016.

Spring

1 May **Labour Day (Fête de Travail)**

May-June **Essaouira Festival of Gnawa & World Music**
Essaouira
0522 27 26 03, www.festival-gnaoua.net.
Every June, around 200,000 people rock up to Essaouira for this festival – four days and nights of a carnival-like atmosphere. See also box p146.

Summer

July **Marrakech Popular Arts Festival**
Théâtre Royal and Badii Palace
0524 43 201 21, www.marrakech festival.com.
A week-long festival with bands and dancing, and the largest music festival in Marrakech. Most events, staged at the Théâtre Royal and the Badii Palace, are free. Different regional folk styles are represented including *ahouache*, *issawa*, *hamadcha*, *gnawa*, *ahidous*, Arabo-Andalucian and Marrakech's own percussive *deqqa*.

30 July **Feast of the Throne (Fête du Trône)**

Aug **Moussem of Setti Fatma**
A well-attended four-day *moussem*, both a religious celebration and a sociable fair. It's held at Setti Fatma (p131).

14 Aug **Allegiance Day**

Autumn

Late Oct-early Nov **Festival des Andalousies Atlantiqes**
Essaouira
Association Essaouira Mogador, 10 rue du Caire 'Dar Souiri', Essaouira (0524 47 52 68, www.facebook.com/FestivalDes AndalousiesAtlantiques).
Arabo-Andalucian, Sephardic and flamenco music festival held in Essaouira amid a host of workshops and debates.

Winter

6 Nov **Day of the Green March (Marche Verte)**

18 Nov **Independence Day**

Dec **Marrakech International Film Festival**
Various venues
0524 43 24 93, http://en.festival marrakech.info.
A multifaceted festival with a global remit. Nine days of screenings, competitions and lavish parties showcase dozens of films and attract star names. Francis Ford Coppola, Martin Scorsese, Oliver Stone, Sharon Stone, Catherine Deneuve and Juliette Binoche have all graced its red carpets. Screening venues include Jemaa El Fna. Tickets are available for almost all films on a first-come-first-served basis from cinema box offices.

1 Jan **New Year's Day**

Late Jan **Marrakech Marathon**
Ramparts of Marrakech
0524 31 35 72, www.marathon-marrakech.com/presa.php.
January sees perfect running weather in Marrakech. Pull on your trainers and run with 6,000 others around the outside of the city's ancient ramparts. The full marathon (42km/26 miles) and the half-marathon (21km/13 miles) start within 45 minutes of each other. There's also a children's race.

Feb-Mar **Marrakech Biennale**
Various venues
www.marrakechbiennale.org.
The fifth edition of the Marrakech Biennale was held to much acclaim in 2014, in venues and public spaces across the city. See box p28.

Marrakech Marathon

Marrakech Biennale

The success of the Biennale has boosted culture in general.

Since it was founded in 2005 (2014 was the fifth edition), the Biennale, founded by Vanessa Branson, has become an important event, covering not just art, but film, literature and music too. It attracts visitors from all over the world, as well as an increasingly high-profile roster of exhibitors. But it's also been hugely influential in putting Moroccan artists on the map, and generating a buzz around Moroccan culture generally, including a recent surge in interest in photography and film. The Biennale played an important part in ensuring the success of the **Museum for Photography & Visual Arts** (box p97).

It's a sea change for a country that, until Branson appeared on the scene, had only a marginal contemporary art scene. Conservative elements felt that the only 'true' art nearly always came in painted form, but the remit of the Biennale is to promote dialogue between all the disciplines, as an expression of artists' responses to the Red City and its environs. The 2014 theme, 'Where are we now?',

was a showcase of the emerging arts scene in Morocco, staged in spaces as diverse as the Jemaa El Fna, the Badii Palace and the Royal Opera House and Theatre.

One of the attractions of the festival is the unique opportunity to get a glimpse of some of the city's hidden treasures, including a wealth of small-scale dars and riads scattered through the Medina – among them Branson's own guesthouse, **Riad El Fenn** (p161), and the arts and culture residence **Le 18** (www.facebook.com/dardixhuit, see also p162 **Dar 18**) set up by Laila Hida. What's more, the Biennale has paved the way for year-round activity at numerous galleries and several major hotels, such as the Four Seasons and Sofitel. It's rare you'll show up in Marrakech and find nothing on.

Pitching acclaimed international and national names together with young, up-and-coming talent makes for a highly stimulating environment. Rarely do you get to see an art movement blossoming before your very eyes, and that makes the Marrakech Biennale so very exciting.

Itineraries

Bab es Salam market

Corners & Courtyards

Marrakech doesn't claim to be a city overflowing with must-see sights; there's joy in simply wandering in the Medina, enjoying its hidden corners and discovering tranquil courtyards. This full-day itinerary takes in some of the Red City's museums and historic buildings but it also helps you discover some of its less-known corners and courtyards, markets and synagogues.

Begin in the southern part of the Medina at the **Badii Palace** (p87). Constructed by the Saadian dynasty at the end of the 16th century with wealth accrued through victories over the Portuguese, the once opulent palace (its walls and ceilings were once covered in gold) is now an atmospheric ruin. It is also the temporary home of the **Marrakech Museum for Photography & Visual Art** (MMPVA). Return to the place des Ferblantiers at the

front of the palace, admiring the work at the ironworkers' stalls in the square. Walk north, passing a park on your left, and follow the road to the right to face the entrance of the Bahia Palace (we'll return here later). Look to your right and duck south under the arch into the **Bab Es Salam Market** (p91), also known as the Jewish market. You are now in the Mellah, marked by narrow gridded alleys and traditionally the city's Jewish area, though its Jewish population today is tiny. Check out the spices and the higgledy piggledy stalls while following the road to the left before turning right on to derb Tijara and a welcome stop for coffee or mint tea at the letter-box red **Caffe Internazionale** (open 8am-8pm daily). Afterwards, follow the road to the end and turn left along derb Sekaia. Then take the third left where the road forks at derb Manchoura. At no.36 is the

Earth Café

Caffé Internazionale

Slat Laazama Synagogue (p91).
Its Majorelle blue-striped courtyard
is a startling and welcoming sight
in contrast to the rather dour streets
of the Mellah.

Head north out of derb
Manchoura and back to visit the
ornate 19th-century **Bahia Palace**
(p92), known for its rooms, arcades
and courtyards decorated with
exquisite carved stucco and bands
of traditional zelij tiling.

After emerging from the palace,
walk north up rue Riad Zitoun
El-Jedid and head under the arch,
on the right, opposite the small car
park. This leads to the **Maison
Tiskiwin** (p95), one of Marrakech's
hidden gems, on your right. The
small museum in a private house
is home to a fascinating collection
of crafts and decorative arts from
southern Moroccco and the Sahara.
From the museum exit, take a right,
then a quick first left along derb Si
Said, winding through the lanes and
passing and possibly popping into
the **Dar Si Said Museum** (p95)
– a palace with a collection devoted

to Moroccan and Berber artisanship
– before emerging under a tiny arch.

By now, you may be ready for a
rest. Opt for a reviving fruit juice at
the **Earth Café** (1 derb Nakousse;
open 10am-10pm daily) – its entrance
stairs are just on the left before the
arch. Alternatively, wait a few
more minutes for some coffee and
flavoursome ice-cream: turn right,
after leaving the arch, along rue
Riad Zitoun El-Jedid. At the corner
of rue Douar Graoua, on the right,
is a tiny square where **Un Déjeuner
à Marrakech** (open 10am-10pm
daily) serves mint tea and orange
blossom ice-cream at its alfresco
tables, or inside in the air-conditioned
cool. If you're already hungry, it's
also a great lunch spot, known for
its house-baked quiche.

Refreshed, head north again
along rue Riad Zitoun El-Jedid,
past the left-hand fork of rue des
Banques (which emerges on to Jemaa
El Fna), and up rue Kennaria to the
less common eastern entrance to the
Rahba Kedima (p53, the magic
and spice market. Take time

Bags packed, milk cancelled, house raised on stilts.

You've packed the suntan lotion, the snorkel set, the stay-pressed shirts. Just one more thing left to do – your bit for climate change. In some of the world's poorest countries, changing weather patterns are destroying lives.

You can help people to deal with the extreme effects of climate change. Raising houses in flood-prone regions is just one life-saving solution.

Climate change costs lives.
Give £5 and let's sort it *Here & Now*

www.oxfam.org.uk/climate-change

Oxfam is a registered charity in England and Wales (No.202918) and Scotland (SCO039042). Oxfam GB is a member of Oxfam International.

Be Humankind Oxfam

Nomad

to chat to one of the stallholders who'll prescribe a spice or a stuffed reptile for your ailments. Then, if you haven't yet had lunch, head up to the terrace of **Nomad** (p63), on the south-west corner of the square, for a panoramic view and a tasty collection of salads and tagines. Or, for some indulgence in the gorgeous surrounds of one of the city's top riads, book lunch in the lush, wild garden of nearby **Riad Enija** (p166).

Exit the market the way you came, turning left (north) along rue Rhaba Kedima (also known as rue Sidi Ishak at this point), passing the Sidi Ishack mosque on your right; ignore the passage straight ahead and turn right and then quick left up derb Sidi Ishack through the busy fruit and vegetable market. From here, take the left-hand street that emerges at the top end of the souks to a widening road that leads to the **Ben Youssef Medersa** (p59), a Quranic school founded in the 14th century. Its beautiful courtyard is often overwhelmed by tour groups but, nonetheless, it's the most stunningly decorated courtyard

in the city, with intricate stucco, zelije tiling and carved cedarwood. Back outside, turn right and head for the door in the wall ahead – **Dar Bellarj** (p59), which hosts temporary exhibitions and also serves coffee just off its courtyard. It's a moment for repose after battling your way through the crowds at the Medersa.

Emerging from Dar Bellarj, turn left and walk under the horseshoe arch and head straight ahead. You will pass the Fondouk restaurant on your left. Along the right-hand side are old *fundouks*, traditional merchants' hostels built around a large open courtyard, with stabling and storage rooms on the ground floor, bedrooms off the upper galleries, and a single gated entrance to the street that was locked at night for security. Today, they are the province of woodworkers and craftsmen, and visitors are welcome to explore their interiors.

Retrace your steps back to the horseshoe arch of Dar Bellarj but turn right under the arch just before you reach it and head west along the northern perimeter of the souks. Keep walking straight ahead until you emerge from under an arch at a widening of the street, with stalls either side. Here you will see a small crossroads and an arch. Head under the arch, passing the **Shrine of Sidi Abdel-Aziz** on your right. An 18th-century doctor famed for his ability to help the mentally ill, Abdel-Aziz promises help for modern sufferers too and people come here hoping for a cure.

Continue south where, after the Dar El-Bacha crossroads, you'll see **Fundouk Sarsare** (192 rue Mouassine) on your left. Now colonised by artisans, this is where Kate Winslet and her children stayed in the film adaptation of Esther Freud's *Hideous Kinky*.

As you continue further south on rue Mouassine you'll be walking under a picturesque part of the souk – the slatted souk ceiling here was erected for *Sex and the City 2*, when the Manhattan girls decamped to the Middle East – Morocco stood in for Abu Dhabi. You will emerge in front of the Mouassine fountain. If you want to get a glimpse of the bathhouse behind, pay to use the public bathrooms by the arch.

Head under the arch, here (to the right of the fountain), into a tight labyrinth of streets to discover the **Douiria Mouassine** (p68), a reception apartment that has been restored to its 17th-century glory, and is now a small museum.

Return to the fountain, turn left, passing another entrance to the Mouassine Mosque and then left again (in front of Café Bougainvillea), heading south on rue Mouassine. For a quiet drink in tranquil surrounds to finish off a very active day, head right off rue Mouassine under an arch that is signposted for the elegantly beautiful and quiet **Dar Cherifa** (p68). Continuing south along rue Mouassine will take you to place Bab Fteuh and Jemaa El Fna.

Ben Youssef Medersa p33

MMPVA

Art Excursion

Marrakech is emerging as a centre for contemporary art as its artists embrace new forms of creativity, including street art, photography, video and other media with energy and enthusiasm.

The establishment of the Biennale has played a large part in setting this creative spark alight. It has also helped ensure the success of the future Marrakech Museum for Photography and Visual Arts (MMPVA), currently in temporary accommodation, which will showcase historic and contemporary Moroccan and international photography. British architect Sir David Chipperfield's proposed cubist brick structure that had been due to open next to the Menara Gardens has gone back to the drawing board and a site in the Medina is to be considered. Also riding the cultural wave will be the Yves Saint Laurent Museum of Fashion, to be built near the Majorelle Gardens, along with a new art museum, Al Maaden African Contemporary Art Museum (MACAAL), designed by architects Omar Alaoui from Morocco and Nieto Sobejano from Spain.

The next Biennale is in 2016, but there's still plenty to see at other times. This walk (and a few taxi rides) will take you to galleries, street art, hidden riads and emerging cultural hotspots.

Start your contemporary art tour at the temporary home of the **Museum for Photography and Visual Arts** (MMPVA, www. mmpva.org) in the Badii Palace (p87), where rotating exhibitions are staged in the gallery on the eastern side of the atmospheric palace ruins.

Next, head south down rue de la Kasbah to check out the photography on the walls at **Café Clock** (p89). Doubling as a cultural centre, the café provides exhibition

Riad Yima

space for local artists as well as hosting music and storytelling sessions. If you already feel in need of refreshment there's good coffee here, plus date milkshakes and Clock's signature camel-burger.

It's best to jump into a taxi from the Mellah up to the **Mamounia** (p161) for the next part of our day. The hotel hosts temporary exhibitions with an emphasis on photography, while its famous gardens provide a green respite from the Medina streets. After enjoying them, walk through the Koutoubia Gardens, and up into Jemaa El Fna.

Enter the souks from the north-eastern section of the square, taking the route in that's opposite the Café de France (p45). Head north up rue Semarine to the Rahba Kedima magic and spice market (signposted to the right off rue Semarine). From here head south, past the new Nomad restaurant (p63) to the buried (but clearly signposted) studio-gallery-shop of multimedia artist Hassan Hajjaj at **Riad Yima** (p60; if you can't find it, give them a call and someone will come and get you). Hajjaj's vibrant and distinctive pop-art-style photography, with

its sharp and humorous juxtaposition of Moroccan and western themes, has been exhibited internationally. He also repurposes everyday objects, like Arabic-language Coca-Cola crates and sardine cans, into bold, new and desirable pieces.

Return to rue Semarine and head north, emerging from Souk El-Kebir just south of the Ben Youssef Medersa and Mosque. Just beyond the entrance to the Medersa is **Dar Bellarj** (p59), which holds temporary exhibitions.

From Dar Bellarj, walk five minutes east to the absorbing collection of historical photographs of Morocco in the **Maison de la Photographie** (p60). After viewing the photographs, stay around for a peaceful lunch on the shaded roof terrace, with sensational Atlas mountain views and authentic, home-style Moroccan cooking (soups and salads to start, followed by tagines and couscous).

After lunch, retrace your steps skirting north of the Medersa complex along rue Riad Laarouss to locate **Dar 18** (p162), hidden off to the right, and it's Le 18 project (www.facebook.com/dardixhuit).

Galerie Rê

A lively cultural hub hosting film screenings and readings that also functions as a budget hotel, it includes exhibition space for paintings and installations.

Next, retrace your steps to rue Riad Laarouss, passing under the arch, before walking past the shrine of Sidi Abdel-Aziz (on your right) and down rue Mouassine and bearing right (signposted) under an arch to the beautifully restored townhouse **Dar Cherifa** (p68), which has a regular programme of temporary exhibitions. Hassan Hajjaj is among the artists who have exhibited. Dar Cherifa also hosts calligraphy workshops and has an artists' residency programme. Tea, coffee and light lunches are served too.

This may well be enough art for one day, but if you still have time and energy, find a taxi for the short trip to the Guéliz area of the Ville Nouvelle and its cluster of contemporary art galleries. Most are open until 7pm or 8pm. Alternatively, a Guéliz gallery stroll can be a separate morning or afternoon's itinerary. Have the taxi drop you off at the sleek **Galerie Rê** (p111), where the emphasis is on contemporary works by Moroccan and Mediterranean artists. Then head towards the **David Bloch Gallery** (p111) on the chic rue des Vieux Marrakchis, an industrial-style space featuring bold abstract works, sometimes incorporating Arabic calligraphy, by the likes of Larbi Cherkaoui and Mohamed Boustane. LA graffiti artist Augustine Kofie is exhibiting here in spring 2015. Turn back to rue de la Liberté and then right up avenue Mohamed V to **Galerie 127** (p111) for contemporary photography.

Return to rue de la Liberté and turn right. At the junction of boulevard El-Mansour Eddahbi and rue de la Liberté is a startlingly beautiful **mural** by Larbi Cherkaoui.

Then head north up rue de Yougoslavie, taking in the **Noir Sur Blanc Gallery** (p116), featuring Moroccan artists working in all mediums, and opposite it, the **Matisse Gallery** (p112), also a showcase for young Moroccan artists, including those working with calligraphy.

By now, it's time for a drink and/ or something to eat at **Kechmara** (p107), back on rue de la Liberté, before heading back to your riad.

Rahba Kedima p40

Souks Custom-made

It's easy to get lost in the souks. In fact, it's almost inevitable. Wandering randomly, enjoying their maze-like quality and pausing at whatever catches your eye is a lot of fun. But the souks also reward a more determined and proactive approach. There's more happening than meets the eye, and what's on display is only the tip of an artisanal iceberg.

We have put together a walk exploring some of the souks' less obvious corners. Taking about an hour (depending on how long you stop to shop), it concentrates mainly on clothing and accessories, and links shops that not only offer interesting stock of their own, but will also – cheaply, quickly and to a high standard – knock up your designs, modify their own, or copy styles that you supply.

Start the walk at any time of day; the souks are particularly quiet in the early afternoon and most workshops are closed on Fridays.

We begin outside the palace of **Dar El-Bacha** (p76) – there's a Moroccan pâtisserie over the road where you can sit with a freshly pressed juice and dessert to set you up for the shopping ahead.

From Dar El-Bacha palace, follow the pedestrianised section of rue Dar El-Bacha. As the lane begins to narrow, you'll find shoemaker **Sabir Abeljalil** on the right at No.39 (no phone). He has a great choice of quality women's footwear in both local and European styles, and will copy whatever you give him in up to three days.

Carry on down rue Dar El-Bacha, crossing rue Mouassine, and you'll pass a row of men with barrows waiting outside the local hammam. After entering the covered area, take the third left turn. Immediately, there's a fork. Bear left again. You're now walking through the metalworkers' souk, **Souk El-Haddadin** (p59).

Café des Epices p40

To the immediate left is a passage leading to **Ahmed Serjal**'s workshop, where he hammers out the flaws in antique trays and hammam bowls and sells them much cheaper than in the mainstream shops. Back on the main alley you'll walk past old bedsteads and other bits of wrought iron; pass by a few metalworkers' dens where men hammer out their designs, sending sparks shooting into the gloomy workshop interiors.

The lane ends at a busy intersection. Take the second lane, **Souk Cherratine**, on the right (not to be confused with the signed Souk Attarine, the first lane on the right after exiting the metalworkers' area). This one is lined with woollen and leather goods. Walk down, past the right-hand turning leading to the slipper souk, and on the right at No.8 is a friendly beltmaker producing leather and kilim-covered belts.

Continue down Souk Cherratine and take the first right on to **Souk El-Kebir** (p53). Shortly, on the right at No.161, is bookbinder **Hassan Makchad** (0670 72 52 84). He has a

colourful selection of leather- and suede-bound notebooks and picture frames. These can also be made to order, or embossed with the text or design of your choice.

Proceed along Souk El-Kebir until you pass under a square arch (look back and you'll see a sign 'Souk des Sacochiers'). You are now entering the **Kissaria** (p53), heart of the souks, and there are several turnings through arches into parallel lanes on the right.

Turn down the first right-hand lane to **Ahmed El Hallaj**'s workshop (no phone), where he produces leather boots using kilims and hides at the first stall on the left. The place is overflowing with boots in various styles and kilims, but if you don't see what you fancy he'll happily make a pair for you.

Heading back to Souk El-Kebir, continue to the next right and walk through **Souk Herrarine**, the leather souk. The leathersmiths' workshops are dotted among the shops that all tend to carry the same colourful styles. Look for friendly

Abdel's shop (no phone) about halfway down on the right – all the locals know him – for a large selection and a few laughs. If he doesn't have what you're looking for, he'll find it while you sip tea in the shop.

Further on, Souk Herrarine joins the **Souk des Babouches** (p59). Turn left and left again when Souk des Babouches emerges into another lane, **Souk Attarine**, a main throughfare, opposite the door of a mosque. You'll eventually arrive at the junction with another main lane. This one is **Souk Semarine** (p52), and you should bear right to continue in the same southerly direction.

If you need a break, follow the sign pointing to the **Café des Epices** (p63) on the left. This relaxed café is on the left, just after you emerge into open-air **Rahba Kedima** (p53). Ground-floor tables are good for people-watching – this square is full of spice merchants, magic supply shops and women crocheting hats. The first floor is for lounging and the top terrace for looking over untidy rooftops. This square is the place to pick up a straw basket, either plain or with sparkly sequins or needlework.

Back on Souk Semarine, opposite the turning to the Café des Épices, is a sign pointing right to 'Petit Souk' and 'Kissariat Bennis'. At No.4, next to a normal-looking tailor, is the tiny cubicle of **Ali Baddou** (0667 49 27 88). He stocks some traditional clothes, but he's best known for his talent for copying whatever shirts you might want to bring him.

Turn right out of this small arcade and continue down Souk Semarine. At No.12, on the left side is **Youssef Lazrak**'s store (no phone) where he sells traditional cotton men's shirts and *gandouras* (the plainer male equivalent of the kaftan, useful as a luxurious nightshirt). Be prepared for some fairly determined haggling.

Café de France

Continue down Souk Semarine and immediately after the patisserie stalls on the right you'll see an arch with the dates 1357/1938 etched into the plasterwork. This is Kissariat El-Ahbass and at the first stall on the left **Hamid** sells higher-quality tunics and kimono-style jackets than you'll find on the main Souk Semarine.

Souk Semarine ends as it passes under an arch. A left turn here will lead you into bustling **place Bab Fteuh**. Just after Pharmacie Place Bab Fteuh on the right is a narrow passage. Follow this and head up the stairs to the left which lead to a mezzanine. At the back you'll see the **Boutique Bel Hadj** (22-23 Fundouk Ourzazi, place Bab Fteuh). Owner Mohammed Bari is a sweet guy with an overflowing shop filled with bits and pieces of jewellery and tribal pendants, including an enormous selection of beads in every size, shape, colour and material. Pick the beads that you like and he'll thread them into a bracelet or necklace while you wait.

From Bab Fteuh, follow the small passageway south to return to Jemaa El Fna. Mark the end of your souk safari by a cool refreshment and some people-watching at the **Café de France** (p45).

Marrakech by Area

Jemaa El Fna

Jemaa El Fna & Around

The soul of Marrakech lies in the amorphous form of Jemaa El Fna, marketplace and forum to the city almost since its foundation. It's an urban clearing, as irregular in shape as an accident of nature, and thronged day and night with a carnival of local life.

Two hundred metres to the west, the towering square minaret of the Koutoubia Mosque is the city's pre-eminent landmark and most recognisable icon. It is not actually very high (77 metres, 252 feet), but thanks to topography and a local ordinance that forbids other Medina buildings to rise above the height of a palm tree, it towers majestically over its surroundings.

To the west of the mosque lies the La Mamounia hotel and its deservedly famous gardens, which were established in the 18th century and pre-date the hotel.

Jemaa El Fna

The best place to be at any time of the day is in among the mayhem of the square (watch your wallet and bags), but if it's time for a rest and a bird's eye view, several of the peripheral cafés and restaurants have upper terraces with fine ringside seating, among them the **Café de France** and **Argana** and – with the best view of the lot – the **Café Glacier** above the Hotel CTM.

Sights & museums

Jemaa El Fna

Map p43 D2 ➊

The square is as old as Marrakech itself. It was laid out as a parade ground by the Almoravids, the founders of Marrakech, in front of their royal fortress (Dar El-Hajar). When the succeeding Almohads built a new palace

Jemaa El Fna & Koutoubia

Legend
- **1** Sights & museums
- **1** Eating & drinking
- **1** Shopping
- **1** Nightlife
- **1** Arts & leisure

Mosque

RUE DES BANQUES

Mosque

Bab Fteuh

Jemaa El Fna

Sidi Moulay el Ksour

RUE DE LA KOUTOUBIA

Place de Foucault

RUE MOULAY ISMAIL

RUE OQBA BEN NAFIA

RUE BAB AGNAOU

French Consulate

RUE FATIMA ZOHRA

RUE JEBEL LAKHDAR

RUE SIDI EL YAMAMI

Koutoubia Mosque

AVENUE BAB JEDID

Tomb of Youssef Ben Tachfine

RIAD ZITOUN EL KEDIM

RUE IBN RACHID

EL KEDIM

Ensemble Artisanal

AVENUE MOHAMMED V

RUE EL ABBAS SEBTI

Cyber Park
Arset Moulay Abdelsalam

Swimming Pools

RUE ABOU

Mamounia

Mamounia Gardens

200 m
200 yds

© Copyright Time Out Group 2015

One day on the square

Jemaa El Fna from morning to night.

During the early part of the day, the square is relatively quiet. The orange-laden carts of the juice-sellers line the perimeter, but otherwise there's only a scattering of figures, seated on boxes or rugs, under large shabby umbrellas. The snake-charmers are early starters with their black, rubbery reptiles laid out in front or sheltered under large drums. For a few dirhams visitors can have a photo taken with a large snake draped over their shoulders. Gaudily clad water-sellers wander around offering to pose for dirhams. Other figures may be dentists (teeth pulled on the spot), scribes (letters written to order), herbalists (good for whatever ails you) or beggars. Overlooking all, the prime morning spot for unhurried businessmen and traders is the patio of the landmark **Café de France** (p45), on the square for the last 50 years.

The action tends to wilt beneath the heat of the afternoon sun, when snake-charmers, dancers and acrobats can barely manage to stir themselves for camera-carrying tourists. It's not until dusk that things really kick off.

As the light fades, ranks of makeshift kitchens set up with tables, benches and hissing flames, constituting one great open-air restaurant where adventurous eaters can snack on anything from snails to sheep's heads (see box p49).

Beside the avenues of food stalls, the rest of the square takes on the air of a circus. Visiting Berber farmers and their families join Medina locals in crowding around the assorted performers. These typically include troupes of cartoon-costumed acrobats, musicians and their prowling transvestite dancers, fortune tellers, henna artists, magicians, and underage boxers. The visitors who provided the *raison d'être* for the afternoon entertainers are less dominant in this more surreal evening scene. Come midnight the food stalls begin to pack up, the performers wind down, and the crowds thin. Along with some gay cruisers, only the musicians remain, attended by wild-eyed devotees giddy on hash and repetitive rhythms.

to the south, the open ground passed to the public and became what it is today – a place for gathering, trading, entertainment and even the occasional riot. The name (pronounced with its consonants tumbling into each other to come out something like 'jemaf'na') is said to refer to its former role as a venue for executions, with the decapitated heads put up on spikes for public display.

Uncontained, disorderly, untainted by grandeur or pomp, untameable by council or committee, Jemaa El Fna is nothing less than bedlam. During the 1970s, the municipality attempted to impose order with a scheme to turn it into a car park. This was opposed and defeated. Since then, thanks in part to the lobbying efforts of Spanish writer Juan Goytisolo (who has lived just off the square since the late 1970s), Jemaa El Fna – and its heady mix of commerce and entertainment – has been recognised by UNESCO as part of mankind's cultural heritage and its preservation is secured.

For a day in the life of the square, see box p44. For eating, see box p49.

Eating & drinking

Argana

Jemaa El Fna (0524 44 53 50). **Open** Closed at time of writing. **Café. Map** p43 D1 ❷

Something of a Marrakech icon, even more so after a bomb detonated here in 2011, killing 17, this café on the edge of Jemaa El Fna was a perennial favourite, its terrace providing ringside seats on the action in the square below. At the time of writing, it was set to reopen after repairs. Stairs at the back of the ground-floor café lead up to two floors of terrace serving three-course set menus or à la carte salads, tagines and *brochettes*, but many just call in for an ice-cream and some people-watching.

Café de France

Jemaa El Fna (no phone). **Open** 6am-11pm daily. No credit cards. **Café. Map** p43 E2 ❸

The most famous of Marrakech cafés boasts a prime location and terrace fronting right on the main square. No one knows exactly how old the place is, but it crops up in Peter Mayne's *A Year in Marrakesh*, written in the early 1950s, and it's a classic meeting point for locals from first light to sundown, with tourists stopping in for a breather and a strong shot of *café noir* (espresso Arabica) or *nouss nouss* (half espresso, half steamed milk) throughout the day. Expect surly service.

Pâtisserie des Princes

32 rue Bab Agnaou (0524 44 30 33). **Open** 5am-11.30pm daily. No credit cards. **Café. Map** p43 xx ❹

A weak-kneed wobble from Jemaa El Fna, this place offers gloriously icy air-conditioning in a dim coldstore of a back room. It may sound gloomy, but, the hotel swimming pool aside, there's no better retreat on a sweltering afternoon. The front of house is taken up by glass cabinets filled with fine cakes and pastries, to be accompanied by cappuccino, English tea, orange juice or shakes. There's a large salon upstairs.

Le Salama

40 rue des Banques (0524 39 13 00, www.lesalama.com). **Open** 12.30pm-1.30am daily. **£££.** Alcohol served. **Moroccan & tapas. Map** p43 D2 ❺

Spread over three floors, this is the only spot on the square where you can combine proper cocktails (they make a mean whisky sour) on the rooftop with 360° views over the city, before heading downstairs into a romantic dining room lit by a sea of giant, pierced-metal lanterns. Part of the Fakir Collection, owned by local entrepreneur Nourredine Fakir, this is where you'll find movers and shakers like Paloma Picasso and Roberto Cavalli when they're in town, feasting on superlative traditional Moroccan dishes including a sensational lamb *mechouia* (spiced and slow-cooked over wood) served by handsome waiting staff in velvet robes. There's a daily happy hour (4.30pm-1am).

Tiznit

Souk El-Kassabine no.28 (0524 42 72 04, mobile 0668 10 04 92). Open 8am-midnight daily. **£.** No credit cards.
Moroccan. Map p43 E1 ⑥

Tucked away in the far north-eastern corner of Jemaa El Fna, Tiznit is one of the few deeply authentic places left on the square. Climb the narrow staircase and you'll discover a tiny little dining room clad in white tiles and lit by fluorescent strip bulbs, where photos of the royal family decorate the walls and small mountains of tagines are piled up behind the kitchen counter. The robust flavours of thick chunks of lamb and potato and the house special, rabbit with caramelised onions and raisins, is as authentic as it comes, lovingly prepared by a smiling father and son team. No alcohol.

Around the Koutoubia Mosque

The minaret of the Koutoubia Mosque – Marrakech's most famous symbol – is visible from near and far. It's possible to walk around either side of the Koutoubia, clockwise between the main entrance and the wall that encloses the grounds of the French Consulate, or anti-clockwise along the top of the Almohad ruins. Either route leads into the orange-tree-filled **Koutoubia Gardens**, which spread south and west of the mosque. Across avenue Houman El-Fetouaki, south of the gardens, a high wall cuts from sight a modest crenellated building; this is the **Tomb of Youssef Ben Tachfine**, founder of Marrakech. A padlocked gate ensures that the great desert warrior rests in peace, his mausoleum off-limits to the public.

Sunken areas on the plaza outside the mosque are the remains of

reservoirs that belonged to the Dar El-Hajar, a fortress built by city founder Youssef Ben Tachfine towards the end of the 11th century, and the first permanent structure in the encampment that became Marrakech. The fortress was short-lived, destroyed by the conquering Almohads who replaced it with the site's first mosque. The small white-domed structure on the plaza is the **Koubba of Lalla Zohra**, a shrine that used to be open to the public until the inebriated son of a former city mayor ploughed his car into the structure and, as part of the repairs, the door was sealed up.

Koutoubia Mosque

Map p43 B2 ⑦

The mosque is one of the city's oldest buildings. The original structure, built in 1147, was demolished because it was not correctly aligned with Mecca. It was rebuilt, and its new minaret was constructed more than half a century later under the patronage of the Almohad Caliph Yacoub El-Mansour.

The name Koutoubia is derived from *elkoutoubiyyin* – Arabic for booksellers – since a booksellers' market once filled the surrounding streets. The mosque's exterior is of red stone, but it's thought to have originally been covered with plaster. The tower is 13m (43ft) wide. Six rooms, one above the other, constitute the interior; leading around them is a ramp by way of which the muezzin could reach the balcony – it was supposed to be wide enough for him to ride a horse to the top. The Koutoubia is built in a traditional Almohad style and the minaret is topped with four copper globes; according to legend, these were originally made of pure gold. There were also supposed to have been only three of them: it is said that the fourth was donated by the wife of Yacoub El-Mansour as compensation for failing to keep the Ramadan fast by eating four grapes. As penance, she had her gold jewellery melted down to fashion

Koutoubia Mosque

the fourth globe. Hardly more credible is the claim that only blind muezzins were employed because a sighted person would have been able to gaze into the royal harem from the minaret.

Eating & drinking

Gastro MK

14 derb Sebaai, Bab Laksour (0524 37 61 73, www.maisonmk.com). **Open** 7.30-10.30pm Mon, Tue, Thur-Sun. **£££**. Alcohol served. **Modern Moroccan**. Map p43 C1 ⑧

The set-menu-only supper club at funky boutique hotel Maison MK is a breath of fresh air on the Marrakech dining scene and one of the first to embrace a modern Moroccan cuisine. Chef Omar combines the sweet spices and exotic flavours of his native cuisine with contemporary techniques learned at the hands of Andrew West, who trained in Gordan Ramsay's kitchens, resulting in some of the most innovative dining in the Medina. It starts with cocktails and canapés on the roof and segues downstairs into dishes such as cream of artichoke soup swirled with nutty-sweet argan oil, deconstructed chicken b'stilla and pan-fried duck crusted with sweet spices. Food lovers looking for a taste of the new wave need look no further.

Grand Tazi

Hotel Grand Tazi, corner of avenue El-Mouahidine & rue Bab Agnaou (0524 44 27 87). **Open** 7-11pm daily. No credit cards. **Bar**. Map p43 D3 ⑨

The Tazi is something of a Marrakchi institution – it used to be the only place in the central Medina where the weary and footsore could kick back with a cheap beer. Times have changed, but it's still the cheapest place in town for a Special Flag (the local brew) and, despite its rather gloomy interior (the roof terrace is better), it's still has a nostalgic cult following if you're not too fussy about the company you keep and don't care about designer surrounds.

Jardins de la Koutoubia

26 rue de la Koutoubia (0524 38 88 00). **Open** 12.30-4pm, 7.30-10.30pm daily. **££. Moroccan-Mediterranean**. Map p43 C2 ⑩

Tucked away behind the garden centre on the Jemaa El Fna, this modern riad is set around a vast swimming pool (open to non-guests for 200dh per day) and makes a lovely setting for a light lunch that combines traditional Moroccan dishes with French bistro fare. Daily staples such as freshly made soups, a hearty *haricot vert* salad or a classic club sandwich served by liveried waiters lend a *soupçon* of glamour to the whole affair. Details like a single rose on the table, deeply comfortable chairs and a well-stocked bar – remember Dubonnet? – have kept it something of a secret hideaway among resident expats, and there's also a decent Indian restaurant on the roof. See also p161.

Portofino

279 avenue Mohammed V (0524 39 16 65, www.portofinomarrakech.com). Open noon-11pm daily. **££. Italian**. Map p43 C2 ⑪

Located at street level below the Pizzeria Venezia, this contemporary rival to its upstairs neighbour wins out for serving excellent pizzas cooked in a proper, wood-fired oven, along with decent pasta dishes and, occasionally, excellent fresh fish). With large-screen TVs, it's popular for watching sports and wouldn't look out of place in any of Europe's big cities; its hangar-like proportions make it great for gathering a crowd. Service can be painfully slow, but comes with a smile.

Rock 'N' Kech

NEW *Rue Fatima Zohra (mobile 0643 22 14 70).* Open 5pm-2am daily. **Bar**. Map p43 C2 ⑫

This newcomer to the Medina scene is a breath of fresh air among the rather more salubrious places to cadge a beer. The charcoal grey terrace with black planters, parasols and palm trees has

Square meals

How, and what, to eat on Jemaa El Fna.

Dinner on Jemaa El Fna is one of the highlights of any trip to Marrakech. As the sun sets, musicians, snake-charmers, acrobats, dancers, dentists, herbalists and henna ladies shift their pitches to accommodate the arrival of massed butane gas canisters, trestle tables and tilly lamps. With well-practised efficiency, it takes only an hour to set up 100 food stalls in tightly drawn rows, with benches for diners, strings of lights overhead and masses of food in the middle. Stallholders fire up griddles and the smoke drifts and curls to create a hazy pall over what must be one of the world's biggest open-air eateries.

Most stalls specialise in one particular dish. Sveral places do good business in *harira* (a thick soup of lamb, lentils and chickpeas flavoured with herbs and veg); similarly popular are grilled *brochettes* (kebab), *kefta* (minced, spiced lamb) and *merguez* (spicy sausage; stall no.31 apparently sells the best in all Morocco). Families perch on benches around stalls selling boiled sheep heads, scooping out the jellyish gloop with small plastic forks. Elsewhere are deep-fried fish and eels, chickpeas drizzled with oil, and mashed potato sandwiches, while a row of stalls along the south side have great mounds of snails, cooked in a broth flavoured with thyme, pepper and lemon. Humblest of the lot is the stallholder selling nothing more than hard-boiled eggs.

Menus and prices hang above some of the stalls, but not all. It's easy enough to just point, and prices are so low that they're hardly worth worrying about. Etiquette is basic: walk around, see something you like, squeeze in between fellow diners. Discs of bread serve instead of cutlery. For the thirsty, orange juice is fetched from one of the many juice stalls that ring the perimeter of the square.

The food is fresh and prepared in front of the waiting diners. Few germs will survive the charcoal grilling or boiling oil; plates and dishes are a different matter. The single same bucket of water is used to wash up all night, so ask for the food to be served on paper, but don't be put off – this is one experience not to miss out on.

top: Jardins de
la Koutoubia p48;
bottom: Rock 'N' Kech p48

a modest buzz, fabulous views of the Koutoubia minaret and plays decent music, and the drinks are reasonably priced. All of which is something of a rarity in a country where you pay a premium for alcohol. The Magaluf go-kart course fake black rock walls need a serious rethink, though.

Tobsil

22 derb Abdellah Ben Hessaien, Bab Ksour (0524 44 40 52). **Open** 7.30-11pm Mon, Wed-Sun. **£££**. Alcohol served. **Moroccan**. **Map** p43 C1 ⑬

Considered by some to be Marrakech's premier traditional restaurant, Tobsil offers a lesson in local gastronomy. There is no menu. On being led by a uniformed flunkey to the door (the place is otherwise impossible to find), diners are greeted by owner Christine Rio, then seated either downstairs in the courtyard or upstairs in the galleries to await an extravagant and seemingly never-ending succession of courses. Aperitifs (included in the price of the meal, as is the wine) are rapidly followed by a swarm of small Moroccan salads, pigeon *b'stilla* (a crisp, flaky pastry pie dusted with icing sugar and cinnamon), followed by something like a lamb tagine with fresh figs, couscous, and finally fruit and tea or coffee accompanied by an array of cakes or pastries. Chef Fatima Mountassamim's cooking is delicious and the experience is well worth having to get a sense of that legendary Moroccan hospitality, but be sure to come hungry.

Shopping

Ensemble Artisanal

Avenue Mohammed V (0524 38 66 74). **Open** 8.30am-7.30pm daily. **Map** p43 B1 ⑭

The second major tourist stop after photo ops at the Koutoubia, the Artisanal Ensemble is another state-sponsored crafts mini-mall like the Centre Artisanal in the Kasbah district

– but far more popular because of its central location. All the artisans selling within are purportedly here by royal appointment, selected as the best in their field (a licence therefore to charge higher prices, which are non-negotiable). Expect everything from fine embroidered table linen (first floor at the back) to jewellery, clothing, lamps and even knock-off European handbags.

Mamounia Gardens

To the west of the Koutoubia Mosque along avenue Bab Jedid lies the **La Mamounia** hotel (p161) and its beautiful gardens. The world-famous hotel began its life with just 50 rooms, but expanded and was remodelled over the years. Its last grand renovation was in 2006, and now it's back to attracting Hollywood stars (Gwyneth Paltrow and Nicole Kidman, to name just two). The hotel takes its name from the gardens, the **Arset El-Mamoun** (Mamounia Gardens), which pre-date it by more than a century.

Mamounia Gardens

Admission free with hotel lunch, dinner or refreshments. **Map** p43 A3 ⑮

The Mamounia Gardens were established in the 18th century by Crown Prince Moulay Mamoun on land gifted to him by his father, the sultan, on the occasion of his wedding. A central pavilion served as a princely residence, occasionally lent out to visiting diplomats. The gardens are designed in traditional style, on an axis, with walkways, flowerbeds, orange groves and olive trees. Non-residents who want to enjoy their splendour can visit for a buffet lunch at the poolside restaurant, take afternoon tea at Le Menzeh tea and ice-cream pavilion in the gardens, or on the back terrace overlooking the gardens, stop by the Majorelle or Churchill bars for cocktails, or indulge in an expensive dinner in French, Italian or Moroccan style. No jeans or shorts.

Souks & Northern Medina

North of Jemaa El Fna are the souks, with alleyway upon alleyway of tiny retail cubicles. This is commerce at its most intoxicating – a riot of strong colours, seductive shapes and rampant exoticism. In the most heavily touristed areas, the overwhelming number of shops is offset by the fact that most seem compelled to offer the same goods. But the further into the souks you venture, the more interesting they become – our reviews here pick out some of the highlights.

The two main routes in are rue Semarine and rue Mouassine; the former offers a full-on bazaar blast, the latter is a more sedate path leading to choice boutiques. In fact, Mouassine is now the smartest part of the Medina. To the north are several of the city's holy shrines; to the west, the high walls of the Dar El-Bacha lead on to rue Bab Doukkala and one of the Medina's gates. To the east, a very different experience awaits: the sights and (strong) smells of the tanneries.

The souks

The entrance to **rue Semarine** (aka **Souk Semarine**) is via an elaborate arch, partially obscured by tat, one block north of Jemaa El Fna – reached via either the spice market or the egg market, both pungent experiences, one pleasant, the other not. Semarine is a relatively orderly street, broad and straight with smart new overhead trellising dappling the paving with light and shadow.

Every section of the souk has its own speciality and here it has traditionally been textiles, although these days cloth merchants have been largely supplanted by souvenir shops. About 150 metres (500 feet) along, the first alley off to the east leads to a wedge-shaped open area known as the **Rahba Kedima**, or the 'old place'. The way between Semarine and the Rahba Kedima leads to a small court, the **Souk Laghzel**, formerly the wool market but now a car-boot sale of a souk where women – and only women – come to sell meagre possessions such as a single knitted shawl or a bag of vegetables. It is also lined with medicine stalls draped in the dead skins of assorted African animals.

The Rahba Kedima used to be the city's open-air corn market but it's now given over to an intriguing mix of raffia bags and baskets, woollen hats and cooked snails. Around the edges are spice and 'magic' stalls and these days a handful of super-cool Medina cafés such as **Nomad** and the **Café des Epices**, both with roof terraces from where you can watch the action in peace.

The upper storeys of the shops on the northern side of the Rahba Kedima are usually hung with carpets and textiles, an invitation to search for the passageway that leads through to the **Criée Berbère**. These days this partially roofed, slightly gloomy section of the souk is the lair of the rug merchants, but until well into the 20th century it was used for the sale of slaves, auctioned here three times weekly.

Nearby, **Riad Yima** is the shop-cum-studio of Marrakech artist Hassan Hajjaj, now celebrated internationally for his bright, pop-art photography using local Medina hipsters as his models. His latest work is a short film featuring the henna ladies of Jemaa El Fna, but it's worth stopping by here to pick up some one-off originals including pierced beaten metal lanterns, flour-sack babouches and funky tees emblazoned with Arabic calligraphy. You can also arrange to have lunch here with a bit of advance planning, and there's always a pot of mint tea on the go.

Back on rue Semarine, just north of the turning for the Rahba Kedima, the street forks: branching to the left is the **Souk El-Attarin**, straight on is the **Souk El-Kebir** (Great Souk). Between the two is a ladder of narrow, arrow-straight passages, collectively known as the Kissaria. This is the beating heart of the souk. Stallholders here specialise in cotton, clothing, kaftans and blankets.

Further along the Souk El-Kebir are the courtyards of carpenters and wood turners, before a T-junction forces a choice: left or right. Go left and then immediately right at the shop selling predominantly red pottery and with a téléboutique sign above to emerge once again into streets that are wide enough for the passage of cars.

Just north is the dusty open plaza of **place Ben Youssef**, dominated by the Ben Youssef Mosque, which is easily identifiable by its bright green pyramidal roofs. The original mosque went up in the 12th century and was the grandest of the age, but what stands now is a third and lesser incarnation, dating from the early 19th century. Non-Muslims may not enter. However, in the immediate vicinity of the mosque is a cluster of tourist-friendly sights, including the decidedly average **Musée de Marrakech**, the enchanting **Ben Youssef Medersa** and the venerable **Koubba El-Badiyin**.

East of the Ben Youssef Medersa, between the place Ben Youssef and the place du Moqf is the **Maison de la Photographie**, a handsome townhouse that showcases photographic works from the period 1870 to 1950, and serves a top-notch, three-course lunch menu for 90dh.

Back at the fork on rue Semarine, bearing left brings you on to **Souk El-Attarin**, or the Spice Souk. Contrary to the name, this part of the souk no longer deals in spices. Instead, its traders largely traffic

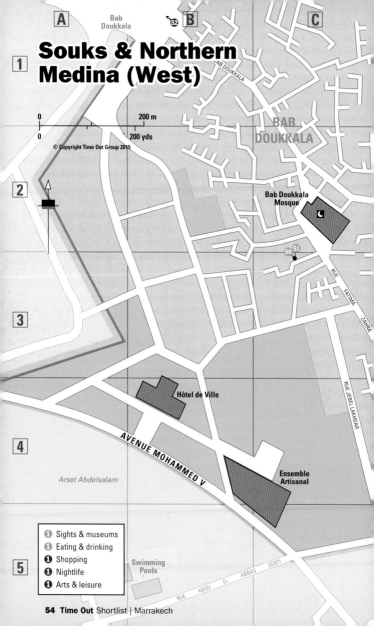

Souks & Northern Medina (West)

A1 Bab Doukkala

B1 52

A2

B2 BAB DOUKKALA

Bab Doukkala Mosque

C2

RUE FATIMA ZAHRA

50 51

RUE JEBEL LAKHDAR

Hôtel de Ville

AVENUE MOHAMMED V

Ensemble Artisanal

Arset Abdelsalam

- ❶ Sights & museums
- ❶ Eating & drinking
- ❶ Shopping
- ❶ Nightlife
- ❶ Arts & leisure

Swimming Pools

RUE ABOU EL ABBAS SEBTI

0   200 m
0   200 yds

© Copyright Time Out Group 2015

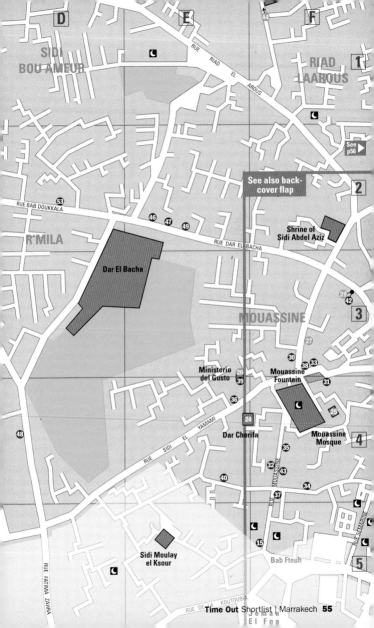

SIDI
BOU AMEUR

RIAD
LAAROUS

RUE RIAD EL AROUS

See ▶
p56

RUE BAB DOUKKALA

53

R'MILA

46 47 49

RUE DAR EL BACHA

See also back-
cover flap

Shrine of
Sidi Abdel Aziz

Dar El Bacha

29
42

MOUASSINE

27

30 38 33

Ministerio
del Gusto

26
39

Mouassine
Fountain

31

36

48

RUE SIDI EL YAMAMI

24

25

Dar Cherifa

35

Mouassine
Mosque

32 43

34

40

37

RUE SMARINE

RUE MOUASSINE

15

Sidi Moulay
el Ksour

RUE FATIMA ZAHRA

Bab Fteuh

RUE DERB EL KOUTOUBIA

Jemaa
El Fna

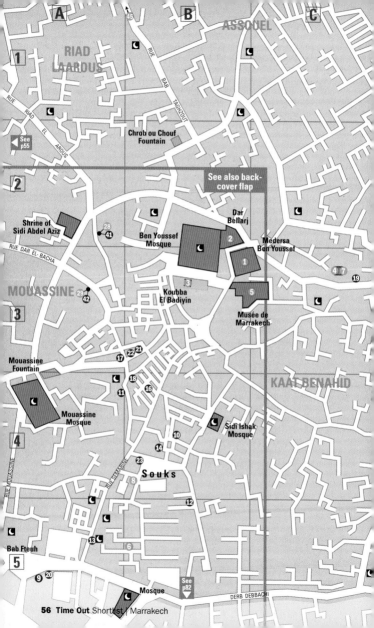

ASSOUEL

A

B

C

1

RIAD
LAARDUS

RUE BAB TAGHZOUT

RUE RIAD EL ARDUS

See
p55

Chrob ou Chouf
Fountain

See also back-
cover flap

2

Shrine of
Sidi Abdel Aziz

Dar
Bellarj

28
41

Ben Youssef
Mosque

2

Medersa
Ben Youssef

RUE DAR EL-BACHA

1

4 7   19

MOUASSINE

29
42

3

Koubba
El Badiyin

5

Musée de
Marrakech

3

Mouassine
Fountain

22 21
17

KAAT BENAHID

18

11

16

Mouassine
Mosque

Sidi Ishak
Mosque

10

4

14

23

RUE SEMARINE

8

Souks

12

RUE MOUASSINE

13

6

Bab Fteuh

5

9 20

Mosque

See
p82

DERB DEBBACHI

56 Time Out Shortlist *Marrakech*

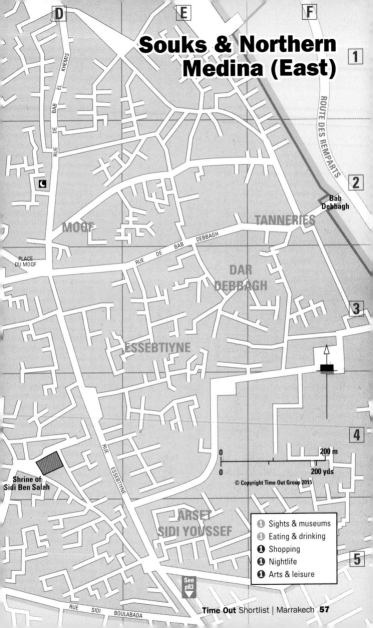

Souks & Northern Medina (East)

D **E** **F**

1

ROUTE DES REMPARTS

RUE DE BAB EL KHEMIS

2

Bab Debbagh

TANNERIES

MOQF

PLACE DU MOQF

RUE DE BAB DEBBAGH

DAR DEBBAGH

3

ESSEBTIYNE

4

| 0 | | 200 m |
| 0 | | 200 yds |

© Copyright Time Out Group 2015

RUE ESSEBTIYNE

Shrine of Sidi Ben Salah

ARSET SIDI YOUSSEF

See p83 ▼

| ❶ Sights & museums |
| ❶ Eating & drinking |
| ❶ Shopping |
| ❶ Nightlife |
| ❶ Arts & leisure |

5

RUE SIDI BOULABADA

top: Souk des Teinturiers;
bottom: spices & metalwork

in tourist tat, from painted wooden thingummies to leather whatchamacallits. Almost opposite the subdued entrance to a workaday mosque is the **Souk des Babouches**, a whole alley devoted to soft-leather slippers – and their almost identical synthetic counterparts. Further along Attarin, distant ringing hammer blows announce the **Souk Haddadin**, the quarter of the ironworkers. One of the most medieval parts of the souk, it's full of dark, cavern-like workshops in which firework bursts of orange sparks briefly illuminate tableaux of grime-streaked craftsmen, like some scene by Doré.

West of Attarin three alleys run downhill into the **Souk des Teinturiers**, which is the area of the dyers' workshops. Labourers rub dyes into cured hides (to be cut and fashioned into babouches) and dunk wool into vats of dark-hued liquids. This results in brightly coloured sheafs of wool that are then hung over the alleyways in a manner irresistible to passing photographers. It also results in the labourers having arms coloured to their elbows. You know you're nearing this part of the souk when you start seeing people with blue or purple arms. The three alleys converge into one, which then doglegs between a squeeze of assorted artisans' salesrooms (lanterns, metalwork and pottery) before exiting under an arch beside the Mouassine fountain and mosque.

Sights & museums

Ben Youssef Medersa

Place Ben Youssef (0524 44 18 93).
Open 9am-6pm daily. **Admission** 50dh; 30dh under-12s. Combined entrance with the Musée de Marrakech 60dh. No credit cards. **Map** p56 B3 ➊
A *medersa* (or *madrasa*) is a Quranic school, dedicated to the teaching of Islamic scripture and law. This one was founded in the 14th century, then enlarged in 1564 by the Saadian Sultan Abdellah El-Ghalib. It was given a further polishing up in the 1990s, courtesy of the Ministry of Culture. Entrance is via a long, cool passageway leading to the great courtyard, a serene place (before the four tour parties arrive) centred on a water-filled basin. The surrounding façades are decorated with zelije tiling, stucco and carved cedar, all executed with restraint. At the far side is the domed prayer hall with the richest of decoration, notably around the mihrab, the arched niche that indicates the direction of Mecca. Back in the entrance vestibule, passageways and two flights of stairs lead to more than 100 tiny windowless students' chambers, clustered about small internal lightwells. Medieval as it seems, the *medersa* was still in use until as recently as 1962. The building stood in for an Algerian Sufi retreat in Gillies Mackinnon's 1998 film *Hideous Kinky*.

Dar Bellarj

7-9 rue Toulat Zaouiat Lahdar (0524 44 45 55, www.darbellarj.org).
Open 9.30am-12.30pm, 2-5.30pm Mon-Sat. **Admission** free.
Map p56 B2 ➋
North of the entrance to the Ben Youssef Medersa is a large wooden door in the crook of the alley emblazoned with a bird's head: this is Dar Bellarj, the 'Stork's House', so called because it was formerly a hospital for the big white birds. The stork is holy to Marrakech. There are countless tales to explain its exalted status. The most commonly repeated is of a local imam, dressed in traditional Moroccan garb of white djellaba and black robe, drunk on wine, who then compounds the sin by climbing the minaret and blaspheming. Man suffers the wrath of God and is transformed into a stork. Even before the arrival of Islam, an old Berber belief held that storks are actually transformed humans.

Restored in 1999, Dar Bellarj now serves as a local cultural centre hosting rotating exhibitions, workshops and musical performances. Unless you're lucky enough to drop in on a happening there's little to see; the chalk white and taupe courtyard is very attractive with seating, and sweet tea is offered to visitors; it makes the perfect respite stop in this busy corner of the Medina.

Koubba El-Badiyin

Place Ben Youssef. Currently closed. **Map** p56 B3 ❸

Across from the Ben Youssef Mosque, set in its own fenced enclosure and sunk several metres below the current street level, is the Koubba El-Badiyin (also known as the Koubba Almoravide). It looks unprepossessing, but its unearthing in 1948 prompted one French art historian to exclaim that 'the art of Islam has never exceeded the splendour of this extraordinary dome.' It's the only surviving structure from the era of the Almoravids, the founders of Marrakech, and as such it represents a wormhole back to the origins of Moorish building history, presenting for the first time many of the shapes and forms that remain the basis of the North African architectural vocabulary. It dates from the reign of Ali Ben Youssef (1107-43) and was probably part of the ablutions complex of the original Ben Youssef Mosque.

The Koubba is currently closed. If it reopens, it's worth descending the brickwork steps and viewing the underside of the dome, which is a kaleidoscopic arrangement of a floral motif within an octagon within an eight-pointed star.

Maison de la Photographie

46 rue Ahl Fès, off rue Bin Lafnadek (0524 38 57 21, www.maisondela photographie.ma). **Open** 9.30am-7pm daily. **Admission** 40dh; free under-12s. **Map** p56 C3 ❹

Patrick Manac'h's passion is plain for all to see. The photography aficionado

has amassed a collection of 8,000 images that span the substantial period from 1870 to 1950; the collection, shown in rotating exhibitions, offers fascinating glimpses into the past. After surveying the collection – all original prints – climb to the top terrace for reviving drinks and a meal before trying to secure that winning shot: the museum's top terrace has a 270° elevated view of the city and the Atlas mountains beyond.

Musée de Marrakech

Place Ben Youssef (0524 44 18 93, www.museedemarrakech.ma). **Open** 9am-6pm daily. **Admission** 50dh; 30dh under-12s. Combined entrance with the Ben Youssef Medersa 60dh. No credit cards. **Map** p56 B/C3 ❺

Inaugurated in 1997, the Musée de Marrakech is a conversion of an opulent early 20th-century house formerly belonging to a Marrakchi grandee. Entering the outer courtyard, there's a pleasant café off to one side. Within the museum, poorly curated and rag-tag exhibits rotate. The star attraction is the building itself, particularly the tartishly tiled great central court, roofed over and hung with an enormous chandelier like the mothership from *Close Encounters of the Third Kind*. The former hammam is lovely, with attractive decorative flourishes. If nothing else, the museum is a cool refuge from the blazing heat.

Riad Yima

52 derb Aarjane (mobile 0667 23 09 95, www.riadyima.com). **Open** 9am-6pm daily. No credit cards. **Map** p56 B5 ❻

The home-cum-gallery-cum-shop-cum-tearoom of acclaimed Marrakchi artist Hassan Hajjaj is tucked away behind the place Rahba Kedima (if you struggle to find it, give them a call and someone will come and get you). Though Hajjaj is primarily based in London, he can occasionally be found at work here, most recently on a film about the henna women of Jemaa El Fna. His

Ben Youssef Medersa p59

Maison de la Photographie p60, & Café

photographs in his trademark striking bright colours and custom-made outfits fashioned from vintage textiles have been the subject of a travelling exhibition that has roved from New York to Dubai. But this is still the best place to see them, or indeed any of his quirky pieces, including pierced sardine-can lanterns, eye-popping plastic kilims and Arabic Coca-Cola crate benches. His pop-art reworking of retro Morocco has been much imitated, but it's still well worth seeking out the genuine article.

Eating & drinking

Café at Maison de la Photographie

46 rue Ahl Fès, off rue Bin Lafnadek (0524 38 57 21, www. maisondelaphotographie.ma). **Open** 9.30am-7pm daily. **£**. No credit cards. **Café/Moroccan**. Map p56 C3 **7**

As well as being an absorbing gallery (p60) showcasing documentary photography in Morocco, this is also one of the Medina's best-kept secrets as a lunch spot. The L-shaped, bamboo-shaded roof terrace has sensational views of the Atlas mountains, and a keenly priced menu du jour offering authentic Berber home-cooking. The menu changes daily and with the seasons, but keeps it simple: soups and salads to start, impeccable tagines and couscous for mains, and lovely desserts such as creamy own-made yoghurt and strawberries.

Nomad

NEW *Place Rahba Kedima (0524 38 16 09, www.nomadmarrakech.com).* **Open** 9am-10pm daily. **££**. No credit cards. Alcohol served. **Café/Moroccan**. Map p56 B4 **8**

Kamal Laftimi's latest project is, like Le Jardin (p70), multifunctional. The ground floor doubles as a modern deli, run by Chabi Chic and selling local ingredients such as preserved lemons and beautifully packaged Atlas olive oil, as well as kitchen tools like olive wood spoons. Upstairs, the space is divided into a chill-out zone under a white rippling roof, and adjacent dining area padded with kilim cushions, while a second storey has shaded dining close to the zigzag-tiled bar. There's also the ultimate crow's-nest perch with fabulous views of the Koutoubia minaret and over the spice market. This time Laftimi's inspiration was groovy 1950s and '60s Morocco, typified by the Harry Bertoia-style diamond chairs on the top terrace. The menu embraces plenty of salads and vegetarian dishes alongside fish, lamb and *kefta* tagines. Profits from the changing dish of the day go to the Dar Bellarj Foundation, to help disadvantaged women in the community. Laftimi also owns the more rustic Café des Epices (on the other side of the square), a top spot for a 40dh breakfast of eggs, traditional breads, fruit, coffee and juice.

Shopping

Akbar Delights

45 place Bab Fteuh (0671 66 13 07, www.akbar delightscollections.com). **Open** 10am-1pm, 3-7pm Tue-Sun. Map p56 A5 **9**

This upmarket French-owned shop deals in luxury clothing and textiles from India, with some items made to their own designs, including a selection of handbags. The sister shop, Moor, in Guéliz (7 rue des Anciens Marrakchis, 0524 45 8274), carries a larger selection of Moroccan home furnishings as well as a clothing line.

L'Art de Goulimine

25 Souk des Tapis (mobile 0661 88 29 06). **Open** 9am-6.30pm daily. Map p56 B4 **10**

For something a little different, try L'Art de Goulimine, which specialises in Rhamana carpets from the plains north of Marrakech. The two young dealers, Rabia and Ahmed, have a small showroom displaying choice pieces just off the main carpet souk (where you'll find plenty of all the more usual carpet types at competitive prices).

L'Art du Bain

NEW *13 Souk El-Labadine (mobile 0668 44 59 42, www.nyushashop.com).* **Open** 9.30am-7pm daily. **Map** p56 A4 **11**

French-Moroccan couple Elsa and Youssef are soap-makers using local and natural ingredients. The line includes a donkey's milk soap that is said to regenerate the skin and slow ageing. Our favourites are Louise, a soap made with verbena and lemon, and Little Fatma, made with argan oil. They make a perfect gift as the packaging is as gorgeous as the product.

Art Ouarzazate

15 rue Rahba Kedima (mobile 0648 58 48 33). **Open** 10am-7pm daily. **Map** p56 B5 **12**

A small, sparsely stocked shop with an interesting collection including upmarket housewares and fashion designs. Carpets and cushions are woven from leather and custom-made for each client. The clothing line is unique and blends a variety of textiles including fur, leather and floral-printed fabric. Handbags start at 600dh; a vest with faux leather starts at 1,700dh.

Au Fil d'Or

10 Souk Semarine (0524 44 59 19). **Open** 9.30am-1pm, 3-8pm Mon-Thur, Sat, Sun; 9.30am-noon Fri. **Map** p56 A1 **13**

It's almost indistinguishable from the multitude of small stores that surround it, but Au Fil d'Or is worth honing in on for quality babouches and djellabas. Also sold are gorgeous lounge/beach wear in the finest fabrics (1,500dh), and finely braided silk-lined jackets (2,200dh) – just the thing should one be invited to the palace. Note that the bulk of the stock is kept in the cellar-like space downstairs, accessed via a trapdoor behind the counter. Watch your head (and your spending).

Bazar du Sud

117 Souk des Tapis (0524 44 30 04, www.bazardusud.com). **Open** 9am-7pm daily. **Map** p56 B4 **14**

This place has possibly the largest selection of carpets in the souk, covering all regions and styles, new and old. The owners say they have 17 buyers out at any one time scouring the country for the finest examples. Although considerable effort goes into supplying collectors and dealers worldwide, staff are just as happy to entertain the novice. Prices range from 2,000dh to 350,000dh. Ask for Ismail, who speaks perfect English.

Beldi

9-11 Soukiat Laksour, Bab Fteuh (0524 44 10 76). **Open** 10am-1.30pm, 3.30-8pm Mon-Thur, Sat, Sun. **Map** p55 F5 **15**

Toufik studied fashion in Germany and now, back in Marrakech, he and his brother Abdelhafid have transformed the family tailoring business into what is probably the most talked-about boutique in town, and one of our favourites. They offer both men's and women's ranges in beautiful colours and fabrics, fashioned with flair and an eye to western tastes. Silk kaftans, velvet vests and cotton tunics are part of the collection that changes seasonally. Custom orders take from two weeks to one month and can be shipped internationally. There's another shop at 19 Souk des Teinturiers.

Bellawi

56 Kessariat Lossta, off Souk El-Attarin (mobile 0668 04 91 14). **Open** 9am-7pm Mon-Thur, Sat, Sun. **Map** p56 B4 **16**

Abdelatif, owner of this closet-like jewellery store, is brother to the famed Mustapha Blaoui (p80). Here, there's just about room for Abdelatif, his workbench and one customer. The walls are hung with beads clustered like berries, along with a fine selection of silver bangles, necklaces and rings set with semi-precious stones, all in traditional styles. The shop is along the same narrow passage as Eva/Adam. There's no sign in English, but just ask for Abdelatif. Everyone knows him – he's been here for over 40 years.

Chez Climou et Ahmed

22 Souk Lebbadine (mobile 0648 50 60 71). Open 9am-8pm daily. No credit cards. **Map** p56 A3 ⑰
Using a small, rudimentary lathe that he spins with his bare feet, Ahmed carves chess pieces from cedar, olive and lemon wood. His designs are pleasingly solid and simple; the black pieces are created using burnt olive oil as a stain. He also sells boards and other woodcraft items, sourced from elsewhere. Step inside his small shop and he'll proudly show you a photo of Ronald Reagan's visit.

Eva/Adam

144 Souk El-Hanna (mobile 0661 08 54 91). Open 10am-1pm, 3.30-7pm Mon-Thur, Sat, Sun; 10am-1pm Fri. **Map** p56 B4 ⑱
Practical, comfortable clothes in neutral colours, made from cotton and lightweight wool, are sold here. The styles are loose-fitting yet elegant, and prices are fair. To find it, walk north up Souk El-Attarin just past the entrance to the mosque on the left. Look to the right for the word 'Lacoste' painted on a whitewashed arch: Eva/Adam is first on the right, with barely more than a door by way of shop frontage.

Faissal Bennouna

25 rue Ahl Fès, off rue Bin Lafnadek (mobile 0664 08 12 87). Open 9.30am-7.30pm daily. No credit cards. **Map** p56 C3 ⑲
The small workshop across from the Maison de la Photographie (p60) is just big enough for a loom and a bit of shelf space to sell the lovely scarves and textiles produced. Soft linen scarves in purples, pinks and oranges are perfect for summer, while heavier cottons are

just right for winter. Prices are reasonable for the quality, with scarves costing from 200dh.

Fundouk Bin Chababa

Place Bab Fteuh (no phone). Open 9am-8pm daily. No credit cards. **Map** p56 A5 ⑳
Just off Jemaa El Fna, heading towards rue Mouassine, is place Bab Fteuh, home to several old *fundouks* (merchants' inns). Our favourite is Fundouk Bin Chababa, piled high with metal platters, hammam buckets, candelabras and other various bits and pieces, some in better condition than others. The prices are fair.

Haj Ahmed Oueld Lafram

51 Souk Smata (0524 44 51 27). Open 10am-6.30pm Mon-Thur, Sat, Sun. No credit cards. **Map** p56 B3 ㉑
Most of the souk's slipper shops are much of a much-ness – look into one and you've pretty much seen them all. But Haj Ahmed Oueld Lafram offers a selection of babouches in a variety of styles from all over Morocco – embroidered leather ones from Tafraoute, for example – and in a variety of materials that include the likes of dyed goat fur, Italian horse leather and python skin. They're not the cheapest ones around, but the quality is excellent.

Mohammed Ouledhachmi

34 Souk El-Hararin Kedima (mobile 0666 64 41 05). Open 10am-8pm Mon-Thur, Sat, Sun. No credit cards. **Map** p56 B3 ㉒
Mohammed does copper – copper trays, copper pots, copper kettles and so on. Only a few of the pieces are new. To find the shop, head north up Souk El-Attarin and take the second right after passing the entrance to the mosque on your left.

Rahal Herbes

43-47 Rahba Kedima (0524 39 03 61). Open 9am-8pm daily. No credit cards. **Map** p56 B4 ㉓

Market forces

Uncover some hidden treasures.

Bab Es Salam market

Away from the souks' main lanes of concentrated commerce, small, specialised markets are worth investigating if you're looking for something a little more striking than a pair of same-same babouches or tadelakt salt-and-pepper shakers.

Just south of Rahba Kedima is **Souk Lagzhel** (map p56 B4). The site of the old slave market, it's now home to a second-hand clothes market. The piles of old garments spread out on the ground don't look like much, but you can uncover vintage kaftans and *ghondora* (robe-like tunics from the Sahara) and some great accessories. Arrive early for the best finds.

At the northern end of the Old City, just inside the Bab El-Khemis gate, you'll find the **Souk El-Khemis**, which spreads chaotically through a quite handsome four-pronged hangar. The main covered area is where you'll find large-scale treasures such as antique cedarwood doors, roll-top baths and wrought-iron windows. Outside, the market spins off down unpaved roads and alleys, with options ranging from

shops selling three-piece suites, to blankets piled high with pitiful cast-offs. Devotees, however, know it as a treasure trove of architectural salvage; when La Mamounia underwent its last refit, the discarded sinks, light fittings and carpets all turned up here.

If you're looking for food, head to the old Jewish quarter of the Mellah, and the **Bab Es Salam** market (map p85 D1), one block east of the lively place des Ferblantiers (a good lunch spot). It's very much a locals' affair, with traders selling jewel-bright fruit and vegetables, piles of herbs and postcard-perfect conical mounds of spices (though traders actually fake it by sticking a small amount of spice on to cardboard cones). It's the best place to stock up on freshly ground spices such as cumin, ground ginger and the legendary spice mix, *ras el-hanout*. Nearby, on the south side of avenue Houmann El-Fetouaki, is the **Marché Couvert** (map p84 C1), where *dadas* (private cooks) and housewives shop for meat and fish; this is where you're most likely to be brought if you sign up for a cookery class.

The west side of Rahba Kedima is lined with herbalists and 'black magic' stores; we recommend Rahal because of owner Abdeljabbar's fluency in English and keen interest in herbal remedies. Abdeljabbar grew up in the shop, which was originally his father's. Today it mostly sells argan oils, but have a seat and Abdeljabbar will soon share the secrets he learned from his father. Chances are you'll leave with a few natural mixtures for any aches and pains you may have.

Mouassine & around

Although it's far from immediately apparent, Mouassine is rapidly becoming the most chic of Medina quarters. West of the main souk area and north of Jemaa El Fna, it's home to a growing number of smart boutiques, interesting galleries and hip *maisons d'hôtes*.

Immediately on entering rue Mouassine from place Bab Fteuh is **Beldi** (p64), a must-stop shop for the likes of Jean Paul Gaultier and sundry international fashions. West of the junction with rue Ksour, three elaborate brass lanterns above the alleyway mark the doorway of Ksour Agafay private members' club.

At the point where the street widens to embrace the walls of the **Mouassine Mosque** (which lends its name to the quarter and was erected in the 1560s by Saadian Sultan Abdellah El-Ghalib), a side street (signposted) off to the west winds left then first right to reach a large wooden doorway with a signplate reading **Dar Cherifa**. Inside is a stunning late 16th-century riad with filigree stucco and beautiful carved cedar detailing. It operates as a gallery and performance space, doubling as a café during the day.

Where rue Mouassine hits rue Sidi El-Yamani, a dim little archway under a sign reading 'A la Fibule' jogs left and right to the fantastical

façade of the **Ministero del Gusto**, an extraordinary gallery-cum-sales space executed in an architectural style that co-creator Alessandra Lippini describes as 'delirium'.

Following rue Sidi El-Yamani west leads to the city gate Bab Laksour, in the vicinity of which is the Moroccan restaurant **Tobsil**. In the opposite direction, a few paces east of the mosque along Sidi El-Yamani is the **Mouassine fountain**, with quadruple drinking bays, three for animals and one – the most ornate – for people. It's here that the character Louis Bernard is fatally stabbed in Hitchcock's 1955 version of *The Man Who Knew Too Much* – although not so fatally that he can't first stagger half a mile to Jemaa El Fna to expire in the arms of Jimmy Stewart.

Beside the fountain is an arched gateway, beyond which is the **Souk des Teinturiers**. A couple of rooms within the gateway, above the arch, are now part of a boutique called **Atelier Moro**, run by Colombian Viviana González. It's a good place to buy funky decorative items, clothes, glass and beadwork.

Between the mosque and the fountain, the road weaves south to the new **Douiria Mouassine** (a *douiria* is a traditional reception area of a house for male guests with a separate staircase) that shelters exquisite examples of decorative arts that were buried, before restoration, under layers of plaster.

Further north up the street are a couple of good examples of *fundouks*. A *fundouk* – in Marrakech – is the distant forerunner of the modern hotel. It was a merchant hostel, built to provide accommodation and warehousing for the caravan traders who had crossed the desert and mountains to the south to bring their wares into the marketplaces of Marrakech. A *fundouk* offered stabling and storage rooms on the ground floor, bedrooms off the upper galleries, and a single gated entrance to the street that was locked at night for security.

Most of the city's surviving *fundouks* now operate as ramshackle artisans' workshops, such as the one at 192 rue Mouassine, **Fundouk Sarsare**. It also featured in the film *Hideous Kinky* as the hotel where Kate Winslet and her daughters lodged. Another grand *fundouk* across the street is thought to be the oldest surviving example of this building type in Marrakech.

At the junction of rue Mouassine and rue Dar El-Bacha, take a right and then the first right, which opens out into **Souk Cherifia**, a multistorey venture with chic designers and creators based on the first floor, and the **Terrasse des Epices** restaurant on the top terrace.

A few steps north of the *fundouks* is a crossroads: go left for the Dar El-Bacha and Bab Doukkala or right for the dyers' quarter, but only adherents of Islam should proceed straight ahead, according to a sign that reads 'Non Moslem interdit'. Up this particular alley is the Shrine of Sidi Abdel-Aziz, resting place of one of the seven saints of Marrakech. Collectively known as 'El-Sebti', this group of holy men have been venerated for centuries as guardians of the city. Each has a shrine erected by Sultan Moulay Ismail in the 18th century. All the shrines are within, or just outside, the walls of the Medina and once a year they are the focus of a seven-day *moussem* (pilgrimage).

Sights & museums

Dar Cherifa

8 derb Charfa Lakbir (0524 42 64 63, www.marrakech-riads.net). **Open** 10am-7pm daily. No credit cards. **Map** p55 E4 ㉔

This gorgeous townhouse is the Medina's premier exhibition space. Parts of the building date from the 16th century and it has been lovingly restored by owner Abdelatif Ben Abdellah, who's taken great pains to expose the carved beams and stucco work while leaving walls and floors bare and free of distraction. Regular exhibitions lean towards resident foreign artists, but there have also been shows by Moroccan artists Hassan Hajjaj and Milaudi Nouiga, and recently an interesting roster of cultural events as well, ranging from live music to poetry readings. The space also includes a small library, tea and coffee are served, and there's a light lunch menu too.

Douiria Mouassine

NEW *5 derb El-Hammam (0524 38 57 21, www.douiria.com).* **Open** 10am-6pm Mon-Thur, Sat, Sun. **Admission** 30dh. No credit cards. **Map** p55 F4 ㉕

Patrick Manac'h and Hamid Mergani of the Maison de la Photographie have restored this petite reception apartment to its 17th-century glory. As you descend into a warren of alleys behind the Mouassine Mosque, little prepares you for the exquisite decorative work within: a stunning symmetry of masterful pigmented stucco, double-stacked, decorated lintels on one side, and horseshoe doors on the other. A side room is enhanced by an arch of *muqarnas* (honeycombed architectural ornamentation) illuminated by vibrant pigments, including an irridescent peacock blue. The top terrace is a quiet refuge from the souks.

Ministero del Gusto

22 derb Azouz El-Mouassine, off rue Sidi El-Yamami (0524 42 64 55, www.ministerodelgusto.com). **Open** 10am-1.30pm daily. By appointment 4.30-6.30pm daily. **Map** p55 E4 ㉖

Showroom for the design talents and eclectic tastes of owners ex-*Vogue Italia* fashion editor Alessandra Lippini

Hammam heaven

Super spas and traditional baths.

La Mamounia

Selman Hotel

Another one of those Moroccan 'must-do' experiences, hammams can be a bit of a disappointment. Public hammams in Marrakech are a pedestrian lot, in most cases, and often not terribly warm or clean.

However, there are plenty of fairly priced day spas around town, where a *gommage* (scrub-down with black soap) in a steam room, *rhassoul* (a white clay body mask infused with essential oils) and a massage on a marble slab will cost in the region of 200dh. You'll also get warmer temperatures and maybe an ice-cold plunge pool, a prettier environment and someone to look after you properly, though the ritual and etiquette remain much the same: men and women strip down to their pants/boxers and your attendant provides the rest: a new mitt for scrubbing, black olive-oil-based soap and clay, shampoo and a plastic comb. Bring your own towel and a pair of flip-flops, and expect to spend at least an hour having your dead skin sloughed away to squeaky-clean, baby-soft smoothness, and allow some time to chill out afterwards. The more boutique places often serve tea and a biscuit.

Probably the best-known traditional hammam in town, **Hammam El-Bacha** (p76) has a six-metre (19-foot) cupola, and the men and women who work here do a fantastic scrub-down. Just remember it's as real as it gets: grit, grime and all, with entry a mere 7dh for men and 7.50dh for women, and massage at 50dh.

Pretty newcomer to the Bacha area **Hammam de la Rose** (p79) feels more luxurious, with candle-lit steam rooms, scented with rose and orange blossom oils and scattered with rose petals.

Down in the Kasbah, **Les Bains de Marrakech** (p91) has dual massage and steam rooms so couples can enjoy that floaty experience together. It's built around an exterior courtyard with a swimming pool at its heart. Cream-coloured tadelakt, stained glass and gold-threaded textiles create a luxurious atmosphere.

At the top end of the scale, **La Mamounia** (p161), the **Royal Mansour** (p162) and the **Selman Hotel** (p177) have eye-popping design on a fantastical scale. They offer good-value day passes with lunch from around 1,500dh.

and Fabrizio Bizzarri, this eccentric space also hosts occasional exhibitions; when they're finished Alessandra and Fabrizio continue stocking work by the artists and designers they like. These include Essaouira-based English artist Micol, American photographer Martin H M Schreiber, the Italian multimediaist Maurizio Vetrugno, Indonesian painter Ribka and Marrakchi pop artist Hassan Hajjaj. Lippini also has a large collection of vintage fashion, much of it worn by the stars and salvaged from film sets after the wrap.

Eating & drinking

Café Arabe

184 rue Mouassine (0524 42 97 28, www.cafearabe.com). **Open** 10am-midnight daily. **Bar**. **Map** p55 F3 ㉗
A good cocktail is not an easy thing to find in the Medina, but the Café Arabe delivers the goods. What a bonus, after dinner on the Jemaa El Fna (about five minutes' walk away), to find yourself perched at a half-moon bar on a rooftop, or kicking back on the low-slung sofas beneath the stars on a balmy night. Providing you stick to the classics – a gin and tonic, an americano, maybe a shot of Fernet Branca – you'll find this a welcome splash of Europe with a thoroughly North African vibe.

Le Jardin

32 Souk El-Jeld, Sidi Abdelaziz, nr Souk Cherifia (0524 37 82 95, http://lejardin. ma). **Open** 10am-10pm daily. **££**. Alcohol served. **Moroccan bistro**. **Map** p56 A2 ㉘
Local restaurateur and all-round hotshot Kamal Laftimi opened Le Jardin as an extension to his growing restaurant empire and as an opportunity to make the most of local talent. A small grocery store at the entrance sells organic fruit and vegetables from local farmers, and one of the balcony rooms overlooking the courtyard has been taken over by Norya ayroN's

glamorous kaftan shop (p74). In the restaurant, the food focuses on fresh, lively dishes over the more ubiquitous stodge. Think marinated sardines (roll-mop style), a 'garden' burger, or rare-grilled duck with caramelised figs accompanied by a crisp Moroccan white. The green-tiled oasis with primrose accents is full of banana palms, lemon trees and bamboo, plus chattering canaries and resident tortoises, and makes for cooling respite from the clamour of the souks.

Terrasse des Epices

15 Souk Cherifia, Sidi Abdel-Aziz (0524 37 59 04, www.terrassedesepices.com). **Open** 11.30am-11.30pm daily. **Main courses** 90dh-145dh. **Moroccan bistro**. **Map** p55 F3 ㉙
When this rooftop restaurant opened a few years ago it revolutionised life in the Marrakech Medina. All of a sudden there was somewhere quiet and hidden away to sit out of the sun; natty shaded dining booths are plumbed to spritz fresh, orange-scented water on to guests. Elephant grass down the middle of the terrace softens its edges, and the food represents an early attempt at modernising the classics. A John Dory fillet with fresh ginger and lemon is typical, but simpler dishes such as a bowl of cooling gazpacho or a caesar salad are good too. No alcohol.

Shopping

Abdelhakim Keddabi

115 rue Mouassine (mobile 0670 21 68 48). **Open** 9am-7pm daily. No credit cards. **Map** p55 F3 ㉚
This is one of the few storefronts with display windows in the area. From here Abdelhakim, a local Marrakchi, sells his simple handbag designs made from soft leathers. The focus is on functional designs produced in his nearby workshop. The collection includes carry-alls and totes, as well as smaller bags – all come in a range of colours.

Le Jardin

Atelier Moro

114 place de Mouassine (0524 39 16 78, mobile 0660 54 35 20). **Open** 9am-1pm, 3-7pm Mon, Wed-Sun. **Map** p55 F4 ③

This L-shaped first-floor space by the Mouassine fountain contains a cool, eclectic selection of homeware, clothes, accessories and carpets chosen by Viviana González. Some of the clothes are designed by Viviana herself and a few other items are from her native Colombia, but most of the stock is Moroccan, often the work of nameless artisans that would otherwise be lost in the souks. There's everything from inexpensive handmade scissors and Tuareg cutlery to pricey rugs, lamps made from ostrich eggs, and suede or Egyptian cotton tops. The door is to the west of the fountain, just right of the arch that leads into the Souk des Teinturiers.

Caverne d'Ali Baba

17A derb Fhal Chidmi (0524 44 21 48). **Open** 9am-8pm daily. **Map** p55 F4 ㉜

This huge shop is stocked with an incredible array of goods, from egg cups to lamp bases, in all imaginable colours. In fact, just about any pottery trend that has hit the Medina will very quickly be copied and put on sale here. Especially attractive are the tadelakt-finish items, which have an almost soft, leather-like appearance.

Cherkaoui

120-122 rue Mouassine (0524 42 68 17). **Open** 9am-8pm daily. **Map** p55 F3 ㉝

Opposite the Mouassine fountain is this glittering Aladdin's cave, full of everything imaginable in the way of home decoration Moroccan-style (with the exception of carpets). The proprietors, one local (Jaoud) and one German (Matthias), use local artisans, 120 in fact, working in various media including wood, leather, metal and clay, to supply the store. Customers include famed hotels La Mamounia and Royal Mansour, as well as film glitterati including Gwyneth Paltrow. Any piece

can be made up in eight weeks, and shipping can be arranged.

Chez Alaoui

52 rue des Ksour (mobile 0662 08 48 71). **Open** 9am-8pm daily. **Map** p55 F4 ㉞

A great place to look for ceramics in a variety of styles including Berber (which looks very African, with bold, clean shapes) and both old and new pieces from Safi, one of Morocco's main pottery-producing centres. Our favourites are the traditional green ceramics from Tamegroute near Zagora. The green glaze never comes out quite the same, so each piece is unique.

KIS Boutique

NEW *36 derb Fhal Chidmi (0524 37 82 52, www.kismarrakech.com).* **Open** 10am-2pm, 3-7pm Tue-Sun. **Map** p55 F4 ㉟

KIS (Keep it Secret) is a cute little hideaway. The turquoise premises hold the fashions and accessories of a handful of select designers. Up the tiled stairs, you'll find Fleur de Pirate's neon shirts, manager Abdel's 'funky Marrakech' mugs and fridge magnets, Salam's sweet pompomed children's slippers, Siroko's stuffed camel toys in bright prints, Brahim's bags and leather-fringed beach blankets, and Caroline Constancio's fashions. Not to mention potato-sack bags emblazoned with the Hand of Fatima in silver sequins. Need time out from the souks? Head for the café on the top terrace, with turquoise tables, tiki parasols and pink cushions.

La Maison du Kaftan Marocain

65 rue Sidi El-Yamani (0524 44 10 51). **Open** 9am-7.30pm daily. **Map** p55 E4 ㊱

La Maison may have the unloved, rundown look of a charity shop, but it also has the widest selection of Moroccan clothing for men, women and children in the souk, housed in what sustained exploration reveals to be a vast mausoleum of a place. Stock ranges from pantalon turque (traditional men's trousers) to beautiful velvet jackets and vintage kaftans that go for 20,000dh. Clothing can be made to measure; it typically takes up to a week to create a tailored garment. Stock has expanded to include cushions, poufs and textiles decorated with traditional Moroccan embroidery styles.

Maktabet El Chab

Rue Mouassine (mobile 0667 23 25 27). **Open** 9am-8.30pm daily. **Map** p55 F4 ③
Aka the 'FNAC Berbère' bookshop, this corner kiosk claims to be 'La première librairie à Marrakech', founded in 1941. The stock of coffee-table books is largely in French, but includes tomes on Moroccan interior design, cookery and the arts. Upstairs is a small café with views over the Medina.

Maktoub by Max & Jan

NEW *128 Souika Fontaine Mouassine (0524 37 55 70, www.maxandjan.ma).* **Open** 9.30am-8pm daily. **Map** p55 F3 ③
Just across from the Mouassine fountain, this concept store largely sells modern Moroccan styles in bright colours created by Agadir-based designers Max & Jan. Bright oranges, fuschias and greens, together with softer blues and browns, are common colours for the fitted dresses, sarouel pants, flowing kaftans and one-piece suits. The collection changes seasonally and a range of accessories is available to complete the look.

Ministero del Gusto

22 derb Azouz El-Mouassine, off rue Sidi El-Yamani (0524 42 64 55, www.ministerodelgusto.com). **Open** 10am-1.30pm daily; also by appointment 4.30-6.30pm daily. **Map** p55 E3/4 ③
Ministero is a surreal space – a sort of Gaudi goes Mali with a side trip to Mexico. As well as filling the role of informal social centre for friends and assorted fashionistas and creatives blowing through town, the two floors also act as an occasional gallery as well as a shop and showcase for funky

'found' objects (sourced from house clearances) such as African-inspired furniture, Eames chairs and Bernini glassware, plus a vintage fashion collection, some of it salvaged from film sets.

Al Nour

NEW *57 rue Laksour (0524 39 03 23, www.alnour-textiles.com).* **Open** 9am-2pm, 3-7pm daily. **Map** p55 E4 ④
Socially responsible shoppers will want to check out Al Nour, which provides an embroidery workshop for disabled women, who are happy to chat as they work away on home accessories including place mats, napkins and tablecloths in colourful patterns. The children's clothing is adorable; the women's fashion line is simple and reasonably priced.

Pop-up Shop – Norya ayroN

NEW *32 Souk El-Jeld, Sidi Abdel-Aziz, nr Souk Cherifia (mobile 0661 29 59 90, www.norya-ayron.com).* **Open** 11.30am-9.30pm daily. **Map** p56 A2 ④
Located up some stairs inside Le Jardin (p70), Algerian-French designer Norya ayroN's Moroccan-inspired womenswear is becoming a hit with the stars. Trendy, yet comfortable, colourful kaftans and one-of-a-kind robes are what Pop-up Shop is known for. Sharon Stone stopped by on a recent visit to Marrakech and her photo sits on the desk. Kaftans start at 690dh and gandouras cost from 1,090dh.

Souk Cherifia

Sidi Abdel-Aziz (http://souk-cherifia. com). **Open** 10am-7.30pm daily (some shops closed Tue). **Map** p55 F3 ④
Some of the city's most exciting designers and artists have opened small, fixed-price boutiques in Souk Cherifia to sell their alluring wares and hip creations. Come with plenty of cash (only some of the boutiques take credit cards) – or steely resistance.

Beautifully soft leather handbags are sold at Lalla (0524 38 36 85, www. shop-lalla.com) – check out the classic

Habibi and the fringed Hippy Habibi (1,500dh), which come in a range of colours. At Sissimorocco (mobile 0615 22 65 20, www.sissimorocco.com), French designer Sylvie Pissard has a range of funky, stylish cushions (750dh). Also here are Artsi Ifrach's fabulous, innovative designs under his Art/C label – cartoon flamingo print kaftan, anyone? Hassan Hajjaj has a small outlet here too, selling his wheat-sack babouches, couscous-sack totes and a reworked Barbie in a box, Moroccan style. For men, there's Randall Bachner's Marrakshi Life (mobile 0659 79 73 54) with its natty threads – smart shirts and stylish scarves set against a gorgeous backdrop of blue-hued tiles.

Tapis Akhnif

6 rue Mouassine (0524 42 60 96).
Open 9am-9pm daily. **Map** p55 F4 ㊳
A small family business, run by a father and his two sons, Akhnif offers a wide array of carpets, raffia and wool rugs and large poufs. There's no sales hassle and prices are fair.

Arts & leisure

Dar Cherifa (p68) hosts exhibitions and cultural events.

Northern Medina

North of the shrine of Sidi Abdel-Aziz in Mouassine, the road zigzags east then north, then east and north again on to rue Bab Taghzout, which runs north to the resting place of another of the city's renowned saints, the Shrine of Sidi Bel Abbas. En route is the stately **Chrob ou Chouf** – 'Drink and Look' – a monumental 18th-century fountain.

Soon after widening to accommodate a local bus stop and scrubby park, the street narrows again to squeeze through the ornate gateway known as **Bab Taghzout**, with its 15-centimetre (six-inch) thick wooden doors. This was

one of the original Medina gates until the walls were extended in the 18th century to bring the shrine within the city.

Through the gateway and a few steps to the right is an even more elaborate arched gateway, executed in carved alabaster. Beyond is an arcade that was once lined with herbalists, faith healers and quack doctors here to minister to/prey on the sick drawn to the tomb to bask in its saintly *baraka* (blessings). Such beliefs remain strong, and the courtyard of the shrine – adorned with supposedly Marrakech's only sundial – is always filled with the crippled and infirm. If things don't work out, a shaded arcade on the south side harbours a decrepit gathering of largely blind characters, all of whom belong to a sect specialising in the ministering of last rites. The sanctuary itself is off-limits; instead, depart the courtyard on the western side where a large open plaza provides a photogenic view of the shrine's pyramidal green roofs.

Returning back through Bab Taghzout, a right turn leads to the **Shrine of Sidi Ben Slimane El-Jazuli**, another of the patron saints of Marrakech. Active in the 15th century, he was a Sufi mystic and his *Manifest Proofs of Piety* remains a seminal mystical text.

Eating & drinking

Dar Yacout

79 rue Ahmed Soussi, Arset Ihiri (0524 38 29 29, http://yacout.ma).
Open 7pm-1am Tue-Sun. **£££**. Alcohol served. **Moroccan**.
Map off p55 F1 ㊹
Yacout's fame rests more on its decor and sense of theatre than it does on the food it serves, but for design lovers it's completely worth it. The building is all show, a madcap mansion designed by American interior designer Bill Willis,

who lived in Marrakech for 40 years prior to his death in 2009. There are flowering columns, candy striping and fireplaces in the bathrooms. Guests are invited up to the yellow crenellated rooftop terrace or into the first-floor lounge for pre-dinner drinks, before being taken down, past the swimming pool and across the courtyard, to be seated for dinner at great round tables, which are inset with mother-of-pearl. Reservations are essential.

Dar Zellij

1 Kaasour, Sidi Ben Slimane (0524 38 26 27, 0524 37 54 41, www.darzellij. com). **Open** 7.30pm-1.30am Mon, Wed, Thur; 12.30-2.30pm Fri-Sun. **£££**. Alcohol served. **Moroccan**. **Map** off p56 A1 **45**

More pared-back than many of the traditional riad restaurants, Dar Zellij has four dining rooms arranged around a regal courtyard of cool white plaster columns and orange trees, and an open-air lounge on the roof (for pre-dinner drinks). Dinner is a romantic affair; tables are scattered with rose petals, painted wood ceilings add colour to the minimalism, and fireplaces and candles create a warm glow. The food is excellent too, and attracts a mix of well-heeled Moroccans and discerning travellers. They come for Moroccan cuisine that goes beyond the usual tagines and couscous to include pristine seafood *b'stilla* and a memorable *trid royale* (plump pigeon wrapped up in tender, buttery pastry leaves), and an excellent wine list. Discreet local musicians add to the vibe without dominating it.

Dar El-Bacha & around

West of the Mouassine quarter and the city's holy shrines is the high-walled former residence of the most unsaintly Thami El-Glaoui, self-styled 'Lord of the Atlas' and ruler of Marrakech and southern Morocco throughout much of the first half of the 20th century. Known locally as **Dar El-Bacha** ('House of the Lord'), and also as Dar El-Glaoui, the residence dates from the early 20th century and is where the Glaoui entertained luminaries such as Churchill and Roosevelt, as well as the women his agents collected for him, scouring the streets for suitable prizes.

Shopping

Librairie Dar El Bacha

2 rue Dar El-Bacha (0524 39 19 73, www.darelbacha.com). **Open** 9am-1pm, 3.30-7pm daily (occasionally closed Sun). **Map** p55 E2 **46**

This small shop mostly stocks coffee-table books about Morocco and Marrakech, but there's also a decent selection of guidebooks and reproductions of old tourist posters. Books are available in both French and English.

Topolina

NEW *134 rue Dar El-Bacha (mobile 0651 34 57 95).* **Open** 9.30am-2pm, 3-7pm daily. **Map** p55 E2 **47**

This store is popular with shoppers who like one-of-a-kind fashion. Made with retro fabrics and bold patterns, the boho-chic collection includes colourful dresses and vintage handbags. Dainty pastel and floral patterned loafers are available for women (starting from 750dh), with more masculine colours available for men. A small seating area at the entrance is perfect for contemplating purchases.

Arts & leisure

Hammam El-Bacha

20 rue Fatima Zohra, Dar El-Bacha (no phone). **Open** *Men* 7am-1pm daily. *Women* 1-9pm daily. **Rates** 7dh men; 7.50dh women. *Massage* 50dh. No credit cards. **Map** p55 D4 **48**

See box p69.

Topolina

Stir it up

Learn to cook Moroccan-style.

One of the best ways to get to know a culture is through its food. Moroccan culinary culture is extremely rich and signing up for a cookery class offers the opportunity to spend quality time with someone from Marrakech and to view the city and its food through their eyes. Nearly all teachers are happy to take students on a shopping expedition to local markets before starting the class, to provide tips on selecting spices and buying produce, for a first-hand explanation of traditional cooking equipment, such as the *gsaa* used to knead bread, or to visit the *ferran* (community oven) where it is baked.

Maison Arabe

The cooking classes at **Maison Arabe** (p79) were the first to arrive on the scene and remain among the best for getting a handle on the preparation and cooking of traditional Moroccan dishes. Classes are structured around traditional Moroccan feast classics: a couple of starters (soups and salads) and a main course (tagine or couscous), or a main course and a dessert. Prices start at around 600dh per person for a group of four to ten (800dh for smaller groups; private one-on-one classes are also available). Classes are held in the hotel's swanky new culinary studio in a lush garden just outside town.

The new kid on the block is Clock Kitchen at **Café Clock** (p89), a modern, light-filled space on the roof terrace and it brings a fresh angle to the established cookery class routine. Because it's some distance from the main produce markets, shopping trips can be done by calèche (horse and carriage) and there's lots of opportunity for more specialised workshops, including bread-baking, pastry-making and foods cooked in community ovens. Most classes (maximum eight students) take a half day.

The tailor-made private classes with chef Omar at **Maison MK** (p161) are a boon for enthusiasts who have already worked their way around the various salads, couscous and tagines, though you can learn about these too. Because classes are limited to two people, there's more flexibility, and Omar is happy to consult about the kind of things you're interested in making, and to put together a customised menu that might include dishes such as a deconstructed pigeon *b'stilla*, or a contemporary dessert of spiced cucumber sorbet with mint foam. The price for a morning of cooking with lunch is 2,000dh for two.

Hammam de la Rose

130 rue Dar El-Bacha (0524 44 47 69, www.hammamdelarose.com). **Open** 10am-8pm daily. **Rates** *Hammam* from 250d. *Massage* from 500dh. **Map** p55 E2 ㊾ See box p69.

Bab Doukkala

From Dar El-Bacha, rue Bab Doukkala runs due west for 800 metres (half a mile) to the gate of the same name. At nos.142-144 is **Mustapha Blaoui**, venue for some of the best shopping in the Medina, and diagonally across the way is a recovery and refreshment stop, the **Henna Café** (www.hennacafe marrakech.com, open noon-evening), with profits being reinvested in the local community.

The major monument round here is the **Bab Doukkala Mosque**, built in 1558 by the mother of the Saadian sultans Abdel-Malek and Ahmed El-Mansour. It's fronted by the Sidi El-Hassan fountain, now dry, fenced around and under restoration. Behind the fountain a hand-painted 'WC' signposts the city's oldest toilets, built at the same time as the Doukkala Mosque opposite. They're still in use.

Across from the fountain, a small rose-pink building houses a 400-year-old **hammam** (men only) with a fantastic cedarwood ceiling in the reception area. Enter an alley, between 141 rue Bab Doukkala and a bike shop, to witness the medieval scene behind the hammam. In a cavernous blackened pit at the end of the alley, men darkened by smoke shovel woodchips into the enormous oven that stokes up the heat for the hammam. The westernmost stretch of rue Bab Doukkala is mostly the domain of the butchers and vegetable sellers. It verges on the macabre, with prominent displays of decapitated heads and mounds of glistening offal. Note that all the hanging bits of carcass display testicles: Moroccans don't eat female meat, so butchers are mindful to prove the masculine provenance of their produce. The massive Almoravid gate of **Bab Doukkala** is now bypassed by a modern road that breaches the city walls. There's a petit taxi rank at the foot of the gatehouse.

Eating & drinking

Maison Arabe

1 derb Assehbe (0524 38 70 10, www. lamaisonarabe.com). **Open** 7-11pm daily. **££££**. Alcohol served. **Moroccan & Asian Fusion**. Map p54 C3 ㊿

The original Maison Arabe was opened by two French women at the end of World War II. It was the first foreign-owned restaurant in the Medina and fast became a social hub for the city's illustrious visitors – film stars, artists and politicians among them. The place has expanded (it's also a hotel, p164) and changed hands a few times since then, but under the directorship of its latest owner, Fabrizio Ruspoli, has regained much of its glamorous lustre. If you can't stay the night, at least come for supper. Exquisite Moroccan haute cuisine is served in a room lavishly decorated with grey tadelakt, antique textiles and filigree lanterns by celebrated local designer Yahya Rouach. Mediterranean and Asian menus, along with Moroccan cuisine, are served alongside the pool. Booking is recommended.

Piano-Jazz Bar

Maison Arabe, 1 derb Assehbe (0524 38 70 10, www.lamaisonarabe.com). **Open** 3-11pm daily. **Bar**. Map p54 C3 ㋛

The leather-panelled walls, club chairs and sofas, tribal rugs, a fire in the hearth, imposing big-game art (an elephant in oils) and a tinkling piano make this bar feel utterly *Out of Africa*. Best of all is Rachid, who's been head barman here since anyone can remember and whose take on service is to make everyone feel like a long-lost friend, whether he's delivering an expertly mixed bloody mary or his secret remedy, hot ginger shot (if he spots you've got a cold). Lebanese bar snacks are a welcome touch too.

Shopping

Aswak Assalam

Avenue du 11 Janvier (0524 43 10 04, www.aswakassalam.com). **Open** 9am-10pm daily. **Map** off p54 B1 ⑤②
Across from the *gare routière* at Bab Doukkala, this decent-sized supermarket offers the closest good grocery shopping to the Medina. There's no booze here, though. It has less choice than Marjane (p129) and Carrefour and is pricier, but it's also much more convenient for anyone without a car.

Mustapha Blaoui

142-144 rue Bab Doukkala (0524 38 52 40, tresordesnomades@hotmail.com).
Open 9am-7pm daily. No credit cards.
Map p55 D2 ⑤③
This is the classiest, most loved 'best of Morocco' depot in town. It's a warehouse of a place: crammed, racked, stacked and piled with floor-to-ceiling irresistibles – lanterns, dishes, pots, bowls, candlesticks, chandeliers, chests, tables and chairs… If Mustapha doesn't have it, then you don't need it. He supplied a lot of the furnishings for the Villa des Orangers (p162) and the Riad Noir d'Ivoire (p167). Even people who don't own a hotel will find it almost impossible to visit here and not fill a container lorry. Added to which, Mustapha is a real sweetheart, his staff are ultra-helpful and shipping here is a cinch.

The tanneries

To experience Marrakech at its most raw, not to mention most pungent, take a taxi to the place du Moqf and walk east along rue de Bab Debbagh to the tannery district. The tanners have been here since the city was founded and legend has it that they are descended from demons who lived under a black king. He condemned them to their vocation for failing to obey his rules. Some workers still believe that the tanneries are inhabited by *jinns* or spirits.

The tanners use hundreds of concrete vats to process the hides, which are mostly sheep and goat, although cow and camel are sometimes used for bigger items. The treatment of the skins – from removal of hair to tanning and dyeing – remains a pre-industrial process that takes 20 days.

The tanneries can be tricky to find, but some loitering youth will always approach unaccompanied foreigners and offer his services as a guide. One is easy to find, though: just before Bab Debbagh, on the right and opposite the Au Rêve Berbère shop, is an arch marked 'Fin XI siecle' and a sign saying 'Association Sidi Yacoub pour les tanneurs'.

The tanneries fill large yards and, with rows of lozenge-shaped pools of various hues, look like giant paintboxes. However, closer up, the bubbling pits are more like cesspools of floating, bubbling crud; the hides piled up beside look like rancid tripe. Pity the poor labourers who wade in the noxious fluids ladling the skins from one pit to another. Guides sometimes hand out sprigs of mint to hold under your nose to block out the reek of pigeon droppings (used to soften the hides).

The results of the process can be seen and purchased at the shops near the gate, but you may prefer to get the hell out of the quarter and purge yourself in the nearest hammam. Taxis can be caught outside Bab Debbagh (where a stair inside leads to the roof of the gatehouse) on the route des Ramparts ringroad.

Bab Agnaou

Southern Medina

Almost since the founding of Marrakech, the area to the south of Jemaa El Fna has been the domain of sultans and their retinues. Today it houses the museum-palaces of the city. The present Royal Palace is built on the site of the earliest Almohad palaces and covers a vast area, equivalent to a whole residential quarter. Morocco's king, Mohammed VI, a little more modest in his requirements, has had a much smaller residence built nearby. Neither of these two modern-day royal precincts is open to the public, but visitors are allowed to explore two 19th-century palaces, the Bahia and the Dar Si Said, as well as the impressive ruins of the Badii Palace, currently the temporary home of the new Museum for Photography and Visual Arts.

Also in the area is the Mellah, historically Marrakech's Jewish quarter, now known as the Hay Assalem quarter.

The Kasbah & around

The pedestrianised rue Bab Agnaou, which runs south-west off Jemaa El Fna, is a honey pot for budget tourists, with banks, ATMs, moneychangers, internet centres and numerous dodgy eateries. At the far end is the **Grand Tazi** (p48), famed for decades as a roost for impecunious travellers and one of the few places in the Medina where it's possible to get a cheap beer. South of the Tazi, the street runs in the shadow of high walls: these are not the city walls, but a wall that formerly sectioned off the royal Kasbah (palace precincts) from the rest of the Medina.

The traditional entrance to the Kasbah is via the gorgeous **Bab Agnaou** (Gate of the Gnawa), named after the black slaves brought from sub-Saharan Africa. The gate was built on the orders of the Almohad Sultan Yacoub El-Mansour in 1185.

A
B
DERB DEBBACHI
C

1

Mosque

RUE DES BANQUES

Jemaa
El Fna

Mosque

RUE BAB
AGNAOU

2

17

DOUAR
GRAOUA

RUE RIAD ZITOUN EL KEDIM

RIAD ZITOUN
EL KEDIM

Dar Si Said
Museum

13

3

15

16

RUE RIAD ZITOUN EL JEDID

14 Maison
Tiskiwin

RUE HOUMANN EL FETOUAKI

Bahia
Palace

4

RIAD ZITOUN
EL JEDID

11

10

Marché
Couvert

Bab Es Salam
Market

MELLAH

5

PLACE DES
FERBLANTIERS

9

PLACE
SOUWEKA

See
p84

Bab
Berrima

D **E** **F**

RUE SIDI BOULABADA

1

ARSET
MOULAY
BOUAZZA

2

RUE BA HMAD

Moulay Idriss
Palace

3

JNANE
BEN CHEGRA

❶ Sights & museums
❶ Eating & drinking
❶ Shopping
❶ Nightlife
❶ Arts & leisure

4

12

RUE IMAM EL RHEZALI

Cemetery

0   200 m

0   200 yds

© Copyright Time Out Group 2015

5

Jewish
Cemetery

See
p85

South Medina
(North)

ARSET
EL MAACH

See
p82

AVENUE HOUMANN EL FETOUAKI

RUE RIAD
ZITOUN EL KEDIM

Marché
Couvert

PLACE DES
FERBLANTIERS

BAB AGNAOU

Bab
Berrima

Bab
Agnaou

Kasbah
Mosque

Badii
Palace

Saadian
Tombs

Market

Centre
Artisanal

KASBAH

Royal
Palace

RUE DE LA KASBAH

RUE DU MECHOUAR

DERB CHTOUKA

RUE OQBA BEN NAFIA

RUE IBN RACLID

Grand
Méchouar

South Medina (South)

D **E** **F**

Bahia Palace

See p83

1

Bab Es Salam Market

MELLAH

Jewish Cemetery

PLACE SOUWEKA

- **1** Sights & museums
- **1** Eating & drinking
- **1** Shopping
- **1** Nightlife
- **1** Arts & leisure

2

BERIMA

Berima Mosque

JNANE EL AFIA

3

Bab Jnane El Afia

4

BAB HMAR

Bab Hmar

Méchouâr Intérieur

0   200 m
0   200 yds

5

1 Agdal Gardens

© Copyright Time Out Group 2015

It's one of the very few stone structures in this otherwise mudbrick city, and has weathered in such a way that the aged limestone now resembles heavily grained wood. Across the street from Bab Agnaou is the original southern gate to the Medina, the Bab Er Rob, now filled by a pottery shop and bypassed by traffic, which exits through a modern breach in the walls.

A short distance inside the Agnaou gate is the **Kasbah Mosque**, constructed in 1190, again during the reign of Sultan Yacoub El-Mansour (hence its alternative name of El-Mansour Mosque). It has been renovated on numerous occasions since (most recently during the reign of Hassan II, father of the current king), but the cut-brick-and-green-tile decoration on the minaret is original. The plaza in front is popular at night with women and playing children and in the day it's busy with guide-led tourist groups. They're not here for the mosque (non-Muslims are forbidden to enter Marrakech mosques), but for what lies hidden in the lee of its southern wall: the **Saadian Tombs**.

In the early 1920s, the French authorities noticed two green-tiled roofs rising above the shanty quarters. Inquiries made of the locals were met with evasive answers. The persistence of one curious official was eventually rewarded when he discovered a narrow dark lane, wide enough for a single person, that ended in a tiny arched door. Beyond lay a sight that apparently no infidel had ever seen before – the holy tombs of the Saadian sultans – now possibly the most-visited site in Marrakech.

Exiting the tombs, a left turn on to rue de Kasbah eventually leads to the **Grand Méchouar**, or parade grounds of the Royal Palace, but the way is closed when the king is in town. Instead it's perhaps more interesting to duck into the warren of alleys behind the tombs, where a small square at the conjunction of four alleys hosts a morning market of fruit, vegetable, meat and fish vendors. A grander market – the **Marché Couvert** – is to the north-east of the Tombs, at the end of avenue Houman El-Fetouaki, opposite the Badii Palace.

The **Badii Palace**, barely 400 metres east of the Saadian Tombs, is the city's other great monument of that era. While secrecy preserved the sultans' mausoleums intact, the scale and ostentation of their triumphal residence marked it out for special attention and it survives only as a denuded ruin. The palace is approached via the open plaza of place des Ferblantiers and a canyon-like space constricted between two precipitous walls; the outer one was intended to keep the Medina at a respectful distance from the royal domains.

In the south-east corner of the Badii Palace, a gate leads through to a newly reconstructed pavilion housing the **Koutoubia Mosque minbar**. This was the original minbar (stepped pulpit) in the city's great mosque. It was fashioned in the early 12th century by Cordoban craftsmen and the 1,000 decorative panels that adorn the sides supposedly took eight years to complete – the word 'ornate' falls somewhere short. It was removed from the mosque in the early 1960s for restoration and after a spell at the Dar Si Said Museum has ended up here.

Next to the minbar pavilion are the excavated remains of troglodytic chambers and passages.

To the south of the Royal Palace lie the **Agdal Gardens**. To get to the Agdal, take the path off the south-western corner of the Méchouar Intérieur, or more sensibly, get a taxi to the entrance on route d'Agdal.

Sights & museums

Agdal Gardens

Open 7.30am-6pm Fri, Sun. Closed if the king is in residence at the Royal Palace. **Admission** free. **Map** p85 D5 ❶

Laid out in 1156-57 by the Almohads, the royal Agdal Gardens are several hundred years older than those most celebrated of Islamic gardens at the Alhambra. They cover a vast 16 hectares (40 acres), stretching south for a couple of kilometres from the back door of the Royal Palace. At the centre of the Agdal is a massive pool, the Sahraj El-Hana, so large that the sultan's soldiers used it for swimming practice. In 1873 Sultan Mohammed IV drowned in it while boating with his son; the servant who managed to swim to safety was executed on the spot for failing to save his lord. The rest of the area is divided into different kinds of orchards and gardens, including an orange grove, vineyards, areas of pomegranates and figs, masses of walnut trees and palm groves. With an eye on safety, we recommend not walking in these groves alone. There are several ornamental pavilions, and it's possible to climb a dilapidated building for an impressive view of the gardens and the High Atlas beyond.

Badii Palace

Place des Ferblantiers (no phone). **Open** 9am-4.45pm daily. **Admission** 10dh; 20dh minbar pavilion. **Map** p84 C2 ❷

Constructed during the reign of Sultan Ahmed El-Mansour (1578-1607), the palace was funded by wealth accrued through victories over the Portuguese. Walls and ceilings were encrusted with gold from Timbuktu (captured by El-Mansour in 1598), while the inner court had a massive central pool with an island, flanked by four sunken gardens filled with scented flowers and trees. At the centre of each of the four massive walls were four pavilions, also flanked by arrangements of pools and fountains. It took some 25 years for the labourers and craftsmen to complete

the palace. Surveying the achievement, the sultan is said to have invited opinion from his fool and received the prophetic response that the palace 'would make a fine ruin'. And so it does. The sultan was spared that vision because barely were the inaugural celebrations over before the ageing ruler passed away. His palace remained intact for less than a century before the Merenid sultan, Moulay Ismail, had it stripped bare and the riches carted north for his new capital at Meknès.

The former main gate is collapsed and gone, and entrance is through a gaping hole in the fortifications directly into the great court. It's a vast empty space the size of a couple of football pitches, ringed around by pockmarked mud-brick walls that act as apartment blocks for pigeons and have stork nests along the battlements. The sunken areas that were once gardens still exist, as does the great dry basin that was the ornate central pool. On the west side are the ruins of the Pavilion of Fifty Columns; a small area of mosaic remains on the floor, but the colours are badly dulled by exposure to the elements.

One of the palace bastions remains intact at the north-eastern corner of the great central court. Steps lead up to a rooftop terrace with fine views of the site and the surrounding quarter. You can also get up close and personal with the many nesting storks. In the south-east corner of the palace, a gate leads through to a pavilion housing the Koutoubia Mosque minbar (p86).

The Badii Palace is also the temporary home of the Marrakech Museum for Photography & Visual Arts. Plans for a new museum by British architect David Chipperfield to open near the Menara Gardens have been shelved, and a site near the Medina is now being considered (see box p97).

Saadian Tombs

Rue de Kasbah, Bab Agnaou (no phone). **Open** 9am-4.45pm daily. **Admission** 10dh; free under 12s. **Map** p84 A2 ❸

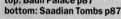
top: Badii Palace p87
bottom: Saadian Tombs p87

Entrance to the tombs is via a constricted passage first 'discovered' 80 years ago and it gives access to an ancient walled garden, the use of which far pre-dates the time of the Saadians. There are a great many early mosaic graves dotted around the shrubbery; the identity of those interned is long lost. Attention instead focuses on the three pavilions constructed during the reign of Saadian Sultan Ahmed El-Mansour. Despite drawing so many visitors, it's far from spectacular, and the setting is so modest that it reminds one of an English parish churchyard.

First on the left is the Prayer Hall, which was not intended as a mausoleum but nevertheless holds numerous graves, mainly of Alaouite princes from the 18th century. Their resting places are marked by what look like marble offcuts from a mason's yard. Next to it is the Hall of Twelve Columns, a far more ornate affair with three central tombs surrounded by a dozen marble pillars. The tomb in the middle is that of Sultan Ahmed El-Mansour, flanked by those of his son and grandson. A third, standalone pavilion has ornate Andalucian-style entrance portals.

Eating & drinking

Café Clock

NEW *Derb Chtouka (0535 63 78 55, http://cafeclock.com).* **Open** 10am-10pm daily. **££**. **Café**. **Map** p84 B4 ❹
See box p90.

Kosybar

47 place des Ferblantiers (0524 38 03 24, www.kosybar.com). **Open** 11am-1am daily. Alcohol served. **££**. **Japanese-Moroccan**. **Map** p84 C1 ❺
One of the early adopters of the Marrakech-chic style, Kosybar has dark, sultry lounges and dining rooms lined in yellow ochre tadelakt with animal-skin rugs on the floor. These spin off a central staircase rising steeply to the roof, where most people spend their time. And why wouldn't you when

it affords such wonderful ringside seats of the antics of the storks who hang out on the ramparts of the Badii Palace, and you get to kick back with a glass of wine over lunch? The place belongs to the son of the owner of some of Morocco's best wine estates, and it has one of the finest wine lists in town (if you're serious, ask to go off-menu). The Moroccan-style meze is perfectly good, but the best thing to order here is spanking fresh, impeccably made sushi and sashimi by chef Nao Tamaki.

Shopping

Lup 31

11 rue Okba bnou Nafia, Sidi Mimoun (0524 39 00 08, www.lup31.com). **Open** 10am-1.30pm, 2.30-6pm Tue-Thur; 10am-1.30pm, 3.30-6pm Fri; 9am-1pm Sat; Mon am by appointment only. **Map** p84 A1 ❻
Stylist, designer and decorator Ludovic Petit is hot property in Marrakech. His work appears at Peacock Pavilions (p177), Le Palais Paysan (p176) and a host of other riads and dars in town. You can have a glorious rummage at his workshop for finds covering the homewares (and financial) spectrum: embroidered cushions, canvas totes, Mondrian-style cushions, oil-drum tables, beaded lamps, poufs made from wheat sacks, scrap metal picture frames and gorgeous brightly coloured laptop bags. You can also find his work at 33 rue Majorelle (p111).

Zwin Zwin

NEW *Place des Ferblantiers (0524 37 83 22, www.zwinzwinmarrakech.com).* **Open** 10am-8pm daily. **Map** p84 C1 ❼
Located in the place des Ferblantiers, just across from Kosybar, this little shop is the place for trendy accessories. Our favourite is the pochette made from recycled grain bags with a vintage photo sewn on the front – funky, yet practical. The pochettes are fashioned in all sorts of colours and sizes – from change purses to laptop bags.

MARRAKECH BY AREA

Clock work

A contemporary cultural space.

The baby brother of the phenomenally successful Café Clock Fez, Mike Richardson's Marrakech branch (p89), housed in an old schoolhouse, opened in March 2014 to widespread cheer. Richardson has made clever use of the building's clean, blocky lines to create a thoroughly contemporary space. As well as providing a great cup of coffee, date milkshakes (no alcohol is served) and his now-legendary camel burger, the café doubles as a cultural centre and exhibition room for local artists and photographers.

Among a roster of constant innovations are storytelling workshops (on Thursdays, with translations) from the *hlaykia* storytellers who once worked on Jemaa El Fna. In the 1970s there were 18 storytellers working on the square, reciting stories from folklore, *A Thousand and One Nights* and the Old Testament to rapt audiences; now you'd be lucky to find one. In a culture where few could read or write, the oral tradition provided more than just entertainment: it was a means of passing down information, ideas, philosophies and values – rather like a newspaper. The workshops are an attempt to breathe new life into this important tradition.

There's more authentic home-grown culture with Sunday music evenings, featuring traditional acts and young local bands, including *gnawa* groups and Berber musicians. In addition, Clock hosts calligraphy, Arabic and cooking lessons (see box p78).

Arts & leisure

See also **Café Clock** (box p90).

Les Bains de Marrakech

2 derb Sedra, Bab Agnaou (0524 38 14 28, www.lesbainsdemarrakech.com). **Open** *9am-7.30pm daily.* **Rates** *Hammam 170dh. Massage 370dh.* No credit cards. **Map** p84 A2 ❽ See box p69.

The Mellah

Hugging the eastern walls of the Badii Palace are the narrow gridded alleys of the Mellah, the old Jewish quarter. The name translates roughly as 'Place of Salt', a reference either to the Jews' historic monopoly on the trade in mineral salts from the Atlas mountains, or to their landing the job of salting the heads of decapitees before they were hoisted on spikes. Although the number of Jews in Marrakech is now negligible following mass emigration, evidence of Jewish heritage is abundant to anyone who knows where to look. Several houses in the neighbourhood have external balconies, which was peculiar to Morocco's Jewish population. Some have Hebrew letters on the metal grills above the doors and there's even an occasional Star of David.

Diagonally across the road from the Bahia Palace entrance, an arch leads through into the **Bab Es Salam Market**, also known to locals as the Jewish market. Following this south and east, past stalls of gaudy beaded necklaces (made in China), bright pyramids of spices (the tallest of them are actually clever cardboard fakes), and windows of the lurid sweets known as Pâte Levy, leads deep into the Mellah. The streets here are some of the narrowest and poorest in the Medina and in places crude scaffolding keeps the houses from collapsing.

In among the narrow lanes, on derb Tijara, is the new **Caffe Internazionale** (mobile 0610 99 89 11, open 8am-8pm daily), a handsome home-turned-café painted in bold letterbox red. At the heart of the quarter is a small square, place Souweka, now disfigured by a badly sited concrete building. At 36 derb Manchoura, along the street that runs north just beyond the square, is one of Marrakech's two last working synagogues (once there were 29). The **Slat Laazama Synagogue** (mobile 0668 95 44 13, open 9am-6pm Mon-Fri, Sun) occupies a large hall off the beautiful open courtyard, striped in Majorelle blue, of a well-maintained community centre. Judging by the plentiful supply of new prayer books and other contemporary trappings, the synagogue is kept alive by remittances from Marrakchi Jews abroad.

On the very eastern edge of the Mellah is the extensive **Miâara Jewish cemetery**; the sheer number of modestly marked graves (tens of thousands) is probably the best remaining testament to the one-time importance of Jewish life in Marrakech.

Shopping

Art C

NEW *Derb Saka (mobile 0660 03 62 46, www.art-c-fashion.com).* **Open** by appointment only. **Map** p82 C5 ❾ Fashion creative Artsi Ifrach has turned his family's old Mellah home into a showroom for his eclectic fashion pieces and collectibles. The former ballet dancer, who was born in Israel after his parents left the Mellah in the 1960s, is self-taught. He has worked in Paris and only visited his parents' home town for the first time a few years ago. His signature style sees him reinterpreting clothes that are one-offs: for example, you'll find a gorgeous deer tapestry in deep bordeaux refashioned as a dress, trousers embellished with handira blanket sequins, shoes made from carpets, a vintage linen piece crowned with a fur collar and the non-kosher pig print dress. Everything in his beautifully tiled Mellah home is for sale. Artsi's work (sold at Anthropologie) is also on sale at his shop in Souk Cherifia (p74).

Aya's

NEW *11 bis derb Jedid Bab Mellah (0524 38 34 28, http://ayasmarrakech.com).* **Open** 10am-1pm, 2.30-4.30pm Mon-Sat. **Map** p82 B5 ⑩
Nestled under the archway leading past Le Tanjia restaurant, Aya's stocks a beautiful collection of kaftans and tunics made from the finest textiles and featuring exquisite embroidery. From evening wear to casual, modern and traditional, the quality of the authentic products is second to none. A photo display of rich and famous customers attests to this.

Dinanderie

6-46 Fundouk My Mamoun (0524 38 49 09). **Open** 8am-7pm Mon-Sat. **Map** p82 B4 ⑪
Moulay Youssef is one of the country's handful of elite artisans. If you need something extravagant wrought from metal – and if you have the money – then Moulay is your man. The bulk of his work is made to order, but adjacent to his workspace is a crowded gallery of smaller pieces. A little difficult to find, the Dinanderie atelier fills an alley immediately west of the small rose garden across from the place des Ferblantiers.

Riad Zitoun El-Jedid

The Mellah is connected to Jemaa El Fna (a distance of just under a kilometre) by rue Riad Zitoun El-Jedid, a name also used for the area. It means the 'new olive garden' but the only olive trees in the vicinity these days are in the modern rose garden at the very southern end of the street.

Just to the north of the Mellah is the Bahia Palace. This place will mean much more to you if you've read Gavin Maxwell's *Lords of the Atlas*, but even if you haven't, its shady courtyards and blue mosaic walls still make a pleasant break from the hot bustling streets outside.

Also down at this end is the Préfecture de la Medina and a narrow arch giving entrance to the derb El-Bahia and **Maison Tiskiwin**, with its collection of southern Moroccan crafts and decorative arts. Following a couple of twists to the north is the **Dar Si Said Museum**, the former home of the brother of Ba Ahmed, builder of the Bahia, and home to another collection.

Sights & museums

Bahia Palace

Riad Zitoun El-Jedid (0524 38 91 79). **Open** 9am-4.30pm daily. **Admission** 10dh; 3dh children. **Map** p83 D4 ⑫
The palace was built principally by Bou Ahmed, a powerful vizier to the royal court in the 1890s and a man of 'no particular intelligence, but of indomitable will, and cruel' (*Morocco That Was*, Walter Harris; 1921). Entered via a long garden corridor, it's a delightful collection of paved courtyards, arcades, pavilions and reception halls with vaulted ceilings. The walls are decorated in traditional Moroccan zelije tiling, with sculpted stucco and carved cedarwood doors. The fireplace off to the right of the main courtyard is quite impressive too. The palace includes extensive quarters that housed Bou Ahmed's four wives and 24 concubines.

On Bou Ahmed's death – probably poisoned by the sultan's mother,

Bahia Palace p92

along with his two brothers – the palace was completely looted by Sultan Abdel-Aziz. Caravans of donkeys staggering under the weight of furniture, carpets and crates made their way the short distance from the Bahia to the Royal Palace. Between then and now it served as the living quarters of the French *résident général*; Edith Wharton stayed here at this time, described in her 1927 book, *In Morocco*, and it's still occasionally used by the current royal family.

Dar Si Said Museum

Off rue Riad Zitoun El-Jedid (0524 38 95 64). **Open** 9am-6.45pm Mon, Wed-Sun. **Admission** 10dh; 3dh children. **Map** p82 C3 ⑬

This palace, whose interiors are a showcase for Moroccan artisanship, is home to a large collection of crafts and woodwork. Among all the ceramics, leather and weapons are beautiful examples of carved cedar, rescued from the city's lost dwellings – among them, polychromic painted doors, window shutters and fragments of ceilings. One room is devoted to 'rural' woodwork, including some primitively worked and painted Berber doors. Such items are very much in vogue with collectors these days and change hands for vast amounts of cash. Captions are mostly in French.

Maison Tiskiwin

8 derb El-Bahia, off rue Riad Zitoun El-Jedid (0524 38 91 92, www.tiskiwin. com). **Open** 9am-12.30pm, 2.30-6pm daily. **Admission** 20dh; 10dh children. **Map** p82 C4 ⑭

On display in this private house, owned by the veteran Dutch anthropologist Bert Flint, is his fascinating collection of crafts and decorative arts from southern Morocco and the Sahara. He has donated all of these artefacts to the University of Marrakech but you can still see them at the Tiskiwin. The exhibition is designed to show Morocco's

connection to sub-Saharan Africa and is a geographically laid-out collection that takes you on a journey across the Sahara, as if you were following an old desert trade route from Marrakech to Timbuktu. Exhibits include masks from as far afield as Mali and an entire Berber tent made of camel hair. This is one of Marrakech's hidden gems.

Shopping

Cordonnerie Errafia

Rue Riad Zitoun El-Jedid (mobile 0662 77 83 47). **Open** 9am-8pm daily. No credit cards. **Map** p82 B3 ⑮

In a little workshop opposite the Préfecture de la Medina, artisan Ahmed cobbles together classic men's loafers out of raffia, with more extravagantly coloured and cut stylings for women. He can also make to order.

Mr Goodyear

26 rue Riad Zitoun El-Jedid (no phone). **Open** 10am-9pm Mon-Sat. No credit cards. **Map** p82 B3 ⑯

Not just Goodyear – there's Firestone, Pirelli and Michelin too. Abdou creates his hardy black accessories – handbags, purses, bracelets, rings and bowls – from rubber tyres. There are actually a couple of 'rubber craftsmen' in the souks but Abdou, 22, who discovered his talent after a woman commissioned him to make a rubber dress, has a very neat and alluring line in earrings, bracelets and hats. He will also make to order.

Warda La Mouche

NEW *127 rue Kennaria (0524 38 90 63).* **Open** 9am-8pm daily. **Map** p82 B2 ⑰

If sarouel pants and flowing tunics are your style, then head to French-owned Warda La Mouche for reasonably priced fashion in a range of bright colours and patterns. Down a few steps is a great sale rack (to the right) and a children's section (to the left), where the girls' sarouels in the sweetest patterns are simply irresistible.

MARRAKECH BY AREA

Carré Eden

Ville Nouvelle & the Palmeraie

Guéliz is the heart of the Ville Nouvelle, or New City, of Marrakech. Built during the French protectorate, with some interesting modernist buildings, it's known for 1930s elegance, though it's marred by concrete blocks, tourist coaches and a McDonald's. With the influx of the tourist euro, however, it's undergoing a renaissance, and is emerging as the most fashionable spot in Morocco, especially around the leafy rue de la Liberté and rue des Vieux Marrakchis, as well as a corner at the southern end of avenue Mohammed V. Today, Guéliz is a vibrant and cosmopolitan neighbourhood, home to the city's most interesting galleries, designers and restaurants, and increasingly, trendy bars and cocktail lounges. To the south, in Hivernage, lie the city's fanciest hotels and dance clubs, while the Palmeraie is home to some of North Africa's priciest real estate.

The 'new city' came into being shortly after December 1913 – the arrival date of Henri Prost, the young city planner imported to assist in the schemes of French *résident général* Marshal Lyautey. One of Prost's early sketches shows how he took the minaret of the Koutoubina as his focal point and from it extended two lines: one north-west to the Guéliz hills; the other south-west to the pavilion of the Menara Gardens. In the pie slice between these lines (which have since become avenue Mohammed V and avenue de la Menara) is the original nucleus of the new colonial city.

One of the first buildings was the church or *église* – a word that was corrupted into the name Guéliz. The **Catholic Church of St Anne** is barely a communion queue from the northern walls of the Medina. It is a modest affair, with a bell tower deliberately overshadowed by the taller minaret of a mosque built next door after independence.

Straddling the Ville Nouvelle and the Medina, the **Cyber Park Arset Moulay Abdelsalam** is a welcome and lushly planted space that provides a peaceful location with plenty of shade and free Wi-Fi.

Guéliz

The focal point of Guéliz used to be the Marché Central on avenue Mohammed V. However, in a mystifying piece of town planning, it was demolished in 2005, and has been replaced by the brand new **Carré Eden** shopping complex, featuring Starbucks and high-street brands, while the fresh produce market has been replaced by a much more sterile affair just east of the nearby place du 16 Novembre.

At the junction of **avenue Mohammed V** and fashionable **rue de la Liberté** is an elaborate colonial building with pavement arcades, art deco lines and Moorish flourishes. Dating from 1918, it's just about the oldest surviving building in Guéliz. This was the address (30 rue de la Liberté) of the city's first tourist office. A fading gallery of ancient hand-painted scenes of Morocco decorates the hallway.

North off the eastern stretch of rue de la Liberté is the chic shopping street, **rue des Vieux Marrakchis**. At its western end, beyond the **Kechmara** bar and where it meets **rue de Yougoslavie**, is a forgotten bit of Marrakech history: a narrow alley planted with mulberry trees and crammed with single-storey dwellings daubed in pink with the odd splash of Majorelle blue and navy blue. This is the old **Spanish quarter**, a reminder of the city's once large Hispanic population.

In the middle of Mohammed V is the **place du 16 Novembre**, which is the main hub of high-street

New museums

A focus on photography, painting and fashion.

With a growing number of artists' studios and the increasing profile of the Biennale (see box p28), Marrakech's reputation as an artistic hub will be sealed by three museums in the next few years.

The popular **Marrakech Museum for Photography & Visual Arts** (MMPVA, www.mmpva.org), showcasing Moroccan, North African and international photography, currently resides in a temporary gallery in the Badii Palace (p87). Proposals for a dedicated museum building, to have been built next to the Menara Gardens, had been shelved at the time of writing, and alternative sites in the Medina were under consideration.

On the other side of town, the **Al Maaden African Contemporary Art Museum** (MACAAL), funded by Fondation Alliances (www.fondation alliances.org), is a new cultural venue designed by architects Omar Alaoui from Morocco and Nieto Sobejano from Spain. The museum's collection will be drawn mostly from the holdings of the foundation's president, Alami Lazraq, a hotels and housing investor.

Exciting news for the world of haute couture is the proposal for an **Yves Saint Laurent Museum of Fashion**, to be built near the Majorelle Gardens, though more information was scant at the time of writing.

Guéliz

- **1** Sights & museums
- **1** Eating & drinking
- **1** Shopping
- **1** Nightlife
- **1** Arts & leisure

To Semlalia &
Route de Casablanca

Cemetery

RUE ABDELOUAHAB DERRAQ

Polyclinique
du Sud

RUE IBN AICHA

BOULEVARD

Cinema
Colisée

CTM
Office

PLACE
ABDEL
MOUMEN

AVENUE MOHAMMED

BD MOHAMMED ZERKTOUNI

ABDELKARIM

EL KHATTABI

RUE DE VIEUX MARRAKECH

RUE TAREK

RUE DE LA LIBERTÉ

RUE DE IBN ZIAD

RUE LOUBNANE

AVENUE

MOHAMMED V

RUE DE YOUGOSLAVIE

BOULEVARD EL

AVENUE MOHAMMED EL BEKAL

MANSOUR EDDAHBI

BOULEVARD MOULAY

RACHID

RUE DE
MAURITANIE

AVENUE HASSAN II

RUE CADI AYAD

See
p118

Théâtre Royal &
Opera House

Jnane
El Harti

Gare

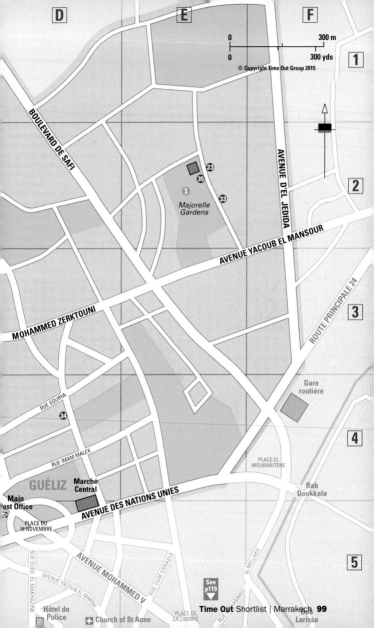

fashion chains and fast food outlets, plus a sprinkling of iconic cafés and bars such as the **Grand Café de la Poste** and newcomer **Level 5**. To the south of place du 16 Novembre, and connected to it by its north-east corner, is the Jnane El-Harti park, originally laid out as a French formal garden and a zoo. The park was relandscaped and now boasts fountains, ponds and a children's play area with two pale blue dinosaurs.

North of place du 16 Novembre, **place Abdel-Moumen** marks the start of the restaurant district proper, with old stalwarts like the **Café les Négociants** where grouchy uniformed waiters serve coffee so strong you can stand a spoon in it, *grande dame* **Al Fassia** serves brilliant traditional Moroccan food, and the **O'Sky Bar** provides a secret hideaway for sundowners.

From place Abdel-Moumen, it's a 20-minute walk to the glorious **Majorelle Gardens**. To get to the gardens, walk from central Guéliz (it's about two kilometres east along boulevard Mohammed Zerktouni) or take a taxi. Note that picnics, unaccompanied children and dogs are not allowed. The area outside the garden entrance on the renamed **rue Yves Saint Laurent** is now buzzing with the opening of the **33 Rue Majorelle** concept store, other boutiques, and the **Café Kaowa** (open 9am-7pm), which serves reviving vegetarian wraps, smoothies and coffees.

Sights & museums

Majorelle Gardens

Rue Yves Saint Laurent (0524 31 30 47, www.jardinmajorelle.com). **Open** 8am-5.30pm daily. **Admission** 50dh; free under-9s. *Berber Museum* 25dh. **Map** p99 E2 ❶

Now privately owned by the Fondation Pierre Bergé-Yves Saint Laurent – but open to the public – the gardens were created in the 1930s by two generations of French artists, Jacques and Louis Majorelle. Although small in scale and out on the edge of the New City, the gardens are often packed well beyond comfort. The juxtaposition of colours is striking; plants sing against a backdrop of the famous Majorelle blue, offset with soft yellows and terra-cottas. Bamboo groves rustle in the soft breeze and great palms tower over all, sheltering huge ancient cacti. Rills lead into pools floating with water lilies and flashing with golden carp, terrapins paddle languidly and frogs croak. Great pots overflow with succulents and birds sing. For the botanically curious, everything is clearly labelled. Yves Saint Laurent's memorial, a rather incongruous and unkempt broken classical column, has been placed against the back wall of the garden.

Jacques Majorelle's former studio has been turned into a beautiful small Berber museum, with well-curated rooms of traditional jewellery, tools, and a fine collection of mannequins draped in traditional dress. Air-conditioned and dimly lit, the museum is a welcome refuge from the intensity of light and colour outside; exhibits have English labelling. Beside the museum is a bookshop (now with its own publishing house), and opposite is the YSL Galerie Love (featuring poster designs from YSL's New Year greetings cards), a small boutique selling 100% Moroccan-made goods: T-shirts, leather goods, babouches, pottery, Majorelle paint, zelije tiles and cushions. The pretty Bousafsaf café behind the museum offers refreshing drinks and snacks.

Eating & drinking

Amaia

84 avenue Hassan II (0524 45 71 81). **Open** 10am-midnight Mon-Sat. **££**. Alcohol served. **French/Italian/South-east Asian**. **Map** p98 C5 ❷

Majorelle Gardens

Association Amal

Usually when a restaurant has such an eclectic menu alarm bells ring, but Eric Garozzo was born in Casablanca to Sicilian parents and his wife has roots in Vietnam, so their menu of French, Italian and South-east Asian dishes is, in fact, completely authentic. Most are based on old family recipes, cooked with lashings of love. The restaurant is an intimate space of rich chocolate browns made sexy by gauzy, champagne-hued cubes that deflect light from chandeliers, and modern wooden table lamps that mean you can actually see what you're eating. Add a little funked-up jazz and a European-Moroccan wine list, all of which is available by the glass, including champagne for 650dh per bottle (very reasonable for Morocco), and this is exactly the sort of neighbourhood joint you'll wish you had around the corner back home.

Amandine

177 rue Mohammed El-Bekal (0524 44 96 12). **Open** 7am-9pm daily. No credit cards. **Café. Map** p98 B4 ❸

This smart pâtisserie is banked on two sides by floor-to-ceiling windows to optimise views of a long, sparkly glass display cabinet piled high with sculpted cakes, highly decorated pastries and pastel-coloured macaroons. You can buy a box to go, but the height of Marrak-chic is to snag one of the candy-coloured armchairs at the front of the shop and order afternoon tea. Also good are the croissants, toasted sandwiches and other savouries.

Association Amal

Corner of rues Allal Ben Ahmed & Ibn Sina, quartier l'Hôpital Ibn Tofail (0524 44 68 96, mobile 0604 23 88 60, http://amalrestaurant.wordpress.com). **Open** noon-4pm daily. **£**. No credit cards. **Moroccan**

Nora Belahcen Fitzgerald's philanthropic project of a women's training centre offers courses in cooking and general hospitality skills, ranging from food hygiene to service, as well as English lessons and a kids' activity centre. The women who come here – many travelling a fair distance from surrounding villages – get paid for their efforts, and punters are treated to some of the best country cooking in the city. Daily specials such as *seffa* (a Fassi dish of steamed vermicelli with chicken, saffron and ginger) combine with lighter meals like niçoise salads and a zingy home-made lemonade.

Azar

Rue de Yougoslavie, corner of boulevard Hassan II (0524 43 09 20, www.azarmarrakech.com). **Open** 12.30-4pm, 7.30-11pm daily. **££££**. Alcohol served. **Lebanese. Map** p98 C5 ❹

The jaw-dropping design of this upmarket Lebanese lounge and restaurant was done by the talented Marrakchi designer Younes Duret, and it's well worth coming for a cocktail just to admire it. Soaring ceilings, lanterns with contemporary Islamic cut-out motifs and custom-made tables and chairs lend a real sense of glamour to the place, and it makes for good eating too, especially for large groups where platters of six to 16 kinds of meze means nobody has to think too hard. Classic crowd-pleasers like houmous, *moutabal* (roast aubergine with lemon and sesame), *tabbouleh* and *kebbe* (minced lamb with pine kernels) combine with more exotic fare like *sawda djaj* (chicken livers in pomegranate juice), *shanklish* (goat's cheese with tomatoes and green onion) and *mouhalabieh* (Lebanese milk pudding with orange syrup and pistachios) to provide a real feast for the senses.

Bar L'Escale

Rue de Mauritanie (0524 43 34 47). **Open** 11am-10.30pm daily. **££**. No credit cards. **Moroccan/Bar. Map** p98 C4 ❺

Beloved by Moroccan men in search of a cheeky cold one, L'Escale is also the best *grillade* (barbecue) in town.

Staff still cook over a wood fire and the lemon grilled chicken is superlative, as are the spicy *merguez* sausages and lamb kebabs, all served with a chopped tomato and onion salad, a dish of shoestring fries and a basket of bread for mopping up. There's a back room specifically for dining, but the top spot is at one of the six sun-shaded tables out on the pavement, where you can happily pass a couple of hours watching the world drift by.

Café du Livre

44 rue Tarek Ibn Ziad (0524 44 69 21).
Open 10am-11pm Mon-Sat; 12.30-11pm Sun. Alcohol served. **Café.**
Map p98 C4 ⑥
Those who know Sandra Zwollo's sophisticated first-floor café/vintage bookshop may feel the Café du Livre has seen better days, but it's still very much the meeting point for newcomers. It's slightly scruffy around the edges, and very smoky at times, but the books and magazines are still here, as are plenty of sofas to sink into, free Wi-Fi and most of the international newspapers. There's also the added lure of a happy hour that lasts from 7pm to 9pm, Tuesday to Sunday. The menu majors in salads and sandwiches. It's one of the few places in town to have beer on tap, and there's often live music or a pop quiz at the weekend.

Café les Négociants

Place Abdel-Moumen, avenue Mohammed V (0524 43 57 82).
Open 6am-11pm daily. No credit cards. **Café. Map** p98 B4 ⑦
Far classier than the endearingly sleazy Café Atlas, which it faces across the road, Les Négociants is a Parisian boulevard-style café with acres of rattan seating and round glass-topped tables crowded under a green-and-white striped pavement awning swinging with chandeliers. It's a glamorous spot for breakfast: *café au lait*, orange juice and croissants, plus papers from the international newsagent opposite.

Catanzaro

42 rue Tarek Ibn Ziad (0524 43 37 31).
Open noon-2.30pm, 7.30-11pm Mon-Sat. **££.** Alcohol served. **Italian.**
Map p98 C4 ⑧
This simple, hacienda-style French-run Italian bistro (red-checked tablecloths, wagon wheel lanterns, wood-beamed ceilings) has a homely air and reliable cooking. It's been going strong for years and remains as popular as ever. White-hatted chefs work in an open kitchen with a big wood-fired oven turning out excellent thin-crust pizzas. There's also lasagne and steaks, as well as slightly more exotic dishes such as rabbit in mustard sauce and a glorious pannacotta. Waiters flit about in red-velvet waistcoats greeting customers old and new with enthusiastic affection, while working a labyrinthine series of dining rooms, though we think the best place to eat is at the heart of the action, in front of the kitchen.

Chez Joel

NEW *12 rue Loubnane (0524 43 15 49).*
Open noon-midnight daily. **££.** Alcohol served. **French. Map** p98 C3/4 ⑨
Chef Jaouad Kazouini learned his trade in Chicago and still has his first restaurant there. He returned home in mid 2013 eager to bring a touch of US laid-back style to Marrakech. This sleek little bistro, with elephant-grey walls framing black-and-white photos from the Chicago restaurant and newspaper print wallpaper, has fast become the haunt of Marrakchi businessmen and savvy expats exchanging gossip over lunchtime specials like mussels and fries with a beer, or platters of Oualidia oysters followed by beef carpaccio and caesar salads at night. A keenly priced wine and beer list is the icing on the cake.

Le Cuisine de Mona

No.115B Résidence Mamoune 5, Quartier El-Ghoul cité OLM (mobile 0618 13 79 59). **Open** noon-3pm, 8-11pm daily. **££.** Alcohol served. **Lebanese.**
Map p98 A3 ⑩

There's no missing the eye-boggling, hot pink and acid apple decor of this cute little eaterie (cross over Mohammed V at Restaurant L'Avenue and walk about ten metres down this residential side street to find it). The doll's-house-sized terrace outside is the top spot on a sunny day, but it gets busy with regulars who come for a dose of Mona's home-style Lebanese cooking. There may be smarter places, but nobody does *baba ganoush*, *tabbouleh* and chargrilled lamb kebabs better.

Al Fassia

55 boulevard Zerktouni (0524 43 40 60, www.alfassia.com). **Open** noon-2.30pm, 7.30-11pm Mon, Wed-Sun. **££**. Alcohol served. **Moroccan**. Map p98 C4 ⑪
Some things never change, and Al Fassia is one of them. Thirty years old in 2015, the restaurant was set up as a women's co-operative headed by chef Halima Chaab and her sisters, and it remains, hands down, the place to find the best traditional food in Morocco. It employs only women, and the business has gone from strength to strength, now having two restaurants and a hotel to its name. The best place to eat, however, is here at the mothership, where elegantly sumptuous surrounds and a pretty garden are complemented by a mind-boggling array of dishes from traditional Moroccan salads to steamed vermicelli with pigeon and slow-roasted shoulder of lamb with almonds and caramelised onions. Reservations essential.

Grand Café de la Poste

Place du 16 Novembre, behind post office, (0524 43 30 38). **Open** 7.30am-midnight daily. **Bar**. Map p98 C4 ⑫
Long before the hotels, the fashionable bars and the sexy French bistros there was the Grand Café de la Poste. Situated right behind the post office, with wrap-around terraces shielded by plants and bamboo screens, the Grand Café was a reliable spot for an afternoon snifter, while the black-and-white

Cheers!

Local wines, cool cocktails.

Moroccan wines (predominantly from Meknès) are getting better all the time, and there are some exceptional vintages made by boutique wineries such as Volubilia and the Vall d'Argan, near Essaouira. Among the best accessibly priced reds are Cabernet du Président, Domaine de Sahari and La Ferme Rouge. Gazelle de Mogador (from the Vall d'Argan vineyard) is a deliciously crisp and refreshing white, and the country's very pale rosé wines (known as *gris*), by Larroque and Volubilia, are delightful on a hot day.

In the last couple of years, Marrakech has started to embrace cocktail culture too, and has some decent mixologists. The **Maison Arabe** (p164) is great for a Sunday morning bloody mary, and the bar on the circular rooftop of the **Pearl Hotel** in Hivernage (corner of avenue Echouhada & rue du Temple, 0524 42 42 42, www.thepearl marrakech.com) mixes a mean Moroccan martini. For more sophisticated sipping with a view, the **O'Sky Bar** (p108) above the Rennaissance Hotel offers 360° panoramas across the city and beyond; it's a sensational spot from which to watch sunset.

Alcohol is heavily taxed. Expect to pay above the odds for beer, wine and cocktails (a bottle of Moët champagne, for example, costs easily in excess of €100). And don't forget that standalone bars close for the month of Ramadan, and the less upmarket hotel bars stop serving alcohol.

Djellabar p120

tiled dining room was the smartest place in town for lunch. There's still a decent line in salads, club sandwiches and aperitifs, though the main reason to come today is to soak up the atmosphere of a bygone era and to have cocktails upstairs at the most sophisticated cocktail bar in town. A central fireplace (open on all sides), leather chesterfields, plush woven poufs, animal rugs, African art and lush, deep green plants make it a place in which to linger.

Kechmara

3 rue de la Liberté (0524 42 25 32).
Open 9am-1am Mon-Sat. Main courses **££**. Alcohol served. **International/Moroccan/Bar**. Map p98 C4 ⑬
Café by day and restaurant by night, Kechmara is also a lively bar lacking the kind of wannabe pretension that Marrakech has a certain penchant for. For many, this was the bar that changed Marrakech. For a long time it was the only bar (in the hip, European sense) in the city and wowed locals with its fresh approach. Brothers Pascal and Arnaud Foltran revamped an old villa, turning it into a seductive mid-century modern space, serving beer on the rooftop and top-notch burgers with skinny fries. As the hipsters discovered it, the menu expanded with a celebration of local produce, including a sensational Oualidia spider-crab salad. There's a long bar counter downstairs, a solid drinks list and beer on tap. Top-quality bands play on Wednesdays, many of them guests in from Paris or Barcelona, and there are continuously changing art and photography exhibitions. Drinks on the roof remain a treat in summer. The brothers' refusal to conform to the fickle trends of Marrakech means their place remains as hot as ever.

Le Loft

Rue de la Liberté (0524 43 42 16, www.loft-marrakech.com). **Open** noonlate daily. **££**. Alcohol served. **French**. Map p98 C4 ⑭

Sleek teak panelling, colonial ceiling fans and cane furniture give Le Loft a distinctly colonial feel, although the food is solid French bistro and the aspiration New York. No matter, since it has a lively, lived-in vibe that makes you want to spend time here. The lunch combo is a good deal (110dh) and there's a good range of starters like home-made pâté with cornichons and caesar salad, as well as slowly cooked lamb shank, duck leg confit and grilled prawns.

O'Cha Sushi

43 rue de Yougoslavie (0524 42 00 88, www.ocha-sushi.com). **Open** noonmidnight daily. **£££**. **Japanese**.
Map p98 B4 ⑮
O'Cha has a deserved reputation for serving the best sushi and sashimi in town. The long, glass-fronted chill counter houses impeccable, freshly made pieces. Ergonomic fibreglass chairs, lichen-green leather banquettes, limegreen walls and modern enamelled lanterns lend a contemporary freshness that you'll enjoy if you eat in, but we prefer to take our sushi and picnic in one of the nearby parks.

O'Sky Bar

Renaissance Hotel, 89 boulevard Zerktouni, corner of avenue Mohammed V (0524 33 77 77, www.renaissance-hotel-marrakech.com).
Open 11am-1am daily. No credit cards.
Bar. Map p98 B4 ⑯
Perched at the top of the Renaissance Hotel, O'Sky Bar has one of the best views in the city with a 360° panorama of the mountains that surround Marrakech. It's brilliant for an afternoon pick-me-up, or a drink at sunset, when you'll be left in no doubt how the 'red' city earned its moniker. Comfortable grey sofas sprawl against blood-red terracotta walls and cactuses in planters painted Majorelle blues and yellows. The music is much calmer than the throbbing techno of most nightspots – funk, soul, blues and jazz – and the cocktails aren't insanely priced

either (90dh-100dh for the classics, up to 200dh for champagne cocktails).

Rôtisserie de la Paix
68 rue de Yougoslavie (0524 43 31 18).
Open noon-3pm, 6.30-11pm daily.
££. Alcohol served. **Rôtisserie**.
Map p98 C4 ⑰

Flaming for decades, the 'peaceful rôtisserie' is a large garden restaurant with seating among palms and bushy vegetation. Simple and unpretentious, it's utterly lovely, whether lunching under blue skies (shaded by red umbrellas) or dining after sundown when the trees twinkle with fairy lights. (In winter, dining is inside by a crackling log fire.) Most of the menu comes from the charcoal grill (kebabs, lamb chops, chicken and *merguez* sausages) but there are also delicacies such as quail, and a selection of seafood. We recommend the warm chicken liver salad, listed as a starter but easily a meal in itself.

Snack Al Bahriya
75 bis avenue Moulay Rachid (mobile 0678 76 82 43). **Open** noon-late daily.
£. No credit cards. **Fish**. **Map** p98 C5 ⑱

If a good old-fashioned fish fry is what you crave, look no further than Al Bahriya, a heaving great canteen of a place with wonderfully friendly staff that's always rammed. The draw? Pristinely fresh fish and seafood, clean fryers and a real charcoal grill capable of doing justice to some of the freshest produce in the country. Mixed platters include prawns, mussels, squid and a couple of whole grilled fish that you eat with your hands on a couple of pieces of paper with hot sauce for dipping.

Le Studio
85 avenue Moulay Rachid (0524 43 37 00, www.restaurant-lestudiomarrakech. com). **Open** noon-2.30pm Mon; noon-2.30pm, 7.30-11.30pm Tue-Fri; 7.30-11.30pm Sat. **French/wine bar**.
Map p98 C5 ⑲

On a street better known for grilled meat on a stick, this is a bistro-wine bar but also one of the few places you can go just for a glass of wine. You need to get in early if you want to perch at the bar with a drink, though. By 7.30pm the place is heaving with a largely French contingent merrily drinking, chain-smoking and carrying on. There's a good selection of wines by the glass, and if you just want a small nibble to go with it, there are plates of cheese and charcuterie.

Trattoria de Giancarlo
179 rue Mohammed El-Bekal (0524 43 26 41, www.latrattoriamarrakech.com).
Open 7.30-11.30pm daily. **£££**. Alcohol served. **Italian**. **Map** p98 B5 ⑳

Just about clinging on to its reputation as Marrakech's finest Italian restaurant, Trattoria serves good food in enchanting surroundings. The Felliniesque interiors (lush, occasionally lurid and more than a little louche) were designed by late local legend Bill Willis and are a delight – in fact, it's worth a visit just to see the decor. The best tables are those overhung by oversized greenery out on the tiled garden terrace, beside a large, luminous pool. In the evening the place is lit by lanterns and candles to ridiculously romantic effect. While the menu is hardly extensive, it holds plenty of broad appeal (a variety of salads, several vegetarian pastas, and an array of meat and seafood dishes). Reservations are recommended.

Le Verre Canaille
Corner of route de Targa & rue Capitaine Errigui (mobile 0650 92 97 42). **Open** 12.15-2.15pm, 7.15-11pm Mon-Sat. **£££**. Alcohol served. **French**.
Map p98 A3 ㉑

With its natty, retractable roof-covered terrace, oyster-grey banquettes and olive wood tables and chairs to match the olive tree planters, Bruno Gomes Tmim's little French bistro is a chic addition to the scene. Candles, French crooners on the stereo and a decent French wine list add to the

Guéliz galleries

Contemporary art in the Ville Nouvelle.

The last few years have seen the scope of Marrakech art go from strength to strength. 'It all changed with the launch of Vanessa Branson's Biennale,' says Hassan Hajjaj, one of the country's leading artists. Not only is the Biennale (see box p28) now a serious art event, but artists in Marrakech are also embracing street art, photography, video and other multimedia with a new gusto.

Of all the recent gallery openings, the **David Bloch Gallery** (p112) pushes the envelope the most. Set in a contemporary, industrial-style space, the focus is on Moroccan, North African and Middle Eastern street artists. Large picture windows and whitewashed brick provide the frame for bold works that fuse neon, neo-calligraphy and geometrics by collectable artists like Larbi Cherkaoui, Mohamed Boustane and Yassine 'Yaze' Mekhnache.

Noir Sur Blanc Gallery (p116) is a sprawling townhouse space showcasing the work of mostly Moroccan contemporary artists. It covers all mediums, from painting and sculpture through to photography and video art.

Galerie Rê

When Nathalie Locatelli opened **Galerie 127** (p112) in 2006, it was the first photography gallery in the Maghreb. Locatelli works with big names in contemporary photography, mostly French or France-based, with work including portraits by Carole Bellaiche and Gérard Rondeau, Alejandra Figueroa's images of ancient statues, and Bernard Faucon's 'staged photography'.

Art collector Lucien Viola's **Galerie Rê** (p112) is part gallery, part theatre. The long, tall building has a floor-to-roof glass frontage to maximise natural light, museum-quality lighting and a high-definition sound system. The emphasis is on contemporary works by Moroccan and Mediterranean-rim artists, and aims to open cross-cultural exchange and dialogue.

The **Matisse Art Gallery** (p116) is a decent space devoted to solo shows by young Moroccan artists such as calligraphy painters Nouredine Chater and Nouredine Daifellah, and figurative painter Driss Jebrane. More established names include Farid Belkahia and Hassan El-Glaoui. Upstairs are some vintage Orientalist canvases.

Galerie 127

Sidi Ghanem

Head beyond the souks for some quality merchandise.

If you've fallen in love with everything in your riad, chances are it came from the industrial zone of **Sidi Ghanem** (http://sidighanem. net) – if it wasn't sourced at **Mustapha Blaoui** (p80), that is. With beautiful linens, gorgeous pottery, scented bath products and lanterns, Sidi Ghanem is the place for those who want to take large pieces of Morocco home with them.

About eight kilometres (five miles) north of town, it doesn't have the most romantic of locations, the streets have no names and the showrooms are housed next to busy workshops. But this old industrial/warehouse area, built on an ordered, linear street pattern, offers space that can't be found in the Medina or Guéliz. More and more Marrakech-based designers are establishing studios and showrooms here and most accept credit cards.

Be warned that it's a long walk from one end of the main street to the other, with minimal shade. If you take a taxi out here, you won't want to let it go – it's not easy to find another one in these parts. If you ask a driver to wait or to shuttle you from shop to shop, agree an hourly rate; 50dh-60dh is a fair price. Or book a driver through your riad and expect to pay up to 600dh. Bus no.15 departs Bab Doukkala every half hour (4dh per person), passing by Majorelle Gardens before eventually winding its way through the industrial zone.

We recommend having the taxi drop you off at the roundabout, near Bo Luminaire, where several shops are located. Pick up a copy

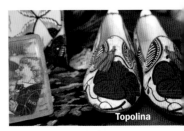

Topolina

of the free map or download it. Most shops are closed Saturday afternoons and Sundays.

Fashion

The Marrakech showroom of Tangier-based fashion designer **Salima Abdel-Wahab** (no.315, mobile 0618 29 90 18, www. salimaabdelwahab.com, open 10am-6pm Mon, Wed, 10am-1pm, 2-6pm Tue, Fri, 10am-1pm Sat) features her fabulous collection of designs created using local textiles including kilims. **Topolina** (p76) has a large, funky workshop and showroom here at no.436 (mobile 0651 34 57 95, open 9.30am-2pm Mon-Fri, afternoons and Sat by appointment), with a huge selection of vintage and vintage-inspired boho-chic styles in bright colours and striking patterns.

Homewares and lighting

If industrial-style interior design is your look, try **Ardevivre** (no.437, 0524 33 66 10, www.ardevivre. com, open 9.30am-12.30pm, 2.30-6.30pm Mon-Fri, 9am-1pm Sat, no credit cards), a large showroom with all kinds of goodies. Next door, **W.Home** (0524 33 61 28, www.w-homemaroc.com, open 9.30am- 1pm, 2-6.30pm Mon-Fri, 9am-1pm Sat, no credit cards) also features a wonderful selection of lamps and interiors pieces. **Design&Co** (no.166b, 0524 33 50 47, open 9am-6pm Mon-Sat) curates artwork, furniture and home accessories and regularly features new artists. **La Boutique de l'Atelier** at no.315 (0524 33 52 67, open 10.30am- 6pm Mon-Fri, 10am-1pm Sat) has a selection of upcycled furnishings in bright metals and one-of-a-kind designs by two interior designers.

For lighting, head to **Henry Cath** (no.139, 0524 33 88 30, open 9am-12.45pm, 2.15-6.30pm Mon-Fri, 9am-1pm Sat), where custom-made lamps and lanterns of the finest quality are produced. Each piece takes five weeks to make.

Cosmetics and perfume

For cosmetics, our favourite is **Les Sens de Marrakech** (no.17, 0524 33 69 91, www.lessensde marrakech.com, open 8.30am-6pm Mon-Fri, 8.30am-4pm Sat). The argan oil sold here is some of the best we've found – expect to pay around 197dh for a 125ml bottle. Visit **Keros** (no.238, 0524 33 63 30, www.kerosfragrances.com, open 9.30am-5.30pm Mon-Fri, 9.30am-1pm Sat) for beautifully scented perfumes and room sprays. **Nour Bougie** (no.231, 0524 33 57 18, www.nourbougie. com, open 8.30am-6.30pm Mon-Sat) provides the ingredients for an exotic ambience: candles in all shapes, colours and sizes as well as cut-out containers for creating magical patterns when lit.

Ceramics

Further up the street, the **Loun** showroom (no.109, 0524 33 60 68, www.lounmarrakech.com, open 10am-6pm Mon-Fri, 10am-3pm Sat, no credit cards) features beautiful ceramics produced in its workshop on the route d'Ourika. There are coffee and tea sets, plus tagines in various sizes and styles, priced from 35dh to 550dh, and vases from 250dh to 1750dh.

One-stop shopping

Fenyadi (no.219, 0524 33 62 01, open 9am-7pm Mon-Sat) has an extensive pottery collection on its ground floor, with modern takes on classic Moroccan shapes, from tagines to tea glasses, as well as pick 'n' mix dinnerware, mostly in fantastically rich colours. It changes the range every year, but keeps older designs in stock so that broken pieces can be replaced. Head upstairs for luxurious Egyptian cotton bedlinen, all in white and embellished with simple, coloured embroidered detailing. You can specify colours with an order, and commission calligraphic embroidery to your specifications. Big white towels and towelling bathrobes round off the range. On a higher floor there is a small selection of scented candles and intricately designed candleholders in leather and metal.

Eating

There are limited options when it comes to eating in the area. **Le Zinc** (no.517, 0524 33 59 69, www. durand-traiteur.com, noon-3.30pm Mon-Sat, open for dinner from 8pm Thur, Fri, no credit cards) is centrally located, serves wine and is popular at lunchtime. **Café Leon** (no.24, 0526 71 65 45, open 9am-4pm Mon-Fri, no credit cards) is perfect for a light lunch (no alcohol) or a wonderful *café au lait*.

priced anywhere between 1,000dh and 25,000dh. There are also T-shirts, bags, slippers and belts for those on a smaller budget, including hats by Le Chapelier.

Naturia Bio Shop

9 rue des Vieux Marrakchis (0524 43 00 00). **Open** 9am-1pm, 3.30-7.30pm Mon-Sat. **Map** p98 C4 ⑫

This small shop is the go-to place for travellers with special dietary requirements. It stocks a selection of natural foods, including gluten-free products, all-natural snacks and herbal teas. Cosmetic, organic argan oils are also available. A naturopath and nutritionist are available for consultation once a week, free of charge, but check with the shop in advance as appointment times vary.

Noir Sur Blanc Gallery

A l'étage 48, Immeuble Adam Plaza, rue de Yougoslavie (0524 42 24 16, www.galerienoirsurblanc.com). **Open** 3-7pm Mon; 10am-1pm, 3-7pm Tue-Sat; by appointment Sun. **Map** p98 C4 ⑬ See box p113.

Place Vendôme

141 avenue Mohammed V (0524 43 52 63). **Open** 9.30am-1pm, 3-7.30pm Mon-Sat. **Map** p98 C4 ⑭

Owner Claude Amzallag is known for his custom-designed buttery leather and suede jackets, and sleek line of handbags and wallets in every colour from forest green to hot pink. The suede shirts for men and stylish luggage are also big hits with the forty-something crowd.

Scènes de Lin

70 rue de la Liberté (0524 43 61 08, www.scenesdelin.com). **Open** 9.30am-1.30pm, 3.30-7.30pm Mon-Sat. **Map** p98 C4 ⑮

A chic fabric store that specialises in linens and also offers a huge range of soft woven cloth or delicate pastel organdie in a range of brilliant hues. Custom-made curtains, tablecloths or

place settings are available. There are plenty of other top-quality textiles, including luxurious bathrobes and towels, cushions with Fès embroidery, and even natural essential oils (including argan oil) and tableware. Downstairs is a small selection of Moroccan couture, including a sale rack with end-of-season stock reduced by up to 50%.

Vita

58 boulevard El-Mansour Eddahbi (0524 43 04 90). **Open** 9am-12.30pm, 3-7.30pm Mon-Sat. No credit cards. **Map** p98 C4 ⑯

A western-style florist and garden centre with a decent stock of cut flowers and ready-made bouquets. It also does delivery (local and Interflora).

Yahya Creation

49 passage Ghandouri, off rue de Yougoslavie (0524 42 27 76, www.yahyacreation.com). **Open** 9.30am-1pm, 3-7.30pm Mon-Sat. **Map** p98 B4 ⑰

Yahya Rouach's mother is English and Christian, his father is a Jew from Meknès, and he's a Muslim convert brought up in the UK and now resident in Marrakech. He designs extraordinary items, such as lanterns, torches and screens, all made from finely crafted metals. His pieces are unique, often stunning, one-offs. Most of them are big too: conversation pieces for a chic sheikh's Dubai penthouse, perhaps? This arcade outlet is a showroom rather than a shop, where customers drop in to place commissions, joining a client list that includes Harrods and Neiman Marcus.

Arts & leisure

Cinéma le Colisée

Boulevard Mohammed Zerktouni (0524 44 88 93). **Tickets** from 25dh. **Map** p98 B4 ⑱

This place trumpets itself as the 'best cinema in Morocco' and it's certainly the best in Marrakech – a comfortable modern venue with excellent sightlines.

Hivernage

South-west of place Abdel-Moumen, Guéliz peters out at the expanse of **avenue Mohammed VI** (formerly known, and still often referred to, as the avenue de France). Here, and to the south, is the area known as Hivernage. A showcase of colonial planning, it's a garden city for winter residence. On curving suburban streets, hidden in greenery, luxury hotels sit next to modernist villas. In the shade of a well-groomed hedge, soldiers indicate a royal in residence.

The junction with avenue Hassan II is lorded over by the monumental **Théâtre Royal**, designed by local star architect Charles Boccara. An open-air theatre here is used for occasional performances but the opera house, behind, remains a shell.

Hivernage is where you'll find popular nightclubs and the **Menara** Gardens. To reach the gardens, take a petit taxi, which should cost about 30dh from anywhere in the Medina. They'll try to charge you more to come back.

Sights & museums

Menara Gardens

Avenue de la Menara (0524 43 95 80).
Open 7am-5pm daily. *Picnic pavilion*
9am-5pm daily. **Admission** free.
Picnic pavilion 10dh. **Map** off p118C5 49
Coming in to land at Aéroport Marrakech Menara, alert passengers may notice a large rectangular body of water to the east. This is the basin of the gardens from which the airport takes its name. They've been there since around 750 years before man took to the air – like the Agdal, the Menara Gardens were laid out by the Almohads in the 12th century. Later they fell into neglect and their present form is a result of 19th-century restoration by the Alouites. The

highly photogenic green-roofed picnic pavilion that overlooks the basin was added in 1869. Climb to the upper floor for a wonderful view over the water or, better still, stroll around to the opposite side for the celebrated view of the pavilion against a backdrop of the Atlas. Great ancient carp live in the basin; buy some bread, toss it in and watch the water churn as the fish go into a feeding frenzy. Soft drinks and ice-creams are available.

Eating & drinking

La Casa

Hotel El-Andalous, avenue Président Kennedy (0524 44 82 26, www.elandalous-marrakech.com). **Open** 8pm-2am daily. **Bar**. **Map** p119 D4 50
A bar that thinks it's a club, La Casa mixes food, music and dance to great effect. It is primarily a bar, dominated by a huge central serving area, surrounded on all sides by tables and seating. Above the counter hangs a giant rig of multicoloured lights fit for a Pink Floyd gig. Much flashing and strobing occurs in an accompaniment to a heavy Arab and Latin beats soundtrack. There's no dancefloor, but then there's none needed, as everyone just lets go where they are. Around the stroke of midnight expect an 'impromptu' performance of dancing from the chefs in the corner kitchen area. Berber columns cloaked in purple drapes and characters from the ancient Tifinagh alphabet highlit in ultraviolet add the thinnest veneer of Moroccan theming.

Comptoir Darna

Avenue Echouada (0524 43 77 02, http://comptoirmarrakech.com). **Open** 4pm-1am Mon-Thur, Sun; noon-1am Fri, Sat. **Bar**. **Map** p119 E4 51
Marrakchi socialites will tell you that Comptoir is sooo over, but on the right night it's still the best party in town. From the outside, it's a well-behaved little villa on a quiet residential

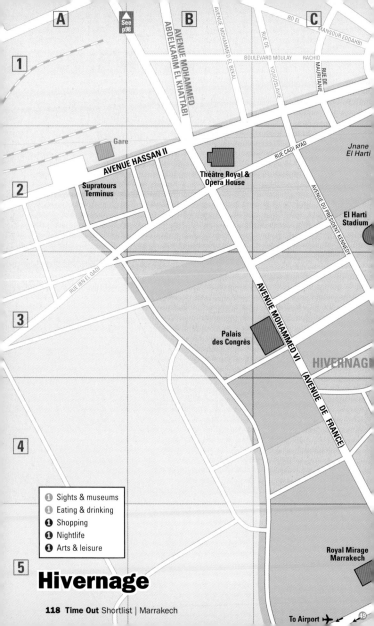

A **B** **C**

See p98

1

AVENUE MOHAMMED ABDELKARIM EL KHATTABI

AVENUE MOHAMMED EL BEKAL

RUE DE YOUGOSLAVIE

BO EL

MANSOUR EDDAHBI

BOULEVARD MOULAY RACHID

RUE DE MAURITANIE

Gare

Jnane El Harti

AVENUE HASSAN II

RUE CADI AYAD

2

Supratours Terminus

Théâtre Royal & Opera House

AVENUE DU PRÉSIDENT KENNEDY

El Harti Stadium

RUE IBN EL QADI

3

Palais des Congrès

AVENUE MOHAMMED VI (AVENUE DE FRANCE)

HIVERNAGE

4

- ❶ Sights & museums
- ❶ Eating & drinking
- ❶ Shopping
- ❶ Nightlife
- ❶ Arts & leisure

5

Hivernage

Royal Mirage Marrakech

To Airport ✈ ⤷ 49

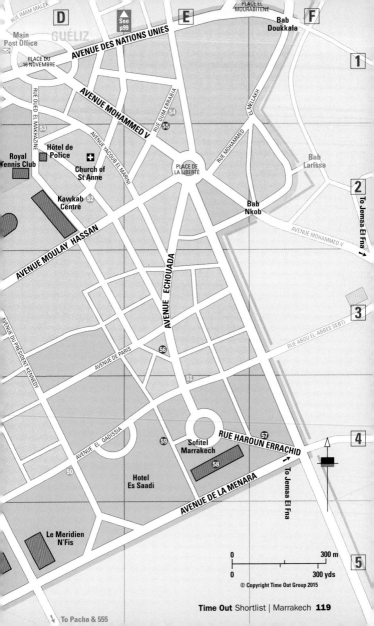

street, but inside the place buzzes with dressed-up diners on the ground floor, while upstairs is a sizeable lounge filled each weekend night to within a whisper of a health and safety crisis. The crowd is a mix of good-looking locals, sharper expats and wide-eyed tourists delighted to have stumbled on the Marrakech they'd always heard about. Drinks are pricey but the nightly belly dancers are hilarious.

Djellabar

2 rue Abou Hanifa, Villa Bougainvillée (0524 42 12 42, www.djellabar.com). **Open** 7.30pm-late daily. **Bar.** **Map** p119 D2 ➎➋

This rather bonkers-looking converted wedding room literally drips in garish colour, carved plaster, fake jewels and Moroccan pop art featuring everyone from Elvis and Ray Charles to the present-day King Mohammed VI in a fez. The music strays wildly from Arabic pop to Latin tunes and 1970s disco and funk but it's reliably fun night of dancing and decent cocktails – and there's always the possibility of an appearance by the bar's creator, Claude Chaulle, formerly of the Buddha Bar in Paris, in a madcap outfit.

Jack is Back

10 rue Oued El-Makhazine (0524 43 38 90). **Open** 8pm-2am daily. **Bar.** **Map** p119 D2 ➎➌

Technically, Jack is Back is more restaurant than bar. The food, such as a bone marrow and parsley salad and artichoke-topped pizzas, is superb, with about two-thirds of the space given over to a mixture of round and oblong tables, slouchy booths and sofas, and a high table presided over by a portrait of a fried breakfast. That's Jack, his tongue firmly in cheek and a regular for years on the Marrakech night scene. This is his latest offering and the little bar at the front of the house teems with regulars, fellow bar owners and scenesters, who all come for a taste of his special brand of unpretentious, grown-up fun,

a funky sound track, killer cocktails and reliably good company.

Katsura

Rue Oum Errabia, behind Hotel Le Marrakech (0524 43 43 58, mobile 0667 12 68 63). **Open** noon-midnight daily. **££.** Alcohol served. **Pan-Asian.** **Map** p119 E1 ➎➍

The best of a number of pan-Asian restaurants in town, Katsura's funky geometric design splashed with vibrant orange, combined with a lively atmosphere and good cooking at reasonable prices, ensures it always draws a crowd. California rolls, *ikura* (salmon roe) maki, top-grade tuna and *chirashi* (sashimi-topped bowls of rice) as well as some pleasing Moroccan twists such as *temaki* (seaweed cones) stuffed with eel, avocado and mint combine well with decent *yakitori* (Japanese skewers) and nicely made Thai noodles and curries.

Nightlife

African Chic

6 rue Oum Errabia (0524 43 14 24, www.african-chic.com). **Admission** free. **Open** 7.30pm-3am daily. **Map** p119 E2 ➎➎

Not a nightclub as such, but a bar with late live music and a thumping dancefloor – and, in 2014, much improved from previous years. A Latin and salsa ensemble from Spain, Morocco and Venezuela rocks the house from 11.30pm Monday to Saturday. A backing-track singer warms up the crowd, and a DJ takes over at 1.30am. Dark wood, zebra-painted niches and carved masks create the 'African' effect, but the 'Chic' is sadly lacking.

Lotus Club

Rue Ahmed Chawki (0524 42 17 36, www.lotusclubmarrakech.com). **Open** 7.30pm-2am daily. **Dinner ££££.** **Show** 9pm. **Map** p119 E3 ➎➏

Costumed dancers with feathers aplenty take to the stage in a Las Vegas-style

Garden city

Marrakech's urban oases.

Menara Gardens

In a hot, dusty city where the predominant colours are pink and red, it's a relief to contemplate water and see serene greens and blues. Some of the classic picture-postcard photographs of Marrakech are taken in two of the city's most famous gardens, the **Menara** (p120) and the **Majorelle** (p100). These little urban oases – and others around the city including the well-tended gardens of hotels in the Palmeraie – provide peace and calm away from the buzz of mopeds, the fumes of exhausts and the chatter of street hawkers.

The Menara Gardens date from the 12th century, as do the royal **Agdal Gardens** (p87). However, gardens were not the preserve of royals. Wealthy merchants, judges, master craftsmen and petty officials dwelt in riads (townhouses built around courtyard gardens). These were usually symmetrical in design: four beds planted with trees, underplanted with perfumed flowers, and arranged around the all-important central fountain. The microclimate thus created provided shade, cooled the air, smelled sweet and encouraged songbirds.

The French continued the horticultural tradition under the Protectorate. In Guéliz, many of the boulevards are lined with jacaranda trees that bloom in electric blue. Bougainvillea and vines clothe the boundary walls of villas, and hibiscus flowers add vibrant colour. Then there are the orange trees. The streets of Guéliz are lined with them. The combination of blue sky, pink walls, green leaves and orange fruit is a knockout; it's like walking through a landscape by Matisse. Unfortunately, the oranges are too sour to eat or juice. Instead, the prize is the blossom, highly valued for its scent.

In recent years the municipality has embarked on a scheme to green the city even more. Large-scale planting of trees and flowers along the airport and Medina ring roads has been completed and the ramparts are now surrounded by beds of roses, hibiscus and jasmine. The **Jnane El-Harti park** (p100) in Guéliz has been totally replanted and relandscaped, as was the **Arset Moulay Abdelsalam** (p97) on the edge of the Medina, now with free Wi-Fi.

Outdoor adventures

Activities around Marrakech.

No trip to Marrakech is complete
without a camel ride. A half-day trip
plus mint tea pit stop in a village
can be arranged through **Touareg
Quad** (Bab Atlas, route de Fès,
opposite Hotel El Dorador, mobile
0660 64 64 92, www.maroc-quad-
buggy.com) at 250dh per half-day
(no under-10s). Its Touareg Day
package includes camel, quad and
buggy riding with lunch, for 1,100dh
per driver, 450dh per passenger.

Camel treks are also available
through **Dunes & Desert
Exploration** (route de Palmeraie,
0524 35 41 47, www.dunesdesert.
com). The company also offers
quad bikes and buggies, for half-
day trips around Marrakech to
multi-day adventures further afield.

Grand Prix champion wannabes
can try go-karting. **Atlas Karting**
(route de Safi, km8, Ouhat Sidi
Brahim, 0524 33 20 33, 650dh
for 1hr) is a challenging course on
the city outskirts. Day packages,
with karting, quad-biking and lunch,
cost 2,100dh.

Horse-riding is popular among
expats and wealthy Moroccans.
Les Cavaliers de L'Atlas (mobile
0672 84 55 79, www.lescavaliers
de latlas.com) is a French-run
equestrian centre five kilometres
(three miles) out of town on the
route de Fès. A half-day ride in the
Palmeraie costs 350dh; a trek
in the countryside near Lalla
Takerkoust is 770dh per person.

Stunning scenery and clear skies
make ideal conditions for aerial
adventures. Hot-air ballooning
is organised by **Ciel d'Afrique**
(Immeuble Ali A, route de Targa,
Guéliz, 0524 43 28 43, www.

Ciel d'Afrique

ceildafrique.info). For paragliding,
try **Evolution2 Marrakech**
(Résidence Ali B, avenue
Mohammed VI, Guéliz, 0524 45 76
88, www.evolution2ma.com).

Back down to earth, golfers are
well catered for on the plentiful
newly manicured courses
surrounding the city. These include
the **Royal Golf Club** (ancienne
route de Ouarzazate, km2, 0524
40 47 05), the oldest course in
Morocco, built in the 1920s, and
the **Al Maaden Golf Resort** (Sidi
Youssef Ben Ali, 0525 065 065,
www.almaaden.com), which
flaunts its modernity with angular
bunkers, water features and
outdoor sculptures. Golf package
agencies include **Golf in Morocco**
(www.golfinmorocco.co.uk). Green
fees are usually around 800dh for
18 holes, with club hire on top and
optional caddy service.

Make sure you have adequate
travel insurance and that the
operator provides training, safety
gear and a good guide and has civil
responsibility insurance.

revue called Oh La La at this dinner cabaret venue. There's also a pop, soul and funk band from England, and Moroccan virtuoso guitarist Mahmoud 'Mood' Chouki. 'Mood' gives a captivating performance in a kaleidoscope of world music styles. The intimate restaurant-bar area has an elegant art deco feel. Turn up after 9pm to view the performance from the bar, but if you want a table near the stage, you'll need to book for dinner (there are Mediterranean, Japanese and Moroccan menus).

Silver

Downstairs at Jad Mahal, 10 rue Haroun Errachid (mobile 0663 73 15 42, www. silvermarrakech.com). **Admission** 200dh. **Open** midnight-5am daily. **Map** p119 F4 ⑰

If you've spent the evening at Jad Mahal restaurant and bar (with house covers band), head underground for after-hours into the shiny, industrial space of Silver. Glittering disco balls, pumping techno and soulful house remixes fill this former cabaret venue and attract a youthful, blinging crowd of partygoers. Guest DJs from Europe regularly perform. Free entry if you've come from Jad Mahal.

So Lounge

Sofitel, rue Haroun Errachid (mobile 0660 12 34 10). **Admission** 250dh (free to hotel guests and restaurant clients). **Open** 11pm-4am daily. **Map** p119 E4 ⑱

The So Lounge space in the Sofitel is carved up into four sections: restaurant So Food; chill-out lounge So Zen; So Nice, an alcohol-free outdoor shisha garden; and So Fun, the dancefloor and music stage. On Wednesdays there are belly dancers and an 'oriental' theme until 1am. Otherwise, there's live soul, R&B and a funk band, plus DJs. The decor is contemporary and cool and the place attracts a more mature crowd of tourists, expats and locals. For groups, it can work out cheaper to make a dinner reservation.

Théâtro

Rue Ibrahim El-Mazini (0524 33 74 00, www.theatromarrakech.com). **Admission** 150dh. **Open** 11.30pm-5am daily. **Map** p119 E4 ⑲

Going strong since 1952, the dramatic Théâtro was originally a variety theatre, attracting such illustrious names as Maurice Chevalier and Josephine Baker. Completely revamped in 2005, it is still the best place in the city for proper dancing. The vast space makes room for all sorts of shenanigans from pole dancers to cabaret-style performances, men on stilts, jugglers and fire-eaters. As well as Morocco's funkiest DJs, the venue attracts guest stars from abroad. There are different themed parties every night of the week; Tuesday is (free for) Ladies Night.

The Palmeraie

Legend has it that the huge Palmeraie north-east of the Medina was born of the seeds cast away by date-chomping Arab warriors centuries ago. A nice story, but it fails to accord due credit to the clever minds that designed an underground irrigation system to carry melted snow water all the way from the High Atlas to enable a palm oasis of several hundred thousand trees to grow. The ancient *khettra* system now has only historical curiosity value because the water supply is guaranteed by several reservoirs and a network of artesian wells.

It's not what you'd call a pretty oasis: many of the palms are the worse for wear and the ground is dry, dusty and lunar-like, with much of the scrappy land turned over to building sites. Even so, this is some of the most desirable real estate in all North Africa. Ever since the 1960s, when King Hassan II first granted permission for it to be sold, Palmeraie land has been the choice for the rich – it's the Beverly Hills of

MARRAKECH BY AREA

Beldi Country Club p126

Morocco. Land is available only in parcels of more than one hectare and buildings must not interfere with the palms. Narrow lanes slalom between copses, occasionally squeezing beside high walls surrounding the typically massive grounds of very discreet residences.

Other than pricey homes, there isn't much to see in the Palmeraie (other than the odd ramshackle village, grazing camels and building sites). You might venture out here for a combination lunch and swim (see box p127), or you might choose to stay in this part of town, taking advantage of the luscious gardens of some of the city's most luxurious hotels (pp173-174).

Sights & museums

Musée de Palmeraie

NEW *Dar Tounsi, route de Fès (mobile 0661 09 53 52, www.museepalmeraie.com).* **Open** 9am-6pm daily. **Admission** free.
Abderrazzak Benchaâbane's museum is rather like a small sanctuary. His private collection of modern and contemporary art from the 1950s to the present hangs in large, bright galleries. Benchaâbane has collected the work of painters, photographers, sculptors and calligraphers, and showcases the work of Moroccan artists including Larbi Cherkaoui and Nourredine Chater, with stunning calligraphy and henna work on paper by Nourredine Daifallah, paintings by Hassan El-Glaoui and Farid Belkhahia, and more. Considering there is no contemporary art museum in Marrakech, it's worth the trip out here, although labels are in French, so if you're not fluent it might be better to organise a tour in advance. Benchaâbane, a university ecology teacher with a science and botanical background, runs a small perfume atelier in his garden with one-hour workshops (50 euros per person). After that you can swan around the cactus garden and take tea in a little domed pavilion in the grounds.

Eating & drinking

Jnane Tamsna

Douar Abiad (mobile 0661 24 27 17, www.jnane.com). **Open** 12.30-2.30pm, 7-9.30pm daily. **££**. Alcohol served.
Moroccan.
It's well worth making the trek out to the Palmeraie from the Medina for lunch and a prowl around the gardens at Jnane Tamsna. It's much more than just a restaurant. Meryanne and Gary Loum-Martin built the house back in the early 1990s and set about creating their very own Garden of Eden with acres of native plants, home-grown fruit and vegetables, olive groves and, of course, those all important palms. With so much pristine fresh produce at her fingertips, chef Bahija, who's been with the family since the start, offers an inventive and healthy spin on traditional Moroccan dishes from a menu that changes twice daily. She also does cooking classes. After lunch, bask by the pool for a couple of hours, but don't forget to pop into the gallery-cum-tearoom to admire Meryanne's own collection of homewares (her scented candles are droolworthy) and works by some of the country's best artists.

Palais Namaskar

88/69 Route de Bab Atlas, Province Syba (0524 29 98 00, www.palais namaskar.com). **Open** 12.30-2.30pm, 7pm-late daily. Bar opens 5pm. **£££**.
Modern Moroccan.
Heading deeper into La Palmeraie, you'll find this aptly named, contemporary 'palace' hidden away behind thick pink pisé walls and surrounded by perfectly manicured gardens and reflecting pools. Complete with turrets and golden domes, sweeping staircases and swimming pools peeking out from frilly arches, it's one of the prettiest restaurants in the city, and chefs Antoine Perray's and Nicolas Warot's modern Moroccan cooking is some of the country's best. Have a sundowner before dinner at the Nomad bar to enjoy

magnificent views across the oasis to the Atlas, though fashionistas may prefer to don their summer dresses and head out for the Sunday Garden Party (788dh excluding drinks).

Nightlife

Le Blokk

Lotissement Ennakhil (mobile 0674 33 43 34, www.leblokk.com). **Open** 8pm-1.30am daily. **Dinner** £££. **Show** 8.30pm.

Blues, jazz and R&B singers take to the stage to accompany dinner before the acrobats start falling from the rafters at around 11pm. Then the party gets in full swing, with a mix of Arabic and western pop music drawing punters to the small dancefloor. The chic restaurant attracts smartly dressed Moroccans and foreigners, but non-diners are also welcome to drink at the bar and dance to the live acts and DJs.

Fuego Latino

Hotel Palmeraie Palace, Circuit de la Palmeraie (mobile 0619 27 29 45, www.palmeraiemarrakech.com). **Open** 7pm-2am daily. **Dinner** £££. **Show** 11pm.

After you've eaten your fill of barbecued *churrascaria* meat and fish at the Brazilian-style buffet, it's carnival time. Sip a caipirinha as you watch the *capoeiristas* perform the traditional Brazilian martial arts dance. And there's more Latin-themed entertainment with samba drummers and exotic dancers. Book for dinner to get the best view of the catwalk stage. Entry to the bar area is free, but the drinks are expensive.

On the southern outskirts of town, this area, home to new hotels and clubs, centres around avenue Mohamed VI.

Nightlife

555 Famous Club Marrakech

Hotel Ushuaia Clubbing, boulevard Mohammed VI (mobile 0678 64 39 40, www.beachclub555.com). **Open** 11pm-5am daily. **Admission** 200dh.

New kid on the block 555 opened in 2012, playing house, R&B and hip hop. Seemingly desperate to attract female clientele, Ladies Nights run Monday to Wednesday, with no charge for groups of four or more. The huge dancefloor only really fills up at weekends. Expect loads of dry ice and ultraviolet beams, exuberant young Moroccans and pounding decibels. While drinks prices may be excessive, free nibbles are provided, and the rooftop Sky5 bar is a popular spot where you can also eat tapas.

Pacha

Boulevard Mohammed VI (0524 38 84 00, www.pachamarrakech.com). **Open** midnight-5.30am Tue-Sun. **Admission** 200dh; 250dh Fri, Sat.

Pacha is an enormous complex which, apart from the club itself, also includes two restaurants, a chill-out lounge and swimming pool. The dancefloor and bars can accommodate up to 3,000 smiley souls. International guest DJs play at weekends, but resident DJ Daox is one to watch out for too. The club is some 7km (4.5 miles) south of town, so getting there and back can be pricey.

Out of town

Eating & drinking

Beldi Country Club

Route de Barrage km6, Cherifia (0524 38 39 50, www.beldicountryclub.com). **Open** noon-1am daily. £££. Alcohol served. **Mediterranean**.

There's no shortage of places just outside Marrakech serving up bone-jiggling techno pool-side. It's rather more difficult finding a peaceful retreat

Poolside lunch, afternoon dip

Souks overdose? Time to relax with lunch and a swim.

Jnane Tamsna

Stimulating as Marrakech is, there comes a time when you just want to chill out by a pool for the afternoon. Fortunately, there are plenty of country options within a half-hour taxi ride from the Medina, as well as a couple of lesser-known getaways within the city itself.

If it's views of the Atlas you seek (particularly sensational in spring, when snow still caps those powerful peaks), head down the route d'Ourika. Here you'll find the **Touco Café** (p129), at the unique Fellah, a hotel that's also part arts centre and part philanthropic project. The restaurant and bar are set around the deep-blue pool with the Atlas mountains as a backdrop and, unusually, non-resident dining guests are welcome to take a dip for free.

Le Bled (p129) is located within several acres of olive and citrus groves. The former farmhouse is now a simple country hotel, painted in bright Majorelle blues, buttercup yellows and hot pinks, and its swimming pool is open to day guests (200dh lunch plus pool

pass). It's blessedly free of the thumping techno that besieges many of Marrakech's so-called beach clubs; and you can have lunch anywhere you fancy. Wine and beer are served, and a petit taxi will bring you here for 50dh if you negotiate hard.

More upmarket is the **Beldi Country Club** (p126). With several long, deep, midnight-coloured pools surrounded by salmon pink pisé buildings, richly scented rose gardens and pergolas shaded in jasmine and bougainvillea, it's every inch the Arabian Days fantasy and doesn't cost the earth (370dh lunch plus pool pass).

Heading into the Palmeraie, **Jnane Tamsna** (p125) is a true oasis filled with soaring palms and native Moroccan and Mediterranean species including aphrodisiac and healing plants. Stroll around before indulging in one of chef Bahija's creative healthy lunches before collapsing by the pool (300dh lunch plus pool pass). The pool house has rotating art exhibitions and its own shop.

In the Medina, the **Jardins de la Koutoubia** (p161) is one of the city's best-kept secrets for an elegantly peaceful lunch and a dip (200dh for lunch plus pool pass). The courtyard swimming pool is vast but often busy with families, so head to the smaller rooftop pool.

Finally, for a real taste of the high life, treat yourself to a day or weekend Spa Pass (500dh-1,800dh, not including lunch) at **La Mamounia** (p161), which gives access to the spa (not including treatments) and the outdoor pool.

Touco Café

for the afternoon where you can combine a swim with a top-flight lunch. Beldi Country Club scores highly on all counts as a suave, sophisticated, summer hangout. Impeccably landscaped rose gardens provide the backdrop for three generously proportioned pools (one for kids, one heated year round, one for everyone) and several different alfresco dining areas dishing up healthy Mediterranean-inspired fare such as spinach, tomato and basil tart, spaghetti vongole and vanilla-strawberry pannacotta. See also box p127.

Le Bled

Douar Coucou, Oasis Hassan II, Taseltanet (0524 38 59 39, www. lebledmarrakech). **Open** 10am-10pm daily. **Pool & lunch** 200dh. Alcohol served. **Moroccan**.

About 20 minutes from Marrakech, this low-key, organic farm hotel and swimming pool set amid citrus orchards and olive groves is a welcome newcomer to the post-lunch scene. It is owned by Dar Moha restaurant in the city and is a popular day out for Moroccans looking for peace and quiet. There's nothing as formal as a restaurant, but the kitchen is happy to lay tables or picnic blankets for you to eat anywhere you like on the grounds: under a shady tree, poolside, or in the cool internal courtyard. The home-grown menu offers authentic home-cooking and fabulous-made ice-cream and pastries. See also box p127.

Touco Café

Fellah Hotel, route de l'Ourika km13, Tassoultante, Canal Zabara (0525 06 50 00, www.fellah-hotel.com). **Open** 8am-11pm daily. **£££**. Alcohol served. **Moroccan**.

It's worth the 20-minute taxi ride out of town to spend time at the Fellah, one of the most inspiring philanthropic projects to hit Morocco in recent years. It wears various hats, as home to the Ma'mun Art Foundation, which runs artists-in-residence programmes, and as a community-based project that employs local villagers to organically farm their land and run the Touco Café, which serves authentic Moroccan street food. The retro, mid-century modern dining room and bar are set around a large, deep-blue swimming pool with the Atlas mountains as a backdrop and, unusually, dining guests are welcome to take a dip for free. If you're staying for the evening bring something sparkly, because Le Salon Mahler is one of the hottest tickets in town, shaking things up with live piano recitals, visiting DJs, film screenings and killer cocktails. See also box p127.

Shopping

Marjane

Route de Casablanca, Semlalia (0524 31 37 24, www.marjane.co.ma). **Open** 9am-10pm daily.

This massive hypermarket is popular with the city's middle and upper classes. It combines a supermarket (food and booze, clothes, household items, electronics, white goods, computers) with a McDonald's, plus Lacoste, Yves Rocher and other franchises, plus ATM machines, Méditel and Maroc Télécom, and a pharmacy. It's about 8km (5 miles) north of town; a petit taxi will cost around 30dh each way from the Medina.

Myriam Roland-Gosselin

6 rue de l'Aéroport, sign indicating La Ferme Zanzibar (mobile 0659 05 31 66, www.myriamrolandgosselin.com). **Open** by appointment only. No credit cards.

Roland-Gosselin has a studio in a tranquil garden just off the airport road, where she makes delicate hand-blown glass objects for the home. Her collection, exhibited at MyArt (place du 16 Novembre, angle rue Tarek Ibn Ziad, Guéliz, 0524 44 91 81, open 9.30am-1.30pm, 4-8pm Mon Sat) includes tumblers, bells, candleholders and small lamps. Colour schemes tend to be warm ambers and oranges that bring to mind fiery Moroccan sunsets.

Ourika Valley

Day Trips

Exciting though the Medina is, after a few days you may feel an urge to chill out somewhere rural for the day. There are plenty of destinations within easy reach of Marrakech. Perhaps the most dramatic and beautiful is the route d'Ourika into the Ourika Valley. Other routes lead to the popular destinations of Barrage Lalla Takerkoust, along the route d'Amizmiz, and the Lac des Aït Aadel and Cascades d'Ouzoud via the route de Fès.

Each of these trips can be done in a day, but we have included a few accommodation recommendations in case you want to linger a little longer. We've also included public transport details, but the downside of using it is that you won't be able to stop whenever you feel like it. A better and more relaxing option is to hire a car and driver for the day. Your hotel should be able to arrange it.

The Ourika Valley

Ourika is a spectacular valley cut deep into the High Atlas. It's not a pass as such – the road stops at **Setti Fatma**, 63 kilometres (39 miles) from Marrakech. Being so close to the city, it's an easy place to get a taste of mountain air and take a break from the summer heat.

Buses and grand taxis leave from Marrakech's Bab Er Rob. Make sure you're getting one that goes all the way to Setti Fatma, as some head only as far as Arhbalou, 24 kilometres (15 miles) short. The journey takes about two hours.

To Arhbalou

The route d'Ourika begins at the fountain roundabout of Bab Jedid, by the Mamounia Hotel. The road follows that stretch of the walls which encloses the Agdal Gardens before crossing 34 kilometres

(21 miles) of hotel developments and agricultural flatland.

There are two possible side excursions. First, **Aghmat** (signposted as Jemaa D'Rhmat) was the first Almoravid capital of the region. It is now a small village, and has a 1960s mausoleum dedicated to Youssef Ibn Tachfine, founder of Marrakech. Secondly, **Tnine de l'Ourika** has a Monday souk and is home to **Nectarome** (0524 48 21 49, www.nectarome.com, open 9am-5pm daily, no credit cards), a charming organic garden of aromatic plants with a shop selling wellness products made from their essential oils. On arrival you're invited to take a tour of the gardens, where the properties of plants are explained. Afterwards, browse the selection of soaps, shampoos and bath, massage, skin treatment and aromatherapy oils. Call ahead to book a foot bath (80dh) or foot massage (250dh), and also for a better chance of getting an English-speaking guide.

Six kilometres (four miles) before reaching Arhbalou from Marrakech, you will find the 'pottery' village of **Tafza**. Leave your car at the roadside by the mosque and then walk 150 metres, following signs, to the centre of the old village and you'll find the carefully curated **Berber Eco-Museum** (mobile 0610 25 67 34, www.museeberbere.com, open 9am-7pm daily, admission 20dh). Housed in an old restored village kasbah, the museum is a treasure trove of artefacts, pottery, ceramics, carpets and rare antique photos depicting local Berber culture and traditions from the past century. The brainchild of Patrick Man'ach and Hamid Mergani, the project aims to promote sustainable tourism and cultural understanding in the village. The museum is a partnership project with their exquisite collection at La Maison de la Photographie (p60), in Marrakech. On-site guide Khalid speaks excellent English and will bring the whole exhibition to life with his thoughtful interpretation.

Beyond here, Berber villages cling to steep valley sides, camouflaged against a red-earth backdrop that forms a brilliant contrast with the deep, luminous greens of the valley.

There's nothing much at **Arhbalou**, except for the turn-off to Oukaimeden. On the stretch beyond, there are a few decent hotels that also double as lunch spots, notably the **Auberge Le Maquis** (0524 48 45 31, www.le-maquis.com, 580dh per room) and **Chez Larbi** (mobile 0661 34 23 92, www.chezlarbi-ourika.com) which has a shaded garden terrace and rooms from 700dh.

Setti Fatma

After a final gorge-like stretch, with cafés and houses along the opposite bank, the road peters out at Setti Fatma. The village is nothing special – lots of cafés and souvenir shops, with satellite dishes on breeze-block houses – but the setting is wonderful, ringed by mountains with lots of streams and grassy terraces. If you arrive in mid August, there's a big four-day *moussem*, an event that's both a religious celebration and sociable fair. The village also has a bureau de guides where you can arrange local hikes.

The shortest and simplest hike is the Walk of the Seven Waterfalls. On the other side of the river from the main body of the village – reached by precarious footbridges made of bundled branches – are a number of small tagine and brochette joints. Concealed behind these is a steep-sided valley, and a climb up it will bring you to the first of the seven cascades. It's quite strenuous, over big river boulders and up a cliff or two. Anyone will point (or lead) the way, and there is a basic café at the foot of the first waterfall where you

Argan for everything

Morocco's miracle oil.

Goats clambering about in argan trees is part of tourist mythology in south-west Morocco. And you may actually see them doing it. Round here grow the world's only argan trees – between Essaouira and Sidi Ifni, in an area that has been declared a UNESCO Biosphere Reserve.

Thorny and knotted, the trees look similar to olive trees and also bear a fruit from which oil can be extracted. The goat's digestive system was the means by which the tough fruit was stripped from the recalcitrant nut. The nuts were then collected from goat droppings before being split to expose the kernel, which was pulped and pressed – it takes 30 kilogrammes of nuts to make one litre of oil. Thankfully, these days the process is mechanical and hygienic and the goats have been sidelined.

Argan oil is highly prized. Rich in vitamin E, it's good for the skin and has become a staple of Moroccan massage and beauty treatments. It's efficacious in reducing cholesterol and countering arteriosclerosis. The culinary variety, where the kernels are toasted, is very tasty. Moroccan 'peanut butter' is called amlou and the best mix is with almonds, argan oil and honey. Culinary argan oil costs around 400dh per litre. Cosmetic oil should be a clear pale yellow, odour-free and absorbed easily into the skin. Expect to pay around 150dh per 100ml.

can rest with a cool drink. The other six are a more serious climb.

Accommodation ranges from the rustic charm of **Au Bord de L'Eau** (mobile 0661 22 97 55, www.obordelo. com) near the falls (rooms from 400dh; no credit cards), to the boutique chic of the fully licensed **Kasbah Bab Ourika** (mobile 0668 74 95 47, www.kasbahbabourika. com, doubles from 1,650dh). Ideal for a few days' escape or even just for an afternoon, it's located around 12 kilometres (eight miles) beyond the turn-off to Oukaimeden.

Activities

The twisting mountain tracks from village to village mean cycling is a popular sport. Operator **Epic Morocco** (www.epicmorocco.co.uk) runs an exhilarating six-day High Atlas Traverse on mountain bikes and mules. Trekking in the Ourika Valley can be booked with local mountain guide Mohammed Aztat of **Atlas Trek Shop** (www.atlastrekshop. com). Alternatively, book a day-hike and lunch direct from **Auberge le Maquis** (p131) near Arhbalour, or **Kasbah Bab Ourika** (above). There is also a bureau des guides at Setti Fatma (mobile 0668 56 23 40).

For skiing, head to Oukaimeden and hire your own equipment, instructor or guide at the base of the slopes or at **Chez Juju** (0524 31 90 05, www.hotelchezjujo.com). Professionally organised canyoning and rafting in the rivers and gorges of Ourika can be booked through **Splash Morocco** (www.morocco adventuretours.com) and usually includes transport from Marrakech.

Route d'Amizmiz

Leave Marrakech as if heading for Asni, and then fork right soon after Oasiria water park. After ten kilometres (six miles), take a right

top: Cycling in the Atlas
Mountains; bottom: Cascades
d'Ouzoud p134

turn for **Tamesloht**, home of a potters' co-operative. The village also boasts ancient olive oil presses with gigantic grindstones driven, until recently, by mules. There's also a rambling kasbah still partially occupied by descendants of the village founders, and next to it a **shrine of Moulay Abdellah** with a minaret that appears to be toppling under the weight of an enormous storks' nest. Call in at the offices of the Association Tamesloht (place Sour Souika) for additional info.

South of Tamesloht, the fertile landscape becomes a brilliant patchwork of greenery. Visible to the left is **Kasbah Oumnast**, a location for films *The Last Temptation of Christ* and *Hideous Kinky*. Eight kilometres (five miles) further south, the road swings on to a narrow bridge over the **Oued N'fis** before looping around to hug the shore of the **Barrage Lalla Takerkoust**, a sizeable reservoir with the mountains as backdrop.

A number of lakeside restaurants line the road; **Relais du Lac** (0524 48 49 43, www.relaisdulac marrakech.com) is the most popular (and noisy) and from here you can also arrange horse-riding with **Les Cavaliers de L'Atlas** (see box p122). Next door is **Le Flouka** (mobile 0664 49 26 60, www.leflouka. com), which has tastefully decorated rooms (from 660dh double). Jet-skiing on the lake can be booked with **Jet Atlas** (0524 30 30 22, www.jet-atlas.com).

The road ends at **Amizmiz** (pronounced 'Amsmiz'), 55 kilometres (34 miles) south-west of Marrakech. Nearby, the luxurious contemporary Moroccan-style **Capaldi Hotel** (0524 48 47 59, www.thecapaldi.com, from 170 euros double) has lovely gardens and an outstanding restaurant open for non-residents; staff can arrange guided hiking in the nearby foothills.

The town has a ruined kasbah and a former *mellah* (Jewish quarter), as well as a Thursday market that's one of the biggest in the region.

There are regular buses and grand taxis between Marrakech (from Bab Er Rob) and Amizmiz. The journey takes just over an hour.

Cascades d'Ouzoud

The route de Fès runs east out of Marrakech. After ten kilometres (six miles), there's a right-hand turn on to the road for Demnate and Azilal. After 40 kilometres (24 miles) skirting the foothills of the Atlas, look for a right turn to the village of **Timinoutine**, which is on the edge of the **Lac des Aït Aadel**. Also known as the **Barrage Moulay Youssef**, this is another large reservoir with a High Atlas backdrop. The scenery is gorgeous and it's a popular picnic spot for Marrakchis. At Demnate, a side road runs south to **Imi-n-Ifri**, which scores with a natural rock bridge, a slippery grotto and fossilised dinosaur footprints. Boutique guesthouse **Tizouit** (mobile 0658 34 61 48, www.tizouit.ma, 600dh double) offers lots of activities, and is an ideal base for a longer stay.

East from Demnate on the way to Azilal is a signposted turn-off north for the **Cascades d'Ouzoud**: the biggest waterfall in Morocco, it plunges 110 metres (360 feet) in three tiers down to a picturesque pool overlooked by cafés. You arrive at the top, where people will want to 'guide' you down, though help isn't really necessary. If you don't fancy going straight back to Marrakech, the **Riad Cascades d'Ouzoud** (0523 42 91 73, www.ouzoud.com, 600dh double) is rustically tasteful.

Two buses a day run from Marrakech to Azilal, and from here you can hire a grand taxi for the 20-minute backtrack to the falls. Market day is Thursday.

Essaouira

Southern Morocco's most interesting coastal town – and the one most easily reached from Marrakech – offers both a contrast and an escape. Here, the pink and green of Marrakech are replaced by blue and white, and the town is cooled by refreshing Atlantic breezes. It's around three hours away by bus, quicker by car or taxi, and, while just about doable as a day trip, travellers tend to stay a while enjoying its chilled-out charms.

Sandy-coloured ramparts shelter a Medina built around French squares, carved archways and whitewashed lanes and alleys. The fishing port provides a constant fresh catch for local restaurants, while the wide, sandy beaches to the south – combined with high winds – have put Essaouira on the international windsurfing map. Essaouira can also claim to be one of the cleanest Moroccan towns, with no vehicles in the Medina and regular street sweeping.

Like Marrakech, Essaouira has next to nothing in the way of formal sights such as monuments and museums. The Medina itself is one big sight, with highlights including the ramparts, the souks and the Mellah. You can march from one end to the other in ten minutes; a more leisurely exploration, however, can take days and the influx of cool little places to eat and drink makes it ever more attractive as a place for R&R.

The port is a separate entity, worthy of at least a stroll. Connecting the two is the place Moulay Hassan, the town's social nexus, which you'll pass through at least a dozen times a day.

The town

Arriving by car from Marrakech, you'll most likely enter the Medina through the arch of **Bab Sbaâ**, one of five gates. (By bus, you'll enter

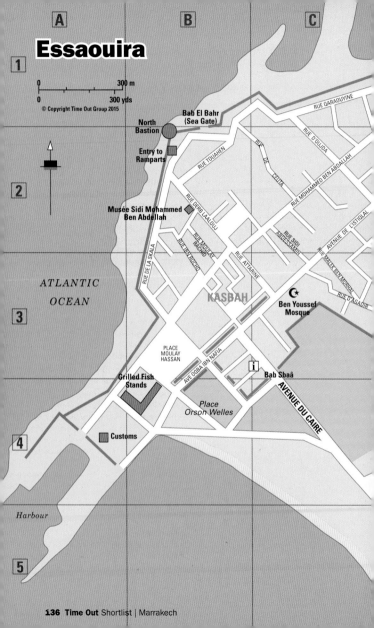

Essaouira

© Copyright Time Out Group 2015

A **B** **C**

1

300 m
300 yds

Bab El Bahr
(Sea Gate)

RUE DARAOUYINE

North
Bastion

RUE D'OUJDA

Entry to
Ramparts

RUE TOUAHEN

RUE DE CEUTA

2

Musée Sidi Mohammed
Ben Abdellah

RUE DERB LAALOUJ

RUE MOHAMMED BEN ABDALLAH

RUE MOULAY RACHID

AVENUE DE L'ISTIQLAL

RUE SIDI ABDESSAMIH

RUE IBN ROCHD

RUE ATTARINE

RUE MALEK BEN MORBAL

RUE DE LA SKALA

ATLANTIC
OCEAN

KASBAH

RUE D'AGADIR

3

Ben Youssef
Mosque ☪

PLACE
MOULAY
HASSAN

AVE OQBA IBN NAFIA

ℹ

Bab Sbaâ

Grilled Fish
Stands

Place
Orson Welles

AVENUE DU CAIRE

4

Customs

Harbour

5

through **Bab Marrakech**.) Beyond Bab Sbaâ, avenue du Caire has the town's fairly ineffective tourist information office on the left, and the police further down on the opposite side. The few cross-streets around here also contain several hotels, galleries and restaurants and a rowdy Moroccan bar, but it's a strangely detached corner of town, separate from both the Kasbah area and the rest of the Medina.

The narrow, shady **avenue du Caire** intersects the broad, open **avenue Oqba Ibn Nafia**, the spine of the Medina. Left, this leads out to the port. Right, it dips under an arch, changes its name to **avenue de l'Istiqlal**, and becomes Essaouira's main commercial thoroughfare. Opposite avenue du Caire, the arch in the wall leads into the Kasbah district and, bearing left, to **place Moulay Hassan**.

Near the Bab Marrakech you'll find the **Artisan Centre** (1 rue Ibn Batouta) – being renovated in mid 2014, providing a solid overview of what crafts are available locally and what you should be paying for them. And near Bab Sbaâ, **Dar Souiri** (avenue du Caire, www.association-essaouiramogador.org, open 9am-12.30pm, 3-7pm) is a cultural centre with a permanent exhibition of Gnawa Festival posters plus first-floor changing exhibits of exceptionally high-quality local photographers.

Place Moulay Hassan & the port

Connecting the Medina to the port, **place Moulay Hassan** is Essaouira's social centre. You can sit at any of the cafés and watch the theatre of the town unfolding. Early in the morning, fishermen pass by on their way to work, and the first wave of itinerant musicians and shoe-shine boys appears. By 10am

MARRAKECH BY AREA

or 11am the café tables have begun their secondary function – as alfresco offices from which most Souiris conduct business at some time or another. Purveyors of sunglasses, watches and carpets sweep from table to table, only occasionally selling something. By now tourists have started to appear, buying the previous day's international newspapers from **Jack's Kiosk**.

Apart from the cafés at street level, place Moulay Hassan is also overlooked by the terrace of **Taros**, the city's premier spot for a sundowner overlooking the ocean. The port comes to life in the late afternoon when the fishing fleet rolls back into the harbour and the catch is auctioned between 3pm and 5pm at the market hall just outside the port gates. Fresh fish are grilled and served up at **stalls** on the port side of place Moulay Hassan and makes for fun picnicking.

If you want to go boating yourself, **Essaouira Sailing Tour** (mobile 0661 62 63 13) is located on the quayside near **Chez Sam** and organises trips of one and a half to three hours (300dh per person; minimum two people).

Skala de la Ville

The narrow **rue de la Skala** leads from place Moulay Hassan along the inside of the sea wall. It's also possible to get here by ducking through the spooky tunnel-like alley that leads off place Moulay Hassan by the **Café de France**.

Rue de la Skala leads to the **Skala de la Ville**, where you can walk on top of the ramparts. There is one ramp up to the top near the junction with rue Ibn Rochd at the southern end, and another near the junction with rue Derb Laâlouj at the northern end. Locals gather here to watch the sunset and lovers cuddle in the crenellations, where ancient

cannon offer places to perch. At the far end is the tower of the North Bastion, the top of which offers good views across the Mellah and Kasbah.

Painters lay out their work for sale on and around the ramparts. Artisans sculpting *thuja* – a local coniferous hardwood with a smell like peppery cedar – have their workshops in the arches below and here you can find all manner of carvings and marquetry.

From near the North Bastion, rue Derb Laâlouj leads back into the heart of the Medina, past a variety of handicraft and antique shops, a handful of restaurants, and Essaouira's lone museum, the **Musée Sidi Mohammed Ben Abdellah**.

At one time Essaouira was known as the Sanhedrin (Jewish cultural centre) of North Africa. As recently as the 1950s the city still claimed 32 official **synagogues**. One that still functions remains at 2 Derb Ziry Ben Atiyah, which is the last lane on the right off rue Derb Laâlouj before it intersects with avenue Sidi Mohammed Ben Abdellah. The synagogue was founded by British merchants from Manchester; at the height of Essaouira's importance this section of the Kasbah was the location of various consulates and administrative buildings.

The Mellah

British merchants outnumbered other nationalities during the 19th century to the extent that 80 per cent of the town's trade was with Britain and sterling was the favoured currency. The sultan brought in Jews from all over the kingdom to deal with trade with Europe; by 1900 they outnumbered the locals. All but the wealthiest lived in the Mellah district between the North Bastion and Bab Doukkala, an area that has been neglected

since most of the Jews emigrated to Israel in the 1950s and '60s.

The Mellah can be found by following the alleys just inside the ramparts beyond the Skala de la Ville – turn down rue Touahen off rue Derb Laâlouj – or by following avenue Sidi Mohammed Ben Abdellah. When the shops and businesses start to peter out, the Mellah begins. These days its alleys are grubby and dilapidated; some houses look ready to fall down. It was always a gloomy quarter; until the end of the 19th century it was even locked up at night and it's still not a place to wander alone. These days there are at most perhaps two dozen Jews left in Essaouira.

At the northern end of the Mellah is **Bab Doukkala**. Just outside of the gate is the Consul's **cemetery**, another reminder of the town's cosmopolitan past. It's crammed with the graves of British officials from the days when Mogador (the old Portuguese name for Essaouira) had as many links with Manchester as with Rabat. Over the road, tombstones are packed tightly together in the old **Jewish cemetery**, where graves are reputed to be five layers deep.

The souks

Leading south-west from Bab Doukkala, **avenue Mohammed Zerktouni** is a busy commercial street of butchers and vegetable stalls. The narrow lanes of the Chabanat district on the eastern side are full of tiny workshops.

In the centre of the Medina, the souks are in cloistered arcades around the intersection of avenue Mohammed Zerktouni and avenue Mohammed El-Qouri, another busy street leading at right-angles towards Bab Marrakech and the hotels **Casa Lila** and **L'Heure Bleue**.

First on the left as you come under the arch from avenue Mohammed Zerktouni is the cobbled grain market. Slaves were auctioned here until the early 20th century. Now it's brimming over with hip, sunshine-filled café terraces where visitors and Souiris bask in the sun. The next cloistered square along, the Joutiya, comes to life between 4pm and 5pm for a daily auction hawking the detritus of daily life: old alarm clocks, fishing reels, slippers and transistor radios.

On the other side of the avenue, the fish and spice souk is a fascinating insight into long-held and lingering Moroccan beliefs. It is here that Souiri women come to buy chameleons, hedgehogs and various weird and wonderful plants for use in sorcery and magic, and where you can buy your own fish and vegetables and have **Chez Karim** across the street cook them for you (simply leave your haul with him and tell him what time you'll be back to eat).

Beyond this point, avenue Zerktouni turns into **avenue de l'Istiqlal**. The jewellery souk is on the left, curling around the outside of the mosque. It's a surprisingly quiet corner where it's possible to browse in peace. Avenue de l'Istiqlal offers Essaouira's most upmarket stretch of shopping, where you'll also find **Mogador Music**. Turn down rue Malek Ben Morhal to find the traditional pharmacy, Azurette, and left into rue d'Agadir to find the **Elizir** restaurant.

After the arched Kasbah gate, avenue de l'Istiqlal changes names again, becoming **avenue Oqba Ibn Nafia**. We are now back in the neighbourhood around Bab Sbaâ. **Galerie Damgaard**, a commercial gallery that has nurtured Essaouira's naïve school of painters, can be found on this stretch.

Sights & museums

Musée Sidi Mohammed Ben Abdellah

7 rue Derb Laâlouj (0524 47 23 00).
Open 8.30am-6pm Mon, Wed-Sun.
Admission 10dh. **Map** p136 B2.
This renovated 19th-century mansion was used as the town hall during the Protectorate and hosts a fairly boring collection of weapons, woodwork and carpetry. There are also *gnawa* costumes and musical instruments and a few pictures of old Essaouira.

Eating & drinking

Traditionally, the best budget lunch was fresh fish from a stall, charcoal-grilled and eaten outside on the quayside, but these days you'll rarely see locals eating there. They will tell you to go to the fish souk, nab a catch of your own and take it to a local café, such as **Chez Karim** (open 10am-11pm daily) and have them cook it for you. It's extremely popular with large Moroccan families and one of the most authentic dining experiences in Essaouira.

If you can't resist the allure of the **fish stalls**, a list of fixed prices is posted on a signboard (it's at the end furthest away from the water and includes a number for complaints, 0524 78 40 33) – it's all much of a muchness. Prices range from 10dh for a plate of sardines to 400dh per kilo of lobster, with squid, sole, shrimp, bass, red mullet, urchin and crab costing anything in between and includes a slice of lemon and half a baguette. A 60dh set meal includes a selection, plus salad, but no alcohol is served. Stalls are open from 11am until 4pm every day.

On place Moulay Hassan, the **Café de France** (open 9am-late daily) has an interestingly dated interior and you can get a decent ice-cream at **Gelateria Dolce Freddo** (open 11am-10pm daily). Groovier

these days than the place Moulay Hassan is the walled, cobbled Grain Market square, a sun-trap with good protection from unrelenting winds, filled with hip little cafés like **Safran** (mobile 0600 60 50 31, open 11am-late daily), a sunny spot for fresh, simply grilled fish, salads, tagines and pastillas.

Les Alizés Mogador

26 rue Skala (0524 47 68 19). **Open** *Lunch* noon-3pm daily. *Dinner* 7pm, 9pm, daily. **£. No credit cards. Moroccan**. **Map** p136 B2.
Opposite the wood workshops under the ramparts, and blessedly sheltered from the winds that lend the restaurant its name, Les Alizés has a stone-arched interior, a friendly, candlelit atmosphere, and hearty portions of good, reasonably priced Moroccan home-cooking from a set menu. This place has a reputation as one of the best budget restaurants in town. You can't reserve, so there may be a wait for a table.

La Cantina

66 rue Boutouil (0524 47 45 15).
Open 10am-5pm Mon-Sat. **Closed** most of Jan. **£. International/ Mexican**. **Map** p136 C2.
Situated on shady place Taraa, the English-owned La Cantina has a vaguely Mexican edge and is a good bet for true vegetarians, with a solid range of meat-and-fish-free dishes including a properly spicy vegetarian chilli and veggie burgers. Breakfasts are excellent too, as are the home-made cakes and scones for an afternoon pick-me-up.

Caravane Café

2 bis rue du Qadi Ayyad (0524 78 31 11).
Open 12.30-2.30pm, 6.30-10.30pm Tue-Sun. **£. No credit cards. Moroccan/ French**. **Map** p136 C2.
The former home of artist Didier Spindler and his partner Jean-François – a traditional house with a central

MARRAKECH BY AREA

top: Elizir;
bottom: Taros p144

courtyard – was converted into a restaurant a couple of years ago. It now comprises several eclectically decorated dining rooms packed around a lushly planted patio and roof terrace, with Spindler's trademark brightly coloured oils on the walls, romantic lanterns on every table, and vases festooned with flowers. The food on a regularly changing menu is always excellent and might include king prawns in a saffron sauce, tender beef *brochette* dressed with argan oil, blood sausage on baked apples, and a brilliant lemon meringue pie. But there's more: a dangerously strong house punch of rum, pineapple and cinnamon, nightly live music from local bands, a convincing magician and fire jugglers.

Chalet de la Plage

1 boulevard Mohammed V (0524 47 59 72, www.lechaletdelaplage). **Open** 6.30-10pm Mon; noon-2.30pm, 6.30-10pm Tue-Sat; noon-2.30pm Sun. **££. French/ seafood. Map** p136 B4.

Built in 1893 entirely out of wood, this iconic beachside institution serves a solid, unfussy menu. The fish is good, there's beer and a small wine list, and the overall vibe is friendly and efficient. Best of all, you can sit outside on the terrace and admire that tremendous panorama of the bay all the way around to the ruins of the Borj El-Berod on the headland.

Chez Jalila

Avenue de l'Istiqlal (mobile 0606 84 53 01). **Open** 9am-late daily. **£. No credit cards. Café. Map** p136 C3.

Situated on the main drag, this cheery little place is a delight. Filled with turquoise chairs topped with tangerine-coloured cushions, it provides a veritable splash of sunshine to accompany your breakfast omelette and morning coffee. The rooftop is a perfect sun-trap if you want to escape the souks with a book, and the homemade ice-cream served in summer is the best in town.

Chez Sam

Port de Pêche (0524 47 65 13, mobile 0661 15 74 85, chez_sam@live.fr). **Open** noon-3pm, 7-10.30pm daily. **££. Seafood. Map** p136 A4.

Abutting the harbour walls, this waterside wooden shack is designed like the hull of a ship, with a wood-panelled interior, portholes that allow you to see the fishing boats bringing in the catch, and a small conservatory dining room that seems to float out over the water. The fish and seafood is decent enough, particularly the sea bass or bream baked in salt so it stays succulent and juicy, but the main reason to come here is the atmosphere – a throwback to the Essaouira of yore.

Elizir

1 rue d'Agadir (0524 47 21 03). **Open** from 6pm daily. **££. No credit cards. Moroccan/ Mediterranean. Map** p136 C3.

One of the first of the hip newcomers, Elizir opened back in 2006 with a Moroccan-Mediterranean menu and an atmosphere of idiosyncratic cool. Slink up the narrow staircase from the street and you'll find yourself in a pair of dining rooms that combine traditional Moroccan tiles with vintage finds from local flea markets. Striking portraits adorn the walls, and the food is straight out of the early 1990s, piled up in moulds with glazes streaked like paint across the plate, but it can be very good. The fish of the day is always excellent, as is the richly flavoured balsamic beefsteak. In winter, ask for a table in the room with the open fire; in warmer months, go for the sheltered roof terrace. The louche, jazzy playlist sounds good wherever you're sitting.

Fanatic

Boulevard Mohammed V (0524 47 50 08, fanatic-essaouira@menara.ma). **Open** 9am-9pm daily. **££. Moroccan/ seafood. Map** p136 C4.

Located midway along the beach between Essaouira port and Diabat,

Fanatic is a slightly smarter beach bar than the rest, with esparto grass sunbeds and shades laid out neatly in the sand, a comfortably shaded terrace dining area and a largely French clientele (always a good sign food-wise). Looking straight across the water to the Purple Isles, it's a blissful spot for a long lunch, especially if you have kids in tow (there's a play park next to the sunbathing areas). Try the mixed fish fry (easily enough for two) with homemade tartare sauce and a bowl of hot, crunchy chips.

One-Up

1 rue Derb Laâlouj (mobile 0610 09 82 03). **Open** 11am-late daily. **££**. **Moroccan/Mediterranean**. Map p136 B2.

Housed in what were once offices of the British Consulate, this clubby first-floor restaurant and bar feels light and airy, with a vintage, lived-in look. Dining furniture from the 1940s and '50s, plaid armchairs and turquoise leather sofas mix well with Moroccan crafts against oyster-grey zelije-tiled walls and Vivienne Westwood wallpaper in dazzling red flame. The mix of styles is spread across several rooms, including a lounge with a glittering fireplace. Casual dining – a fusion of Mediterranean and Moroccan tapas, fish and chips in a paper cone and burgers – is paired with killer cocktails. There's a rooftop chill-out lounge too.

La Table Madada

7 rue Youssef El-Fassi (0524 47 11 06, www.latablemadada.com). **Open** 12.30-2.30pm, 7.30pm-late daily. **£££**. **Seafood**. Map p136 B3.

This sleek and stylish restaurant sprawled beneath sturdy stone arches is now widely regarded as the best in town. Giant lampshades direct light over linen-clothed tables, cream-coloured banquettes and comfortable armchairs, a large, corner fireplace keeps chilly nights at bay and the buzz created by popping champagne corks

(110dh a glass), clinking platters of Dahkla oysters and general bonhomie could have you believe you've landed somewhere far more cosmopolitan than little old Essaouira. Local seafood is put to good use here in the form of tiger prawn risotto, grilled John Dory, and sea bream ceviche. The cooking classes at L'Atelier de Madada next door are a great way to fill an afternoon.

Tara Café

5 rue Boutouil, place Taraa (0524 78 30 64). **Open** 8am-7pm daily. **No credit cards**. **International**. Map p137 D1.

Wedged into the arches of a sturdy old townhouse, with tables and chairs spilling out into the square, this is a reassuringly homely little place and a top spot for satisfying breakfasts and lunches. Soothing jazz and piano music emanate from the dining room while the owner, Abdou, floats about in a cream djellaba looking after his customers personally. The food is superb, with a varied menu ranging from boat-fresh fish and seafood to Lebanese meze and a comforting shepherd's pie.

Taros

Place Moulay Hassan (0524 47 64 07, www.taroscafe.com). **Open** 11am-4pm, 6pm-midnight Mon-Sat. **££**. **Bar/ Mediterranean/Moroccan**. Map p136 B3.

Perched above the main square on a corner overlooking the sea, Taros is a multipurpose venue with a prime location. It has a first-floor salon and library, where you can drink tea and read quietly in the afternoons or have a beer and listen to live music in the evenings (Thur-Sat). Then there's a cocktail bar on the fine roof terrace. And, of course, food, with a seafood focus and European and Moroccan dishes.

Vague Bleu

2 rue Sidi Ali Ben Abdellah (mobile 0611 28 37 91). **Open** noon-3pm, 6.30-9pm Mon-Thur, Sat, Sun. **£**. **No credit cards**. **Italian**. Map p137 D3.

Possibly the smallest restaurant in the world, Vague Bleu is built into a triangular recess with just five or six tiny tables. It was formerly owned by an Italian chap who employed local husband-and-wife team Brahim and Fadma to help him, teaching them all he knew before heading back to the motherland. They've gone from strength to strength, serving what is probably the best Italian food in the country. Daily specials such as prawn and courgette lasagne are chalked up on a blackboard, but it gets rammed so get here early or be prepared to wait.

Shopping

As with its bars and restaurants, Essaouira's shops are becoming more diverse and sophisticated. The town has all the variety of Marrakech packed into an infinitely more manageable space, with local specialities such as argan oil (found only in Morocco) and the best wine in the country.

To find these treasures in situ, hop in a taxi to **Lalla Abouch Organic Farm and B&B** (Tidzi, mobile 0661 32 27 91, www.darattajmil.com), which works with local families to make argan oil for both cosmetic and edible purposes, and has simple, charming accommodation too.

Then head to **Le Val d'Argan Winery** (Ounagha, route de Casablanca, mobile 0660 24 18 93, www.valdargan.com) owned by Charles Melia, a respected winemaker in the Châteauneuf du Pape region of France, who's transferred his skills here. Tastings with lunch cost 200dh and showcase a good cross-section of wines from the bright, refreshing La Gazelle de Mogador white to the flagship Le Val d'Argan Rouge. Should the mood take you, you can also snag a room at the vineyard in simple but comfortable stone cottages

Pamperville

The best spas, hammam and massage experiences.

For total indulgence in gorgeous surroundings, visit **Mumtaz Mahal** (5 rue Youssef El-Fassi, 0524 78 53 00, www.riadmumtaz mahal.com), the most lavish and luxurious of all the city's hammam experiences. Jewel-like zelije, marble columns and a vigorous scrub-down will soon have you feeling like new. For a spa experience in contemporary surroundings, **Azur** (place Moulay Hassan, 15 rue Khalid Ben Walid, 0524 78 57 94, www.azur-essaouira.com, open 10.30am-7.30pm daily) is a sleek outfit with state-of-the-art facilities and various beauty treatments. It's also cute place to hangout in the sun when it's all done.

For a more conventional Moroccan experience, **Les Massages Berbères** (135 avenue Mohammed El-Qouri, 0524 47 31 30, www.les massagesberberes.com) has well-trained therapists and offers a two-hour massage in clean, comfortable rooms with deeply moisturising argan oil for 350dh.

And if you really want to keep it real, there's **Hammam Pabst** (rue Ennasr). The oldest public baths in Essaouira, it was used for the murder scene in Orson Welles' *Othello*. It's one of the best places in the country for a scrupulously clean, intensely hot, supremely traditional *gommage* (scrub-down with black soap). It costs 10dh for the hammam, plus 50dh for the *gommage*, and is open daily until 9pm for women, after 9pm for men.

MARRAKECH BY AREA

Gnawa grooves

Celebrating one of Morocco's cultural treasures.

Every May or June, around 200,000 people flock to Essaouira for the **Festival of Gnawa & World Music** – a heady, carnival-like four days and nights. Each year the festival draws together Morocco's most revered *gnawa* masters, or *maâlems*, together with renowned contemporary jazz, world and blues musicians, for what has been described as 'one of the world's biggest jam sessions'.

One year, the acrobatic leaping of *gnawa* dancers was brilliantly mirrored by a balletic troupe of Georgian cossacks; another time, the ecstatic *qawali* trance of Pakistan's Faiz Al-Faiz fused perfectly with the hypnotic *gnawa* groove.

Once looked down upon and regarded with suspicion, the *gnawa* are now seen as one of Morocco's cultural treasures. They are descendants of slaves from sub-Saharan Africa, now constituted as an itinerant brotherhood of healers and mystics. Their music is rooted in trance and possession rituals, where spirits are represented by colours, and colours are represented by music. These spirits, or *mlouks*, are invoked during all-night ceremonies.

It's compellingly rhythmic stuff played on bass drums, clattering iron castanets and a sort of bass lute called a *guimbri*. True *gnawa* music is reserved for spiritual ceremonies and the masters seen performing in Essaouira will be called upon in their home towns when required – they are not professional gigging musicians.

The music was never intended for entertainment, but the festival in Essaouira provides an exception and all the greatest *maâlems* will come to perform.

Young Moroccan artists such as Aziz Sahmaoui have given the tradition a contemporary twist, and DJ-producers like London-based U-cef fuse *gnawa* with hip hop and dub to take it in a new direction.

Essaouira is bursting at the seams with for this annual party. Thankfully, in recent years, crowd safety issues have been addressed and the event is less concentrated inside the Medina. There is one main stage on place Moulay Hassan, another out on the beach, with some ticketed smaller events inside the Medina. In addition, festival-goers can buy stage-passes to allow access to a limited-capacity standing area in front of each stage. Otherwise the big outdoor concerts are still free.

For the latest festival news and programme details, visit www.festival-gnaoua.net.

MARRAKECH BY AREA

(www.riaddesvignes.com) arranged around a swimming pool.

Afalkay Art

9 place Moulay Hassan (0524 47 60 89). **Open** 9am-8pm daily. **Map** p136 B3.
Searching the wood workshops under the ramparts might turn up the odd different item, but pretty much anything they can make out of fragrant *thuja* wood – from tiny inlaid boxes to great big treasure chests, toy camels to bathroom cabinets – can be found in this big place opposite the cafés of place Moulay Hassan. Staff speak English and are used to shipping larger items.

Azurrette

12 rue Malek Ben Morhal (0524 47 41 53). **Open** 9.30am-8pm daily.
No credit cards. Map p136 C3.
At some remove from the hassle and hustle of the spice souk, this traditional Moroccan pharmacy has the largest herb and spice selection in the Medina and also offers perfumes, pigments, remedies, incense and essential oils. The big, cool space is lined with shelves of common condiments, exotic ingredients, mysterious herbs and colourful powders, all in glass jars or baskets. English is spoken by amiable young owner Ahmed, who's happy to explain what's what.

Bokado

Rue Derb Laâlouj. **Open** 8am-8pm daily.
No credit cards. Map p136 B2.
Abdullilah started out as a herbalist, but while waiting for customers he found himself with idle hands and, somewhat unusually for a Moroccan man, got into sewing. The reason, he says, that the Sufis became masters of patchwork is because they travelled from place to place in one djellaba; and the more patched it got, the richer the experience they had to share. He recycles vintage fabrics into a unique collection of hand-stitched patchwork quilts, cushions and bags costing up to 2,400dh for a double bedspread.

Chez Boujmaa

1 avenue Allal Ben Abdellah (0524 47 56 58). **Open** 8am-midnight daily.
No credit cards. Map p136 B3.
The place to stock up on deliciously flaky Moroccan pastries as well as English teas and biscuits. There's also a range of Italian pasta and parma ham, and French cheeses, if you're hankering for a taste of Europe. Staff will make up a sandwich for you at the basic deli counter if you just want something easy to take to the beach.

Elahri Mohamed Tisserand

181 Souk El-Gouzel (mobile 0655 09 74 14). **Open** 9am-8pm daily.
No credit cards. Map p137 D2.
This tiny family-run weaver's shop still has a working loom at the back, where weavers make bespoke textiles as well as their own designs. The influence of European taste is evident in the beautiful soft cotton throws in muted tones of ash green, dusky pink and duck-egg blue, and heavier sheep's wool and camel blankets edged with pompoms, as well as the flashier silk fabrics often favoured by Moroccans.

Espace Othello

9 rue Mohammed Layachi (0524 47 50 95). **Open** 9am-8pm daily. **Map** p136 C3.
The extremely mixed bag of work by artists from Essaouira and beyond includes some small pieces as well as large paintings and sculptures. There's some interesting stuff here, but you have to poke around a bit to find it. The gallery's architecture is worth a look in its own right. It's located behind the Hotel Sahara.

Galerie Damgaard

Avenue Oqba Ibn Nafia (0524 78 44 46, www.galeriedamgaard.com). **Open** 9am-1pm, 3-7pm daily. **Map** p136 B3.
Danish expat Frédéric Damgaard opened the town's only serious commercial gallery in 1988 and helped to develop the work of around 20

local artists – who came to be known as the Essaouira School. It's bright and colourful, almost hallucinogenic work, heavy with folk symbolism and pointillist techniques. *Gnawa* artist Mohammed Tabal is the star: his 'paintings of ideas' are inspired by the *gnawa* trance universe of colour-coded spirits. We also like the paint-splattered wooden furniture sculptures of Saïd Ouarzaz and the dreamlike canvases of Abdelkader Bentajar.

Histoire de Filles Concept Store

1 rue Mohamed Ben Messaoud (0524 78 51 93, contact@histoiresdefilles.com). **Open** 10am-8pm daily. **No credit cards.** Map p136 B4.

Perhaps the smartest shop in the Medina, this top-notch collection of clothing, accessories and interior design items points to a modern Morocco. Quality contemporary kaftans, elegant locally made straw Panama hats, impeccably cut stuffed camels and chic hessian lampshades, leather pouches and scented candles make for easy gift-buying.

Jack's Kiosk

1 place Moulay Hassan (0524 47 55 38). **Open** 9.30am-10.30pm daily. **No credit cards.** Map p136 B3.

In a key location on the square, Jack's is the place to find the previous day's international newspapers and other foreign periodicals, complemented by a small selection of new and second-hand English, French, German and Spanish books – mostly guides and bestsellers. Jack also rents seaview apartments by the ramparts.

Mashi Mushki

89-91 rue Chbanat (www.facebook.com/mashimushki). **Open** 11.30am-6.30pm Tue-Sun. **No credit cards.** Map p137 E2.

An extension of Project 91, located across the way, Mashi Mushki – meaning 'no problem' – sells a carefully selected range of boutique Moroccan handicrafts and trinkets. Many of them are made by local women's co-operatives with the help of local designers who lend the crafts a more contemporary edge. Modern striped cushion covers and throws in browns, creams and charcoals with natty neon zips look just as good when you get them back home as they looked in the shop.

Mogador Music

52 avenue de l'Istiqlal (mobile 0670 72 57 79). **Open** 10am-10pm daily. **No credit cards.** Map p136 C2/3.

Gnawa, Arabo-Andalusian, grika, belly dance, rai, desert blues – Mogador Music is well stocked with all varieties of North African and West Saharan music on CD and cassette. If you can't find it here you probably won't find it anywhere: owners Youssef and Azza know their stuff and distribute to all the other music shops. There's another shop at 1 place Chefchaouen (mobile 0661 72 83 62).

Othman Shop

86 rue Derb Laâlouj (mobile 0666 09 05 28, othmanshopp@hotmail.com). **Open** 10am-8pm daily. **No credit cards.** Map p136 B2.

On first inspection this seems to be a small hole-in-the-wall shop specialising in antique Berber jewellery with the odd bit of nicely made Indian silver thrown in. On closer inspection, however, you'll also discover beaded masks from the Cameroon and owner Kamal Ottmani's lovingly hoarded collection of antique kaftans from 1960s and 1970s. His father, something of a local legend, sells knitted skull caps on the next corner.

Ouchen Mohamed

4 rue El-Attarine (0524 47 68 61). **Open** 9am-9pm daily. **No credit cards.** Map p136 C3.

On a corner by the Riad Al Madina (p153), Ouchen Mohamed is our favourite of the various leatherwork shops. It's good for poufs, bags and belts, but there's also a big slipper selection and a few non-leather items, such as boxes, mirrors and old musical instruments.

Project 91

79 rue Chbanat (www.p-91.com).
Open 11.30am-6.30pm Tue-Sun.
No credit cards. Map p137 E2.
The clever concept here allows visitors to 'leave their wardrobe' and recycle items through this social enterprise shop, which also provides work experience for young people. The UK-based charity was created with the aim of helping young people in Essaouira find jobs and new skills through small grants for schooling, vocational training and supporting other organisations. As well as second-hand clothes, you'll find handwoven blankets and throws, flour sack totes and other low-cost gifts. The full 100% of the shop's profits is invested in the charity.

Riri d'Arabie

66 rue Boutouil (0524 47 45 15).
Open 10am-7pm daily. **No credit cards. Map** p137 D1.
French exile Richard Brecquehais accumulates bric-à-brac, some of which he sells on as *objets trouvés*, some of which he arranges in his own eccentric way, matching pictures to frames or ornaments to shelving units. The result is a small curiosity shop of old postcards, framed mirrors, ancient signs, out-of-date toys and a scatter-brained sense of comedy. If you feel like sitting down, he also sells juices (10dh) and a few hot snacks (35dh).

Trésor

57 avenue de l'Istiqlal (mobile 0664 84 17 73). **Open** 9am-8.30pm daily. **Map** p136 C2/3.
On the Medina's main avenue, jeweller Khalid Hasnaoui speaks good English and offers a more discerning selection than that found in the nearby jewellers' souk. It's a mixture of Berber, Arab, Tuareg and other pieces – some old, some new, and some new but using old designs. Look out for work in the local filigree style, traditionally made by Essaouiran Jews.

Hotels

The bar is continuously being raised for Essaouira accommodation, but if you've got your heart set on a particular guesthouse it's essential to book, especially if you want to secure anything at all over Christmas or Easter and during the *gnawa* festival in June (see box p146). There are rooms to suit all budgets and there's no such thing as a bad location – most places are a few minutes' walk from the central place Moulay Hassan and the fishing port.

Old Essaouira houses are set around open courtyards and tend to be smaller and less fussy than their Marrakchi equivalents, although the boutique hotel is on the rise here. Only a very few places own ocean views or roof terraces with cinematic vistas of sea and sky, which you'll soon come to realise is not such a bad thing once you've battled breakfast in high winds. Those same ocean breezes can make the town cold and damp too, and you will be glad of a log fire or central heating in winter – so double check that heating is provided. Keenly priced apartments of one sort or another can be found via **Jack's Kiosk** (p148).

Casa Lila

94 rue Mohammed El-Qouri (0524 47 55 45, www.riadcasalila.com). **££**. 825dh-1,600dh. **Map** p137 D3.
Halfway between the souks and Bab Marrakech, this tasteful, unfussy *maison d'hôte* has eight rooms and suites, plus one two-bedroom apartment, ranged around the central courtyard. Most of the rooms have baths (three just have showers) and all except the apartment have open fires. Common areas include a salon off the courtyard and a rambling roof terrace. It's all nicely decorated in bold pinks and purples with lots of grey tadelakt in the bathrooms, complemented by a few well-chosen knick-knacks.

Dar Adul

63 rue Touahen (0524 47 39 10, www.dar-adul.com). **£. Map** p136 B2.

Houses on the ocean side of the Medina need a lot of maintenance if they're not to fall into decline, and the four bedrooms of this former notary's house were recently renovated by the house's owners – who also own the Caravane Café (p141). Given a new lease of life thanks to lavish colours, deeply comfortable beds and a quirky roof terrace complete with its own ceramic crocodile, it's a welcome addition to otherwise fairly samey options in this price bracket. Heating is supplied. Downstairs, a restaurant occupies the ground-floor rooms and courtyard, decorated with rich textiles, jugs of roses, flamboyant oil paintings and papier mâché sculptures. Everything's for sale and the daily changing lunch menu (150dh-200dh) is excellent value.

Dar Beida

0667 96 53 86, mobile 07768 352190 in UK, www.castlesinthesand.com. **£. Map** p137 D2.

For something a bit special, consider 'the White House'. Deep in a corner of the Medina, a twist or two off the tourist trail, this is a wonderful 200-year-old house owned by English partners Emma Wilson and Graham Carter. They've renovated and furnished with playful good taste, mixing Moroccan materials and flea-market finds with imported antiques and a retro vibe. The result manages to be both idiosyncratically stylish and unpretentiously comfortable (there are plug-in electric heaters). It can sleep up to four couples, has two bathrooms, two roof terraces, a lounge, a small library, open fires and a well-equipped kitchen, and comes with two amiable cats for £300 per person per week, with a minimum booking of three persons.

Dar Maya

Rue d'Oujda (0524 78 56 87, www. riaddarmaya.com). **££. Map** p136 C2.

Of all the chic newcomers, Gareth Turpin's Dar Maya has the most design gravitas. Rising upwards to an elegant roof terrace with, unusually for Essaouira, a small plunge pool, the soft, sand-coloured hues and gentle curves of the place give it the air of a contemporary sandcastle. Light breezy balconies connect one room to another, and rooms are made interesting by contrasting textures and carefully chosen bespoke pieces of furniture, such as the cube-shaped poufs made of old flour sacks. Bedrooms are pared back, with spacious bathrooms and fireplaces, and while there's no formal restaurant (breakfast is served wherever and whenever you like), there's always someone around ready to help you with a glass of wine and something to nibble.

Dar Mouna Mogador

44 rue Ibn Khaldoun (0524 78 32 56, mobile 0666 40 95 48, www.darmouna. com). **£. Map** p137 D2.

Easily spotted by the colourful mural at the entrance, this cheap and cheerful bolthole is run by gregarious Australian expat Jane Folliott, a fountain of information not just about the local area but for all of Morocco. Her five homey rooms are spread over three fairly steep floors and decorated in a shimmer of purple and orange textiles. There's simple furniture, *objets d'art* by local artisans and gas heating. There's a sweet, sheltered roof terrace where Jane serves a hearty breakfast of fresh fruit, yoghurt, eggs, goat's cheese and olives, along with as much juice and coffee as you can drink.

Dar Ness

1 rue Khalid Ben Oualid (0524 47 68 04, www.darness-essaouira.com). **No credit cards. £. Map** p136 B3.

This is a bright little spot located just off the place Moulay Hassan. Bare brick in places lends a lived-in feel to the place. It has a couple of pleasant living rooms with real wood

Casa Lila p149

Catch the wind

The coast here is perfect for windsurfing.

Ocean Vagabond

Auberge de la Plage

With frequent high winds between March and September, Essaouira is Morocco's capital of windsurfing. Known as the Alizés, the north-westerly winds really are strong; wetsuits and sturdy sails are necessary. In winter, surfers can also be found on the town's broad and sandy beaches.

A 20-minute walk along the seafront (or short cab ride from Bab Sbaâ), **Ocean Vagabond** (boulevard Mohammed V, www.oceanvagabond.com, open 8am-6pm daily, no credit cards) is the best place to hire equipment and receive instruction from a friendly French and Moroccan team. It offers surfing, windsurfing and kite-surfing; windsurfing tuition starts at €120 for a six-hour starter course, including equipment. It's also a good beach café for breakfasts, salads and pizzas with the sun on your face and your toes in the sand.

There is more hardcore windsurfing at **Sidi Kaouki**, 25 kilometres (15.5 miles) to the south of Essaouira, where a broad beach stretches for miles. The village here is also popular with non-surfers in search of peace and quiet. There are several reasonable places to eat such as **La Mouette et Les Dromadaires** (mobile 0678 44 92 12, open 11am-5pm Wed-Sun), or **Beach and Friends** (Corniche Sud Plage d'Essaouira, 0524 47 45 58, www.beachandfriends.com, open 11am-11pm daily), where surfer types gather to chat over beachy chill-out tunes, fuel up on burgers and generally look cool, and small hotels, including the **Auberge de la Plage** (0524 47 66 00, www.kaouki.com), which also has horses and can arrange trekking. Bus 5 runs regularly to Sidi Kaouki from outside Bab Doukkala. You can also get there via grand taxi.

fires off the courtyard, and spotless bedrooms, their only down side being the hand-held showers. Still, it's good value for the price.

L'Heure Bleue

2 rue Ibn Batouta, Bab Marrakech (0524 78 34 34, www.heure-bleue.com). **£££. Map** p137 D3.

Although this has long been considered the poshest spot in town, you can end up feeling just a tad abandoned, thanks to the erratic opening hours of the bars, rooftop terrace and restaurant, and service that ranges from welcoming to aloof. A renovated private mansion of 16 rooms and 19 suites arranged around a lovely, leafy courtyard, its big draw is a rooftop swimming pool with fab views. The standard rooms (on the first floor) are spacious and African-themed – black marble, dark wood, zebra-patterned upholstery. Suites are on the second floor, and have Portuguese (blue and white), British colonial (19th-century engravings) and 'Eastern' (gold and burgundy) themes. The British colonial-style bar has big armchairs and mounted animal heads, but it's pot luck as to whether you'll get served.

La Maison des Artistes

19 rue Derb Laâlouj (0524 47 57 99, mobile 0662 60 54 38, www.lamaison desartistes.com). **£. Map** p136 B2.

A characterful French-run guesthouse that makes the most of its oceanfront location and the slightly eccentric taste of its original owners. It has six comfortable rooms, three overlooking the sea, three facing on to the patio, all furnished differently and some boasting intriguingly odd pieces. The suite is splendid, with the ocean on three sides and, lording over it, the roof terrace like the bridge of a ship. It's pretty exposed, however, and can get a bit rattly in high winds, though there is heating. La Maison seems to be a home from home for an assortment of young and vaguely arty French folks,

and whether you'll like it here depends greatly on whether you get on with the crowd. Manager Cyril is also proud of his 'Judeo-Berber' kitchen and lunch or dinner (150dh per person, 200dh for non-residents, booking necessary) can be served on the roof terrace with the ocean view.

Ocean Vagabond Guest House

4 boulevard Lalla Aicha (0524 47 92 22, www.oceanvagabond.com). **££. Map** p137 D4.

In a modern villa on the seafront, just a short walk outside the old city walls, Ocean Vagabond boasts a few features alien to converted Medina houses, such as a garden and a pool. Opened by the crew from the Ocean Vagabond café and surf station (see box p152), it's a breath of fresh air in all senses. Common areas are bright, stylish and simple, and the place has heating. The 14 rooms are themed ('Bali' is vaguely Indonesian, 'Geisha' vaguely Japanese, and so on). Try to get one of the four ('Dogon', 'Felluca', 'Pondichéry' and 'Inca') that have balconies with an ocean view (two others have balconies with a view of the Medina – and the post office). A garden bungalow is the place for pampering: it houses a hammam and rooms for massage, beauty treatments and a hairdresser.

Riad Al Madina

9 rue Attarine (0524 47 59 07, www.riadalmadina.com). **£. Map** p136 C3.

Once the location of the Hippy Café, this is a good-value hotel that trades on the myth that Jimi Hendrix, Frank Zappa and Cat Stevens all once hung out here. The beautiful courtyard is one of the nicest breakfast spots in town, with wrap-around balconies spilling over with geraniums and ferns, and a restaurant and bar area that hosts *gnawa* musicians on Wednesday and Saturday evenings. The rooms have all been recently renovated so the overall feel is clean and fresh, though if you're tall you might want to avoid the low ceilings of the mezzanine rooms. The hotel has heating.

Riad Remmy

29 Daoud Ben Aicha (mobile 0653 23 61 92, 0676 08 09 55, www.riadremmy. co.uk). £ (whole house rental available). **No credit cards. Map** p137 D2.

Run by gregarious Manchester expat Sandra Cripps, this is a bright, thoughtfully decorated boutique B&B with a chill-out lounge in the courtyard warmed by a big fireplace, and five rooms spread out over the next three floors. A pale palette brightened with colourful local textiles keeps things easy on the eye, and the natural-coloured tiles, stripped-back wood and lush ferns give the place a relaxed ambience. On the second floor a small communal kitchen is available for guests to make their own tea, coffee and light meals, and there's a pleasant roof terrace for catching a few rays.

Villa de l'O

3 rue Mohamed Ben Messaoud (0524 47 63 75, www.villadelo.com). ££. **Map** p136 B4.

Indulge in a little colonial-edged glamour at this richly decorated luxury retreat. From the cane furniture of the planted courtyard to the sultry bar with its leather sofas and Louis XVI-style armchairs, to the ample roof terrace with endless sea views, chill-out areas, sunbeds and a bar, this place feels just as grown up as its competitors, minus the stuffiness. In the rooms, ceiling fans, fireplaces and rich velvet throws contrast pleasingly with fun extras like telescopes for all those sea views. Add impeccable service and a decent restaurant and it's easy to see why this place has fast established itself at the top of the high-end hotel roster.

Villa Maroc

10 rue Abdellah Ben Yassine (0524 47 61 47, www.villa-maroc.com). ££. **Map** p136 B3.

The first boutique hotel in Morocco when it opened back in 1990, the Villa Maroc is now a mature, well-known establishment. It's nicely located just inside the walls of the Kasbah quarter, with its roof terraces conveniently overlooking the square and the fishing port. Twenty rooms and suites are furnished in appealing style and arranged around an intriguing warren of open terraces, narrow staircases and small, secluded spaces – the result of knocking together four old merchants' houses. Dinner costs 200dh; the food, served in one of several small salons, uses ingredients from the owners' farm. Non-residents are welcome for the lunchtime barbecue and access to the pool.

The Beaches & Diabet

Essaouira has wonderful beaches, but the north-westerly winds, known as the Alizés, make it cold and choppy for bathing. It's ideal for windsurfing, though (see box p152). The area to the north of town is fast becoming known as the Guéliz of Essaouira because of its funky beach scene with various cafés and bars like **Beach and Friends** (0524 47 45 58, 11am-11pm daily) and **Tamouziga** (0524 47 45 78), a popular expat haunt for a Sunday lunch of sardine tagine or a great pizza. At this end, the Plage de Safi can be dangerous when it's blowy, but it's nice when it's warm and usually less crowded than the main beach.

The main beach stretches for miles to the south, backed by dunes once the town peters out. Closer to the Medina it serves as a venue for football. There's always a game going on and at weekends there are several played simultaneously, their kick-offs timed by the tides. You'll also find guys with camels,

or they will find you, insistently offering rides. It can be fun to trek around the bay to the ruined old fort of **Borj El-Berod**, but wait until you find a camel guy you feel comfortable with, and agree a firm price before setting off.

The village of **Diabat** is a few miles further south and a little inland, on a ridge overlooking the scrubby dunes. In the late 1960s it hosted a hippie community, and legends of a visit made by Jimi Hendrix abound. Any lingering flavour of those times is, however, rapidly being obliterated by the enormous golf resort between the village and the ocean. Diabat's main street now overlooks one of the fairways, and there is further large-scale development occurring along the coast. For an out-of-town lunch in an open-sided café set in gardens, try the **Tangaro**. Day passes for pool and lunch are 250dh.

A whole new town, **Essaouria Al Jadida** (meaning 'New Essaouria'), is going up near the airport; and the small surfer haven of **Sidi Kaouki** (see box p152), 25 kilometres (15.5 miles) south of Essaouira, has expanded too.

Hotels

Tangaro

Diabat (0524 78 47 84, www.auberge tangaro.com). **££**.
This 100-year-old former farm has recently become the hip hangout of local groovers and shakers. Situated at the top of a hill in Diabat, it has fabulous ocean views, swimming pool access, a yoga studio and a breezy massage room created from pale driftwood, along with a chic, open-sided café for lunch or sunset cocktails followed by electricity-free, candlelit dinners. The handful of rustic rooms are scattered across the rambling eucalyptus-scented gardens, simply decorated but all with working fireplaces.

Guided tours

Morocco Made Easy

mobile 0666 40 95 48, info@ moroccomadeeasy.com.
Jane Folliott runs guided tours of Essaouira and the surrounding area, which will get visitors off the beaten track. She also offers bespoke itineraries across Morocco.

Getting there

By bus

Supratours (0524 43 55 25) runs a bus service from its depot next door to Marrakech railway station; the timetable changes frequently, so check times. In summer, buy tickets (one-way 70dh regular coach, 100dh confort plus) at least a couple of days before travelling as the service for the three and a half hour journey gets busy. You can buy tickets in advance from www.marrakech traintickets.com.

In Essaouira, buses arrive at and leave from the south side of the big square outside **Bab Marrakech**, where tickets are sold at a kiosk (0524 47 53 17) next to the Télécom building. Again, it's best to check times in advance.

By taxi

Shared grand taxis from Marrakech (80dh per person) leave from **Bab Doukkala**. Coming back, they leave from outside Essaouira's *gare routière*. You can also hire your own taxi for around 700dh.

By air

At the time of writing, **Royal Air Maroc** (www.royalairmaroc.com) was running three daily flights from Paris and thrice-weekly flights from Casablanca to the tiny Aéroport de Mogador.

Essentials

Royal Mansour p162

Hotels

The piecemeal conversion of the Medina into a vast complex of boutique hotels continues apace. Marrakech probably boasts more boutique hotels per square mile than any other city in the world. The current number of riads, as they're now generically known, weighs in at almost 1,000. And although rocketing property prices means that there are few real bargains left on the market, all the signs are that this trend is set to continue.

Riads

'Riad' means garden house, though for 'garden' you can usually read 'courtyard'. The city's riad guesthouses are organised around one or more of these courtyards, reflecting the traditions of Moroccan domestic architecture, which are inward-looking with thick blank walls to protect the inhabitants from heat, cold and the attentions of the

outside world. Grander riads involve two or more houses knocked together, but many consist of just half a dozen or so rooms around a single courtyard. Most are privately operated affairs, which generally means excellent personal service and a high degree of individuality. Rooms feature en suite bathrooms in all but the cheapest riads, but in many places TVs, telephones and other mod cons are often dispensed with in the name of authenticity and getting away from it all.

Marrakech can be decidedly chilly during the winter and many riads offer chimneys, central heating and hot water bottles – if you feel the cold, check exactly what's available. Breakfast is commonly taken on a roof terrace shielded from the sun beneath tent-like awnings (and is, in the majority of cases, included in the room price), while lunch and dinner are provided on request. Many riads have excellent cooks, producing food as good as, if not superior to, anything dished up in the city's restaurants.

Most riads forgo any kind of tell-tale frontage or even nameplate. Given that they often lie deep within the obscure twists of narrow alleys, this can make them a swine to locate. Guests are generally met at the airport (for which there may or may not be an additional charge) and riad staff may give you a map with their location marked, but after that it's just you and your sense of direction. With that in mind, it's always wise to carry your riad's business card to show locals in case you get lost.

Staying out of town

Gaining in favour of late is the out-of-town retreat. There are a growing number of villas and new-build compounds, usually with gorgeous gardens, on the outskirts of the city – scattered throughout the Palmeraie and further afield – that serve as retreats dedicated to indolence and pampering. Marrakech is on hand to provide blasts of colour and exoticism between early afternoon waxings and evening cocktails. One way to holiday is to spend a couple of days at a riad in the Medina followed by a couple of days in a self-indulgent retreat.

Whichever way you choose to go, we highly recommend pushing the budget. Marrakech isn't the place to scrimp on accommodation – not when your hotel could turn out to be the highlight of the trip.

Rates & booking

There are significant seasonal variations in room rates. What constitutes the peak period varies by establishment, but generally speaking you'll pay considerably more (and there'll be a minimum stay) for a room any time over

SHORTLIST

Most gorgeous gardens
- Dar Zemora (p173)
- Les Jardins de la Medina (p170)
- Jnane Tamsna (p173)
- La Mamounia (p161)

Best for arts
- Dar 18 (p162)
- Fellah Hotel (p175)

Best for food
- Dar les Cigognes (p169)
- Maison Arabe (p164)
- Maison MK (p161)
- Palais Namaskar (p174)
- Riad Enija (p166)

Best cheap and cheerful
- Dar 18 (p162)
- Equity Point Hostel (p164)
- Hotel Gallia (p160)
- Hotel du Trésor (p170)
- Jnane Mogador (p170)

Most luxurious
- Amanjena (p175)
- Ksar Char-Bagh (p174)
- La Mamounia (p161)
- Royal Mansour (p162)
- Villa des Orangers (p162)

Best rural retreats
- Dar Zemora (p173)
- Jnane Tamsna (p173)
- Ksar Char-Bagh (p174)
- La Pause (p176)
- Tigmi (p177)

Best modern styling
- Palais Namaskar (p174)
- Le Palais Paysan (p176)
- Riad 72 (p165)
- Riad Mabrouka (p171)
- Talaa 12 (p168)

Best courtyard gardens
- Dar Doukkala (p164)
- Riad Enija (p166)

ESSENTIALS

Christmas/New Year and Easter, as well as late September to October, when the fierceness of the summer heat has abated and temperatures are near-perfect. Rooms are scarce at peak times and booking well in advance is a must. Note that some riads close in high summer.

When it comes to making a reservation, even though most hotels boast websites, bear in mind that Moroccan servers are prone to meltdown. Book through the website by all means, but make sure you receive a confirmation email.

For deluxe hotels (**££££**) you can expect to pay from 3,450dh (approx £250); expensive (**£££**) around 2,100dh-3,450dh (approx £150-£250); moderate (**££**) 850dh-2,100dh (approx £60-£150); and budget (**£**) under 850dh (approx £60). Breakfast is usually included. Payment is typically either cash in local currency or by credit card (there's often at least a five per cent surcharge added on to card payments to cover transaction costs). When it comes to paying your bill, you'll also want to know whether VAT (at 20 per cent) and the nightly tourist tax, which varies according to the category of the establishment, are already included.

Dar Attajmil

23 rue Laksour, off rue Sidi El-Yamani (0524 42 69 66, www.darattajmil.com).
££

With just four bedrooms, Dar Attajmil – owned by the lovely English-speaking Italian Lucrezia Mutti – is one of our favourite small riads. There's a tiny courtyard filled with tropical foliage: banana trees and coconut palms that throw welcome shade on to a small recessed lounge and library. Bedrooms overlook the courtyard from the first floor, and are beautifully decorated in warm, rustic tones with dark-wood ceilings and handsome tadelakt bathrooms. Best of all, though, is the astonishingly peaceful roof terrace, which is scattered with cushions, wicker chairs and sofas. Dinner (traditional Moroccan with Italian leanings) is available on request. It's an easy six-minute walk from the house to Jemaa El Fna.

Hotel Gallia

30 rue de la Recette, off rue Bab Agnaou (0524 44 59 13, www.ilove-marrakesh. com/hotelgallia). No credit cards. **£**

The lanes off rue Bab Agnaou – mere seconds from Jemaa El Fna – are thick with budget options, but Gallia comes

Maison MK

top of the class. This small guesthouse ticks all the right boxes: it's smack-bang central, clean and aesthetically pleasing. The 19 ensuite double rooms open on to two picturesque, flower-filled courtyards, where a Moroccan breakfast is served. Bathrooms are big, modern pink affairs with limitless hot water. The well-kept flowery roof terrace is an ideal spot for lounging.

Jardins de la Koutoubia

16 rue de la Koutoubia (0524 38 88 00, www.lesjardinsdelakoutoubia.com). **£££**
With more than 100 rooms, several gardens, indoor and outdoor pools, a fitness room, and a choice of restaurants including Moroccan, Indian and international, this is the place to stay in the Medina if you crave a hotel rather than an intimate guesthouse. The comfortable, well-run establishment is brilliantly located, two minutes from Jemaa El Fna in one direction and two minutes from the Koutoubia mosque in the other. The courtyard pool is heated, staff can shake a proper cocktail in the Piano Bar, the patio restaurant (p48) is a fine spot for lunch, and everything is nicely spacious. The faux traditional design may not bother the major style supplements, but it isn't too shabby, and both bedrooms and bathrooms are large and welcoming.

Maison MK

14 derb Sebaai, Bab Laksour (0524 37 61 73, www.maisonmk.com). **£££**
Maison MK oozes class behind its cool walls close to Jemaa El Fna. Indulge in an intense double session of hammam and massage at the in-house Spa MK before sauntering upstairs to the terrace for the nightly Gastro MK supperclub (p48). Canapés are served on the terrace as the sun sets and the call to prayer echoes around the Medina. Then guests head downstairs to the dining room to complete the gourmet adventure. Menu highlights include a rich cauliflower and leek soup laced with argan oil and a clever apple tart

tagine. Intrigued by the new-wave Moroccan cuisine? Book into one of the cookery classes (see box p78). After dinner, hit the hookah and cigar snug for a late-night rendezvous under the fabulous papier-mâché sculpture of a mounted camel head smoking a Camel cigarette, or settle into the cinema room (popcorn included) for a late-night screening. Rooms are very comfortable with minibars, iPod docks, large tadelakt bathrooms (with an enormous rubber duck for company) and wafting drapes in russet tones.

La Mamounia

Avenue Bab Jedid (0524 38 86 00, www.mamounia.com). **££££**
La Mamounia is seriously glamorous. In early 2014, Nicole Kidman stayed here while filming *Queen of the Desert*, joining a long list of celebrities who've graced its fabled rooms. After an almond-scented milk and platter of dates on arrival, walk through the majestic Bar Italien with its original Majorelle ceiling to the famous gardens (p51). Renovated in 2009, the rooms are smartly elegant with carved stucco horseshoe arches, bands of ziggurat-stacked *zelije* (traditional tiling), painted doors and latticed horseshoe windows in the marble bathrooms (with chocolate-brown Havaianas for sun-tanned toes). And then there are the expansive terraces from which to enjoy the crisp African light and views of the Atlas mountians. You can be pampered in the spa, take tea in the gardens or dine at the multiple restaurants. After a stay here, you'll have a hard time returning to normal life beyond the storied walls.

Riad El Fenn

2 derb Moulay Abdallah Ben Hezzian, Bab El-Ksour (0524 44 12 10, www. riadelfenn.com). **£££**
This riad has received plenty of media attention, partly because it's co-owned by Vanessa Branson (sister of Richard) and partly because it's such a fine place

to stay. Several historic houses have been joined to create 24 spacious, luscious jewel-coloured bedrooms that are happily lost in a warren of staircases and courtyards. The clutter-free rooms are dominated by an Egyptian cotton-swathed bed, standalone baths in some, camel leather-tiled floors and proper-sized desks. Despite the grandeur of the architecture and some serious modern art on the walls, the mood is relaxed, with plenty of private spaces, three pools and a glorious rooftop terrace.

Riad Omar

22 rue Bab Agnaou (0524 44 56 60, www.riadomar.com). No credit cards. **£**
Omar's cramped but clean, no-frills rooms are the trade-off for budget prices and an excellent location on pedestrianised rue Bab Agnaou. This is a hotel rather than a *maison d'hôte*, with 17 rooms and four suites set around a central courtyard with a small fountain. They're all air-conditioned and have decent-sized bathrooms (though only seven of them have baths). The four suites have small sitting areas.

Royal Mansour

🆕 *Rue Abou Abbas El-Sebti (0529 80 80 80, www.royalmansour.com).* **££££**
The Royal Mansour is a stunner (see box p163). It's fit for a king and was built by one. Morocco's Mohammed VI employed 1,500 craftsmen to fashion the 53 riads, lobby, restaurants and spa within its grounds. Although the Mansour oozes luxury, it's an opulence that somehow doesn't overwhelm. The private riads, topped by terraces with plunge pools and reached by paths that meander through the gardens, are very private. If you want to speak to another human being, head for the library with its retractable roof and telescope, the dessert library with its cabinet of sweet confections, or the spa sanctuary with its indoor pool under a pavilion of glass. Three Michelin-starred chef Yannick

Alléno is consultant for the restaurants, and La Grande Table Marocaine wows with gourmet treats such as spinach salad with orange blossom foam, royal pigeon pastilla, and gold-dusted chocolate fondant dessert.

Villa des Orangers

6 rue Sidi Mimoun, place Ben Tachfine (0524 38 46 38, www.villadesorangers. com). **££££**
Built in the 1930s as a judge's residence, the dreamy Villa des Orangers is in Moorish palatial style, with 27 rooms and suites done out in deep chocolate, bordeaux and stone tones, and arranged around three beautiful courtyards – one filled with the eponymous orange trees, the others lavishly decorated with lacy carved plasterwork. Ten suites have private upstairs sun terraces, and all rooms have access to the roof with matchless views of the nearby Koutoubia minaret. The subterranean spa and beautifully lit hammam – also open to non-guests – is a draw, as are the three swimming pools. Service is outstanding, and breakfast, a light lunch, non-alcoholic drinks, laundry and airport transfers are included in the price.

Souks & northern Medina

A room here puts you right in among the souks and sights, and the nearer to Jemaa El Fna the better. Remember that much of the Medina is inaccessible by car, and it's an advantage to be close to a taxi-friendly main street.

Dar 18

🆕 *18 derb El-Ferrane, off rue Riad El-Arous (0524 38 98 64).* No credit cards. **£**
It's barely possible to find anything cheaper in the Medina, but the real attractions of this artists' hub are the pop-up events, art installations

Pure luxury

Rest assured at Marrakech's grandest grandes dames.

Morocco's most famous 'destination' hotel, **La Mamounia** (p161) was opened in 1923 to coincide with the arrival of the French-built North African railway network. In the inter-war years, it became more or less synonymous with a trip to Marrakech, and an exclusive clientele of writers, artists, colonial rulers and well-to-do adventurers would sip whisky in the piano bar or stroll around its well-watered gardens. Winston Churchill was a regular, painting a number of watercolours on the balcony of his favourite suite; and Doris Day sang 'Que Sera, Sera' in room 414, in Hitchcock's *The Man Who Knew Too Much*.

La Mamounia

For the rich and famous, it carried on being simply the only place to stay well into the late 20th century – until the new boutique hotels started making it feel its age. A kitsch makeover in 1986 didn't help, adding a conference centre but eradicating the cool elegance of the past. Nor did a 2001 overhaul of the rooms. And so, in 2006, it closed again for major renovations, reopening in 2009 following a design revamp by Parisian Jacques Garcia, and boasting no less than 27 fountains, 2,264 doors and 1,000 lanterns. Craftsmen reworked the building's art deco style to a more classically Moroccan one abounding in richly painted wood (*zouaq*) doors, a feast of intricately carved stucco (*ghebs*), walls patterned with *zelije* (coloured decorative tilework) and bathrooms screened with lattice woodwork (*mashrabiya*). Another major change was the conversion of the Moroccan restaurant into a seductive swimming pool chamber.

Across town, the Moroccan king's **Royal Mansour** (p162) opened in 2010 close to Jemaa El Fna with a network of service tunnels as intriguing as the hotel itself. No expense was spared on the 53 private riads built within a walled garden plot that showcases the finest in Moroccan craftsmanship: *zelije* is patterned in beautiful honey and cream in the public areas, Le Bar is clad with rose gold leaf, the spa pool under a glass curved roof is lined with white onyx mosaic, *mashrabiya* screens in dark wood filter the stark light and carved stucco maps the walls.

Both of these stunning hotels deserve a visit, even if you can't afford to book in for the night. While La Mamounia welcomes visitors, the doormen at the Royal Mansour are less keen. So make a booking at one of the in-house restaurants, then you'll pass through a courtyard entirely adorned with midnight blue Brazilian marble on your way to dinner.

in the courtyard such as the emerald green threaded balcony weaving by Hermione Skye, and artwork on the walls, plus the knowledge that your stay supports local Moroccan artists. Upstairs are three comfortable bedrooms – think recycled wardrobe doors as mirrors, French dressers, white drapes, and tadelakt bathrooms. Lounge about on the roof terrace with its potted cactus and flowers or grab a mint tea from the cool black-and-white tiled kitchen while mingling with the residents and visiting artists.

Dar Doukkala

83 Arset Aouzal, off rue Bab Doukkala (0524 38 34 44, www.dardoukkala.com).
££

A handsome mix of English country mansion and Moroccan townhouse pepped up with 1960s and art deco vintage pieces, Dar Doukkala is a very chic, slightly unkempt, homely place to stay. Its five bedrooms and two suites are filled with gorgeous period details and furnishings, including claw-foot tubs and pedestal basins in the bathrooms. Other eccentric touches include Guimard-like glass canopies projecting into the central, lusciously overgrown garden courtyard, and an artful array of lanterns patterning the wall behind the terrace-level pool. It's one of the most fun and delightful maisons d'hôtes in town. Both suites have two extra beds for kids, while one of the doubles also comes with an extra bed. The location is good, too, opposite the wonderland warehouse of Mustapha Blaoui (p80) and close to the main Dar El-Bacha road and its taxis.

Equity Point Hostel

80 derb El-Hammam, Mouassine (0524 44 07 93, www.equity-point.com). **£**

Equity Point has achieved a considerable feat by shoehorning a 147-bed hostel into the heart of the Medina – including a swimming pool. Buried down derb El-Hammam behind the Mouassine fountain, Equity has reinhabited the old Riad Amazigh and built a brand new attached property behind. The original riad has private rooms, but it's all a bit dark and uninviting. The best options are the dorm rooms – girls only or mixed – with lockers that line the pool area in the new building. You'll have to bring your own towel or pay a charge, but with breakfast and Wi-Fi included, and tours and cooking classes that can be booked at the front desk, there's little to complain about – except the awkward location. Sometimes the hostel signs are taken down and once you go under the arch between the Mouassine fountain and the mosque (where there are also signs to the Douiria, p68), the signs peter out. You may be best booking the airport transfer so you're delivered direct to the door.

Maison Arabe

1 derb Assehbe, Bab Doukkala (0524 38 70 10, www.lamaisonarabe.com).
£££

Maison Arabe began life in the 1940s as a restaurant run by two raffish French ladies. It gained fame through its popularity with illustrious patrons such as Winston Churchill before closing in the 1980s. It reopened in 1998 as the city's first *maison d'hôte*. Today, it has expanded considerably and houses 12 rooms and 14 suites, with a hotel feel. Inside, the prevailing style is Moroccan classic with French colonial overtones – with Orientalist paintings and antiques and an elegant cedarwood library. Rooms are supremely comfortable, most with their own private terraces. In addition to the on-site pools guests can use the large swimming pool at Coin Caché, in a luxurious garden setting and a 15-minute ride from the hotel (with a free shuttle service). There's Arab-Andalusian music to accompany dinner in the Moroccan restaurant (p79) and guests can also sign up for Moroccan cookery workshops (see box p78). There are also two hammams and a wellness area.

Maison Arabe

Riad 72

72 derb Arset Aouzal, off rue Bab
Doukkala (0524 38 76 29, www.
riad72.com). **££**
Italian-owned, this is one sleek and
good-looking riad – Marrakech has
it away with Milan. The result is a
traditional townhouse given a black,
white and grey tadelakt makeover.
The structure, space and detailing are
Moroccan, the furniture and fittings
imported. There are just four guest
bedrooms, all up on the first floor
and set around the central courtyard.
Rooms include a huge master suite, 5m
(16ft) or more in height and crowned by
an ornate octagonal fanlight. Guests
have a choice of scented toiletries and
each room has its own Italian espresso
machine. The roof terrace has one of
the best views in town, with the green-
tiled roofs of Dar El-Bacha in the fore-
ground and a jagged mountain horizon
beyond. Being that much higher than
the neighbours means sunbathing is
no problem (many riads are overlooked
and modesty can be an issue). Superior
vehicle access is a further bonus.

Riad Adore

 97 derb Tizouagrine, Dar El-Bacha
(0524 37 77 37, www.riadadore.com).
££

This, the latest in the Pure Riads collection of sleek little properties, is
in the most fashionable part of the
Medina. The contemporary design is
the result of Stuart Redcliffe's passion
for interiors, and he's used clean lines
and soothing, muted tones as a frame
for eye-popping souk finds such as
hand-embroidered bedlinens and
bespoke lanterns. Unusually, each of
the individually decorated rooms has
cable TV, and you'll find stacks of life-
style magazines scattered throughout
the various living areas. There's also a
well-stocked library, television lounge
with fireplace, courtyard plunge pool,
top-notch hammam (book at least one
session, it's one of the best in town) and
romantic canopied roof terrace for
dining. The food
here is excellent.

Riad Azzar

94 derb Moulay Abdelkader, off
derb Debbachi (0661 15 81 73,
www.riadazzar.com). **££**
Owned by a friendly, English-speaking
Dutch couple, Azzar is a neat little
six-room riad with the feel of a B&B.
It's distinguished by a small, emerald-
green heated plunge pool in the middle of the courtyard. Walls are whitewashed and the decor is understated:

Riad Star

it's a very tasteful place. Three of the rooms are suites and come with fireplaces and air-conditioning (as does the twin room); of these, the Taznarth suite also boasts a beautiful mashrabiya (wooden lattice) window overlooking the courtyard and a particularly lovely grey tadelakt bathroom. Riad Azzar supports a local orphanage; guests are encouraged to contribute by bringing children's toys and clothing or school materials for donation.

Riad Enija

9 derb Mesfioui, off rue Rahba Lakdima (0524 44 09 26, www.riadenija.com). **£££**

Riad Enija's 15 rooms and suites variously boast glorious old wooden ceilings, beds as works of art (wrought-iron gothic in one, a wooden ship bed in another), some striking furniture (much of it designed by artist friends of the Swedish/Swiss owners) and grand bathrooms resembling subterranean throne rooms. Central to the three adjoining houses is a lush Moorish courtyard garden gone wild. Distractions such as TVs and telephones are dispensed with, but alternative services include anything from a visiting aromatherapist and masseurs to cookery classes. Food is excellent, and the riad is just a few minutes' walk from Jemaa El Fna. The only downside is the fact that taxis can't get you anywhere very near. Then there's the nuisance of having the latest fashion shoot going on outside your window – we warned you this place was a looker.

Riad Farnatchi

2 derb El-Farnatchi, Kat Benahid (0524 38 49 10, www.riadfarnatchi. com). **££££**

Farnatchi is the creation of Jonathan Wix (42 The Calls in Leeds, the Scotsman in Edinburgh and Hôtel de la Trémoille in Paris). It's now an intimate, top-class hotel run by his son, James. Suites are set around four courtyards, one of which has a modestly sized heated pool. The suites are vast and supremely luxurious, with large sunken baths, shower rooms, under-floor heating, desks, armchairs and private sun terraces. Standout features include a funky patchwork kilim bedspread in one room, and a bathroom with an art deco-style black marble sunken bath and accompanying circular pink marble sinks in another.

The hotel is right in the middle of the Medina, just north of Ben Youssef Medersa; taxis can get to within 200m. A spa and standalone restaurant are in the pipeline. The hotel is closed throughout August.

Riad Kniza

34 derb l'Hôtel, Bab Doukkala (0524 37 69 42, www.riadkniza.com). **£££**
This grand, well-located 18th-century house has belonged to the family of current owner Mohammed Bouskri for two centuries. It's the most Moroccan of upmarket riads, decorated entirely in traditional style. There are seven suites and four rooms, and even the smallest is pretty spacious. The suites all have separate sitting rooms and there are working fireplaces throughout. Mohammed Bouskri has also been a professional guide for more than 30 years, so it's a useful place for anyone who wants to 'do' Marrakech in an old-school way. Rates include a free half-day tour of the Medina and airport transfer. The in-house hammam is large enough for two people – the perfect way to spend a romantic afternoon. No children under 12 allowed.

Riad Noga

78 derb Jedid, Douar Graoua (0524 37 76 70, www.riadnoga.com). **££**
Noga is one of the homeliest of Marrakech's riads. Behind salmon-pink walls lies a bougainvillea- and orange tree-filled courtyard (complete with chatty grey parrot), serving as an antechamber to an inner, more private courtyard centred on a shimmering, tiled, solar-heated swimming pool. Noga is very spacious (it's made up of three old houses knocked into one), and shared by just seven rooms. All of the rooms are bright, bold and cheery, displaying the hospitable touch (small libraries of holiday-lite literature, for instance) of the garrulous German owner, Gaby Noack-Späth. Expansive roof terraces filled with terracotta pots and lemon trees offer terrific views over the Medina and make for the perfect spot to enjoy aperitifs or fine cooking.

Riad Noir d'Ivoire

31 derb Jdid, Bab Doukkala (0524 38 09 75, www.noir-d-ivoire.com). **£££**
Riad Noir d'Ivoire has that gratifying combination of looking spectacular while feeling exceedingly comfortable. Interior designer and former co-owner Jill Fechtmann mixed specially commissioned Moroccan elements with assorted curiosities from sub-Saharan Africa, Europe and India. Six rooms and three suites set around two courtyards have huge beds imported from the US, Egyptian cotton sheets, big bathrooms and pleasingly eccentric furnishings that vaguely exude an animal theme. Off the chandeliered winter courtyard with plunge pool there's a hammam, plus a lounge/library, small boutique, dining area and cosy bar. The vibe is sociable, especially around the summer courtyard pool, but it's also enchantingly serene.

Riad Star

NEW *31 derb Alailich, Kaat Benahid (UK +44 20 7193 7357, www. marrakech-riad.co.uk/riad-star).* **££**
A glittering homage to American starlet Josephine Baker, who stayed in this Medina home in the 1940s while entertaining Allied troops, Riad Star's seven rooms are themed: Josephine's Room is furnished with funky cushions printed with Baker's image, as well as lithographs of Baker on the walls. The Lori Park flying wire and monofilament *Josephine Dancing* sculpture, depicting Baker sporting the iconic banana tutu, makes for a glorious bathroom feature. Downstairs in the dining room, Baker's sequinned gowns are displayed alongside a rail of 1920s clothes for guests to dress up in. Slip into a flapper dress and lounge on the top sun terrace or by the small courtyard fountain amid the silver pouffes, Baker collectibles and silver screen moments projected on to the walls. It's a dreamy place to stay.

ESSENTIALS

Riad Tizwa

26 derb Gueraba, Dar El-Bacha
(0668 19 08 72, UK +44 7973
115 471, www.riadtizwa.com). **££**
Relaxed and comfortable, Tizwa is one
of the friendliest riads in town. Laid
out in the usual fashion on three open-
fronted floors around a central tiled
courtyard, this place is a great anti-
dote to design excess. The six rooms
are white with gull-grey doors and
splashes of colour; some have wood-
beamed ceilings. Design solutions are
simple but striking, such as thick, high
azure tadelakt headboards that con-
ceal clothing rails behind them. Each
room is equipped with an iPod dock-
ing station. There is a hammam, and
the roof terrace has a shaded area for
alfresco dining. Another advantage of
this place is that it's accessible to taxis.
Mornings are a pleasure – early-morn-
ing coffee and tea at your door in tas-
selled Thermoses, and breakfast when
and where you want it.

Riad Wo

41 derb Boutouil, Douar Graoua (mobile
0665 36 79 36, www.riadw.com). **££**
Working on the premise that guests
will get quite enough sensory input
from their forays into the Medina,
Spanish owner Elsa Bauza designed
her five-bedroom riad with a philos-
ophy of simplicity and 'quiet in the
head'. The bedrooms – two huge, two
big, one small – have white walls,
unadorned save for a few framed textiles. Three rooms have fireplaces.
Downstairs, zen-like lines are matched
by some quietly retro furnishings. Up
top are two roof terraces, one of which
is shared by two rooms, perfect for
families or friends travelling together.
Below is a spacious courtyard, a
plunge pool and two sitting rooms (one
with a piano).

Riyad El Cadi

87 derb Moulay Abdelkader, off
derb Debbachi (0524 37 86 55,
www.riyadelcadi.com). **££**

Made up of eight interconnecting
houses, El Cadi is a rambling maze of
a place in which getting lost is a pleasure – which is lucky as it'll happen
quite a lot in your first few days. The 12
well-appointed suites and bedrooms,
as well as the various salons, corridors,
staircases and landings, also double
as gallery spaces for an outstanding
collection of art and artefacts gathered
by late former owner Herwig Bartels.
Despite the rich details, the overall
feel is uncluttered, cool and contemporary. Bartels' daughter Julia now
runs the riad, and standards remain
high. Extensive roof terraces with
tented lounging areas further add to
the appeal of what, for the money, is
some of the classiest accommodation
in town. The two-bedroom Blue House
is available for groups and is part of
the main riad. The only drawback is its
distance from taxi dropping-off points,
though cars can get quite close at the
top end of Jemaa El Fna in the morning.

Talaa 12

12 Talaa Ben Youssef, El-Moqf (0524
42 90 45, www.talaa12.com). **££**
A serene, minimalist-style riad in the
north-east of the Medina, Talaa 12 has
white walls and grey shutters, with
judicious bolts of colour provided by
rugs, furnishings and hangings. The
courtyard is planted with lemon trees,
and Arabic chill-out and gnawa-style
music plays on the CD player. There are
eight comfortable bedrooms, with limestone tadelakt bathrooms. Location is
another plus factor: Talaa 12 is in the
El-Moqf section of the Medina, right
next to the souks, a few doors down
from the Musée de Marrakech and just
a ten-minute walk from Jemaa El Fna.
The roof terrace has a 360° view of the
rooftops of Marrakech and the high
peaks of the Atlas mountains.

Tchaikana

25 derb El-Ferrane, Azbest (0524 38 51
50, www.tchaikana.com). No credit cards.
££

Tchaikana's four rooms are spacious, particularly the two 11m x 5m suites (which can sleep up to four people). The decor is chic, with a nomad/ethnic vibe, and the central courtyard, laid out for dining, is gorgeously lit at night. Soft drinks and orange juice are free for guests, and there's a selection of board games to keep youngsters busy. The owners, Jean-Louis Montilla and Barbara Seine, are French, and Jean-Louis' photographs are displayed throughout the riad. In case you're wondering, a *tchaikana* is a Central Asian teahouse. Closed 15 July to 31 August.

Southern Medina

Dar Les Cigognes

108 rue de Berima (0524 38 27 40, www.sanssoucicollection.com). **£££**

Dar Les Cigognes is two properties combined – and reworked by the architect Charles Boccara – facing the walls of the vast Badii Palace. Above the central courtyard, perfumed with orange trees, are several of the Dar's 11 bedrooms. One features an iron four-poster, creamy drapes, carved stucco ceilings, a sparkling *handira* carpet on the floor and an astoundingly beautiful wardrobe inlaid with mother-of-pearl. In summer, breakfast and dinner are taken on the roof terrace of the 17th-century building, originally a merchant's townhouse. The terrace is so close to the palace walls that you can virtually eyeball one of the famous nesting storks. Les Cigognes is well known for its food and cooking classes – Yotam Ottolenghi filmed an episode of his *Mediterranean Feasts* television series here.

Dar Fakir

16 derb Abou El-Fadal, off Riad Zitoun El-Jedid, Kennaria (0524 44 11 00, www.darfakir.co.uk). **££**

This riad is for the twentysomething crowd. Dar Fakir's central courtyard and surrounding salons are layered with casually strewn rugs and scattered with inviting sofas for lounging with a drink. The heady scent of incense hangs heavy in the air and tea candles illuminate the riad, while the chilled-out beats humming in the background complete the vibe. The eight guestrooms (two on the ground floor, six upstairs) are very simply done but attractive, including tadelakt bathrooms. Owner Noureddine Fakir also runs restaurants Le Tanjia and Le Salama, both within walking distance of the riad.

Riyad El Cadi

Hotel du Trésor

77 derb Sidi Boulokat, off rue Riad Zitoun El-Kedim (0524 37 51 13, www. hotel-du-tresor.com). No credit cards. **£**
The Trésor is indeed a little treasure. Restored by its Italian owner, this small hotel blends Moroccan features with mid-century accessories to create a retro look across the building. The chic, white-tiled patio, dotted with Saarinen tulip chairs and tables, has a deep plunge pool and is shaded by a leafy orange tree. The 12 rooms mix and match: a painted ceiling looms over a mezzanine bed, while a mid-century droplet chandelier illuminates the room. At this price, so close to Jemaa El Fna, it's a steal.

Les Jardins de la Medina

21 derb Chtouka, Kasbah (0524 38 18 51, www.lesjardinsdelamedina.com). **£££**
At the southern end of the kasbah, this former royal residence has been a luxurious 36-room hotel since 2001. You enter a beautiful reception area eccentrically decorated with a tree and wooden birds hanging upside down from a painted dome. From there, you emerge into a wonderfully spacious garden with rows of orange trees and a heated swimming pool actually large enough to swim in – which makes it a great place for families. Comfortable rooms, decorated in a Moroccan-international style, come in three categories. Most are in the middle 'superior' class – big enough to have sofas as well as beds – and all of them have DVD players and iPod docks. A large international restaurant, splendid hammam, gym, beauty salon and cookery school round off the perks.

Jnane Mogador

116 derb Sidi Bouloukat, off rue Riad Zitoun El-Kedim (0524 42 63 24, www.jnanemogador.com). **£**
The Mogador is a small riad with considerable charm and warmth in a prime location – and all for an unbelievable 380dh-480dh per double with en suite bathroom (just don't expect a power shower). The 18 rooms are simple and predominantly pink with tadelakt bathrooms. All have heating, but a few lack air-conditioning, an important factor in summer. Public areas are much more ornate, with fountain courtyards, stucco arches and a large roof terrace used for in-house meals. The spa in the basement is a great place for a cheap and relaxing massage with Rachida. English here is limited and breakfast isn't included in the rates, but it's available for 35dh.

Riad Hayati

27 derb Bouderba, off derb El-Bahia, Riad Zitoun El-Jedid (UK +44 7770 431 194, www.riadhayati.com). **£££**
Could this be the most tasteful riad in town? It's a little piece of visual perfection, with two bedrooms arranged around the courtyard and two set off the galleried first floor of a white courtyard framed by cascading bougainvillea; intricately carved dark wooden doors complete the look. In an adjoining building, reached through a beautiful and tranquil salon, a small staircase leads up to a private garden suite with plunge pool and sunloungers on its own terrace. Complementing the classic Moorish architecture are subtle references to Ottoman Turkey, Persia and Arabia, and mementos of the British owner's many years in news broadcasting from the Middle East (*hayati* means 'my life'). The location is extremely peaceful but only six or seven minutes' walk from Jemaa El Fna.

Riad Kaiss

65 derb Jedid, off Riad Zitoun El-Kedim (0524 44 01 41, www.riadkaiss.com). **£££**
Renovated by the late architect Christian Ferré, the nine-room Kaiss is small but exquisite. Its Rubik's Cube layout has rooms linked by galleries, multi-level terraces and tightly twisting stairs, all set around a central

courtyard filled with orange, lemon and pomegranate trees. The decor is traditional Moroccan: earthy ochre walls with chalky Majorelle-blue trim, stencilled paintwork (including some gorgeous ceilings), jade *zelije* tiling and frilly furniture (including four-poster beds). Guests are greeted by red rose petals sprinkled on the white linen pillows. Modern tastes dictate a handsome, cool plunge pool on the roof and an in-house hammam to relieve aching, souk-sore limbs.

Riad Linda

NEW *93 derb Jamaa, derb Dabachi (0645 91 27 78, UK +44 7812 365 712, www.riadlinda.com).* **£**

This bright and breezy guesthouse is run by the very welcoming Linda, who hails from Edinburgh. The six rooms are named and themed by colour and feature cheery accents, paintings by Linda's husband Gordon Davidson, and plenty of shelf space. One downstairs room is wheelchair-accessible with an adaptable lavatory and shower chair available. Meals are taken on the top terrace with its candy-pink sunloungers, potted bougainvillea and Bedouin tent, or around the central dining table. Staff are very friendly and helpful.

Riad Mabrouka

56 derb El-Bahia, off Riad Zitoun El-Jedid (0612 41 73 21, www.riad-mabrouka.com). **£££**

The Mabrouka is a vision of cool, understated Moroccan-minimalist elegance, with whitewashed walls, black-and-white photography, billowing canvas in place of doors and some fabulous painted ceilings and shutters; kilims add selective splashes of colour. The result is stylish, but also very comfortable. Bathrooms are sensuous; all soft corners and rounded edges, they look as if they've been moulded out of coloured clay. With just four suites and two doubles, the place has a very intimate feel. There's a pleasant roof terrace with a

Hotel du Trésor

canvas-shaded breakfast area, and a good kitchen turning out Moroccan, Mediterranean, French and Italian food.

Riad Souika

6 derb Souika, Berima (www.lawrence ofmorocco.com/accommodation/riad-souika). **£**

This small, quiet riad is close to the Berima mosque in a non-touristy part of town, but it's just a short walk from the monumental Badii Palace and the labyrinthine Mellah. With just three rooms, it's perfect for families or groups of friends who want a place to themselves. The choice room at the prettily tiled Souika faces out out on to one of the top sun terraces, with glass doors leading away from the low-slung bed and cute blue and tadelakt grey bathroom with alcove shower. Aziz, the manager, comes in daily to serve breakfast in the dining room or on the terrace, and is a dab hand at cooking dinner if you fancy a night in.

Riyad Al Moussika

17 derb Cherkaoui (0524 38 90 67, www.riyad-al-moussika.ma). **£££**

One reason laid-back Turinese owner Giovanni Robazza opened this former pasha's palace as a guesthouse was to showcase the superb cordon bleu cooking of his son Khalid. This is a riad for gourmands, dedicated 'to the art of good living', with a comfortable, worn-in feel. The palace has been restored in a relatively traditional style: fountains splash and birds sing in the trees, while six bedrooms are complemented by a hammam, a formal dining room and a small library with some interesting volumes. There are three courtyards, one of which features a long, thin 'Andalucian' pool for swimming, plus two flower-filled roof terraces for dining. The riad also houses the popular Pepe Nero restaurant.

La Sultana

403 rue de la Kasbah, Kasbah (0524 38 80 08, www.lasultanahotels.com). **£££**

The Sultana is astonishing in that it's a completely new-build hotel of considerable size in the middle of the Medina – and you'd never know it was there. It has no frontage to speak of, but beyond the arched street door are 28 guestrooms and suites, connected by arcaded corridors, courtyards, landings and galleries. There's a good-sized swimming pool with beautiful

Jnane Tamsna

turquoise mosaic, a full spa complex, a row of boutiques and a vast roof terrace with a splash pool that overlooks the gardens of the Saadian Tombs. The architecture (Moorish-gothic) and decoration is sumptuous, mixing Indian, African and Oriental touches with Moroccan. Serving French and Moroccan cuisine, the restaurant is open to non-guests who reserve in advance, but the basement bar is residents only. Kitted out to resemble a ship's cabin, the bar even has a window into the deep end of the swimming pool. The hotel closes for two weeks in July.

Ville Nouvelle & Palmeraie

Dar Zemora

72 rue El-Aandalib, Ennakhil, Palmeraie (0524 32 82 00, UK +44 7913 152 195, www.darzemora.com). **£££**
Set in a hectare of lush gardens filled with roses and hibiscus, fragrant bougainvillea and palm trees, Dar Zemora is the Marrakech equivalent of an English country-house hotel – perhaps because it's owned by an English couple, who've remodelled this former private abode beyond all recognition. Apart from two large sitting rooms, a dining room and a library with leather-upholstered armchairs, the main house contains just three rooms and two big suites. The Zahara suite, done out in coffee-coloured tones, boasts a king-size four-poster, a small private terrace with daybed and a sunken marble bath. There's also a two-bedroom pavilion in the garden with a spacious living room and its own private pool. The hotel closes for three weeks in August.

Les Deux Tours

Douar Abiad, Palmeraie (0524 32 95 27, www.les-deuxtours.com). **£££**
Les Deux Tours (named for its distinctive twin towered gateway) is the sublime work of leading Marrakchi architect Charles Boccara. It's a walled enclave of earthen-red villas that together offer 37 chic rooms and suites in a lush blossom-, citrus-, fig- and palm-filled garden setting. No two rooms are the same, but all feature glowing tadelakt walls and *zelije* tiling with stunning bathrooms, several in pink mud-brick domes seductively lit via glassy punch-holes. Guests share the most attractive of outdoor pools, keyhole-shaped and fringed with perfectly maintained grassy lawns, as well as an alfresco restaurant. After a day in the souks, head for the hammam or a massage. The free shuttle bus service into Guéliz (not always a given with Palmeraie hotels) is a definite bonus.

Hotel du Pacha

33 rue de la Liberté, Guéliz (0524 43 13 27, www.hotelpacha.net). **£**
Hotel du Pacha is a fairly standard two-star joint: the only indication that this is Morocco comes courtesy of a handful of aged tourist office posters. Better rooms have small balconies overlooking a pleasant central courtyard, but all are clean with air-conditioning, TV and Wi-Fi. There are plenty of female staff around, making it a comfortable option for solo female travellers. Its position, a stone's throw from the chic shopping street of rue du Vieux Marrakchi and the new Carré Eden shopping centre in Guéliz, is unrivalled. Note that breakfast costs extra (40dh).

Jnane Tamsna

Douar Abiad, Palmeraie (0524 32 94 23, www.jnane.com). **£££**
The creation of designer Meryanne Loum-Martin and her ethnobotanist husband Dr Gary Martin, Jnane Tamsna is a 'Moorish hacienda' with opulent suites and 24 gorgeous rooms, set in five buildings scattered around some beautiful, fragrant gardens, each with its own pool. The architecture is vernacular chic, coloured in the palest tones of primrose, peppermint and clay, and enhanced by Loum-Martin's

ESSENTIALS

own furniture. The surrounding fruit orchards and herb and vegetable gardens provide organic produce for the kitchen. The combination of rural tranquillity, Zen-like aesthetics and ecological beliefs makes for an almost utopian (no locks on the doors) vibe. There's also an art gallery (ask to see Loum-Martin's Meissen porcelain designs) and boutique, gardening and calligraphy workshops, and magic shows and children's activities during the holidays; non-guests are able to take advantage of 'pool, lunch and tennis' packages or visit for dinner (p125). Donations for guided tours of the gardens go towards a charity project to restore Moroccan school gardens.

Ksar Char-Bagh

Djnan Abiad, Palmeraie (0524 32 92 44, www.ksarcharbagh.com). **££££**
Ksar Char-Bagh takes the whole Moroccan fantasy trip to its extreme. The original French owners recreated a Moorish palace nearly defies belief; it's been built from scratch on a kasbah-sized scale. A moated gatehouse with 6m (20ft) high beaten metal doors fronts an arcaded central courtyard with a pool. Extensive grounds contain herb and flower gardens, an orchard, a subterranean rose marble hammam and a palm-lined, heated 34m (112ft) pool. Lunch or dinner can be served out on the terrace or by the pool; the chef previously worked as a sous-chef to Gérald Passédat at Marseille's Le Petit Nice. A champagne bar, library and cigar salon complete the luxury picture. All these treats are shared by just a handful of sumptuous and spacious suites, each featuring its own private garden or terrace, and several with their own exclusive swimming pool.

Mosaic Palais Aziza

NEW *Mejjat 3/38, Cerde Ennakhil, Commune J'Nanate, Palmeraie (0524 32 99 88, www.mosaicpalaisaziza.com).* **££££**
The charming Mosaic Palais Aziza is run by its equally charming manager

Karim El-Ghazzawi. What distinguishes the Aziza from the various other palaces that now dot the Palmeraie are the inventive dishes from its Morolino Moroccan-Italian restaurant, and its decadent spa. With just 12 rooms, the hotel is also an intimate place, with a warm and friendly vibe. Plush white beds are surrounded by soothing aubergine and tangerine tones, and the large grey tadelakt bathrooms feature rain-shower cubicles, jacuzzi baths, and luxury chocolate and poppyseed soaps. The centrepiece of the hotel is the pool surrounded by matt gold sunloungers (with an attached section for the kids). When you're not stretched out in the sun, head for the subterranean spa for a hammam and one of the best massages in Marrakech.

Palais Namaskar

NEW *Route de Bab Atlas, no.88/69, Province Syba, Palmeraie (0524 29 98 00, www.palaisnamaskar.com).* **££££**
The modernist villas at this Palmeraie palace are stylish and secluded. Behind thick, heavy doors, a private heated aquamarine pool, set amid olive trees, unfurls in front of the floor-to-ceiling glass windows of your private hideaway. Minimalist in outlook, there's a chimney for winter days, grey velvet chairs, a vast Minotti double beanbag for watching the Bang & Olufsen TV, a super sleek bathroom with double rainshower cubicle and an outdoor bathtub. There are rooms at the hotel, set behind the spa area, but you'll want to opt for a villa if you can. The Namaskar is known for its Moroccan food (p125), but it's a shame they've taken some of the heat out of the Thai food (pandering to guests' requests).

Further afield

All the places listed below are roughly a ten- to 40-minute drive from the Medina – far enough away to be rural, but close enough to head into town for dinner.

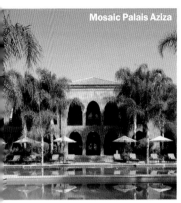

Mosaic Palais Aziza

Amanjena
*Route de Ouarzazate, km12 (0524
39 90 00, www.amanresorts.com).*
££££
The Amanjena is part of Aman
resorts, one of the world's most luxurious hotel chains. What clients get for
their money is an exclusive gated complex a few miles south of town. The
architecture is low-rise palatial, rose
pink and frilly, trimmed with green-
tiled roofs. At the heart of the resort
is the *bassin*, a massive fish-filled reservoir of water that feeds two shallow
canals running between the 32 pavil-
lons and six *maisons*. These are vast
private residences oozing pared-back
luxury. All come with their own walled
gardens, and some have private pools.
Services range from hammams to the
loan of clubs for use on the Amelkis
golf course next door. Yes, that might
be Sting lounging by the pool, but if
you can afford to stay here you're probably as rich and famous as he is.

Chez Max
*Douar Tagadert Ait El-Kadi, route
du Barrage, km24, Tameslouht
(www.lawrenceofmorocco.com/
accommodation/chez-max).* **£££**
As the hills slope up towards the High
Atlas, a scattering of Berber villages

colonise the starkly beautiful plains.
In the midst of the village of Tagadert
lies a stylish country getaway in the
form of Chez Max. Set around a huge
living-dining space accented with stylish mid-century furniture and books,
as well as vintage Berber finds, are five
bedrooms split between two adjoining
buildings. Wander around the village
and the olive groves during your stay
before huddling around the open fire in
winter or taking a dip in one of the two
pools in high summer. Come winter or
summer, though, savouring Saida's
delicious home-cooked traditional
Moroccan dishes will be a highlight.

Fellah Hotel
NEW *Route de l'Ourika, km13,
Tassoultante, Canal Zabara (0525
06 50 00, www.fellah-hotel.com).* **£££**
This desert-chic retreat blended with
urban cool is a big hit with hipsters,
artists and young families alike. The
funky hotel, with a social responsibility ethos, roams over land dotted with
cactii, herbs, a children's treehouse,
sunken gym, gorgeous pool and farmyard. Embedded into the landscape
are villas with spacious rooms and
fabulous half-egg bathtubs, but it's
the restaurant area and pool, the Salon
Mahler for films and talks, and the

ESSENTIALS

on-site cultural centre (http://dam-arts.org) that really stand out. The beautiful 2,500-book library, with a children's section, is a centre for translation; one of the villas is dedicated to an artists' residency programme; there's a fabulous kids' club and cooking classes; and Wat Po masseurs from Bangkok can be found at the spa. The central bar, restaurant and pool section is heralded by a kitsch Arnold Schwarzenegger Santeria-style altar, shabby-chic sofas and a pool table. Beyond lie alfresco restaurant Touco (p129) and an alluring pool with thatched tiki parasols set against the backdrop of the Atlas mountains. A literary project educates women in the village, and local kids can use the children's pool and gym.

Le Palais Paysan

NEW *Douar Akrich, route d'Amziz, km20 (0529 80 16 38, www.lepalaispaysan.com).* **£££**
The 'Peasant Palace', a 16-room hotel with fabulous views of the Atlas, is anything but peasant-like. This chic modernist country hotel stares out across the undulating green-hued foothills of the Atlas, which eventually rear up to the snowy peaks beyond. There's a joyous simplicity to the rooms, done out in taupes and stone with the odd spash of colour – African cherry-coloured feathered circular headdresses are pinned to the bedroom walls. The unheated, oblong slate-grey mosaic pool unfurls alongside parasols and smart forest-green loungers, while the farmyard is a boon for kids who won't sit still. As the sun sets in the evening, the surrounding countryside is filled with shepherds leading their flocks back home, and it's all just a 40-minute drive from the Medina. A spa, cookery classes, Atlas hikes and falconry complete the bucolic picture.

La Pause

Douar Lmih Laroussiène, Commune Agafay (0661 30 64 94, www.lapause-marrakech.com). No credit cards. **££**
La Pause is the closest thing you'll get to a desert experience within the vicinity of Marrakech. At this country retreat it's all about big skies, magnificent sunsets, rolling hills and nothing much else for miles and miles around. Guests are accommodated in beautifully simple, cosy, country-style rooms

Peacock Pavilions

scattered about an oasis that curves around a river. Lunch and romantic, lantern-lit dinner are served in traditional tents. Owner Frédéric Alaime fell in love with the spot while out riding, and outdoor activities are a big part of the La Pause experience. There's horseriding, mountain biking and camel trekking – not to mention an intriguing form of cross-country golf and a swimming pool buried in the olive grove. There really isn't anything else quite like it in Marrakech.

Peacock Pavilions

Route de Ourzazate, km18 (mobile 0664 41 46 53, www.peacockpavilions.com). **££££**

This striking, stylish retreat, located just 20 minutes from downtown Marrakech, is set in an olive grove and scented by flourishing rose gardens. Maryam Montague and her husband Chris host guests in two large pavilions set either side of an inviting, sparkling turquoise pool. The Atlas and Medina pavilions house two and three bedrooms respectively. Another pavilion harbours a library, shop and indoor dining room. All are decorated with Maryam's eclectic global treasures: Moroccan carpets, wooden fertility sculptures, Swan chairs fashioned from petrol cans, and primary-coloured vintage Malian bread baskets. The alfresco cinema with its deckchairs is an indulgent perk (and is accompanied by lashings of hot chocolate in winter). Chris and Maryam run yoga retreats, outreach Project Soar (www.projectsoarmarrakesh.org) for girls in the local village, and also manage an online shop, www.redthreadsouk.com; Maryam's book, *Marrakesh by Design*, is a must-buy for those seeking to recreate the Moroccan look at home.

Selman

NEW *Route d'Amziz, km5 (0524 38 67 18, www.selman-marrakech.com).* **££££**
An extraordinary 80m (265ft) heated pool lined with chic pavilions greets you at the family-run Selman, just a ten-minute drive from the Medina. It's a Moorish-style palace clad with enormous Baccarat chandeliers and luxury fabrics, but it retains an intimate feel. Owners Saida and Abdeslam Bennani Smires are equestrian aficionados and their collection of 12 award-winning Arabian horses, which are paraded for guests on a regular basis, are a real draw. The 56 rooms – think plush suedes in tangerine, taupe and mustard, elegantly lit with Moulay Youssef lanterns, luxury *zelije* bathrooms and in-mirror TVs – overlook the pool, gardens and stables. There are also five individual villas set back behind Assil, the Moroccan restaurant pavilion. The luxury spa, dimly lit and beautiful, pampers with Chenot beauty treatments.

Tigmi

Douar Tagadert El-Cadi, route d'Amizmiz, km24 (0524 48 40 20, www.tigmi.com). **£££**
The ultimate rural retreat, Tigmi is a mud-walled haven of solitude with five suites and 16 rooms lying in the middle of nowhere halfway to the foothills of the Atlas, some 15 miles (24km) south of Marrakech. The hotel's architecture and interiors are rustically simple but fashion-shoot stylish – whitewashed arches, arcades and alcoves, covered walkways and terraces with beguiling views over raw, dusty-pink landscapes; think Sergio Leone with citrus fruits. Most suites have courtyards (one has its own little pool), terraced chill-out areas and sweet, cosy bedrooms with fireplaces that are lit in winter. There's a TV room, hammam, two outdoor pools, food (and wine) when you want it, and a small Berber village for company, but no phones and otherwise little to do but kick back and relax amid the flowers and foliage. A rental car would extend your options, but then again, as David Byrne once sang, 'Heaven is a place where nothing ever happens'.

Getting Around

Arriving and leaving

By air

Aéroport Marrakech Menara

0524 44 79 10, www.marrakech. airport-authority.com

Marrakech's international airport is located just six kilometres (four miles) west of the city. From the airport to the city centre is a ten-minute drive. There is also an airport information desk in the arrivals hall. There are banks offering currency exchange in both the baggage and arrivals hall, open 8am-6pm daily, plus two ATMs.

Taxis wait outside the arrivals building. There are official fixed rates for taxis from the airport, but drivers rarely adhere to these charges: 70dh for a small taxi, 100dh for a big taxi to the Medina or Guéliz; 100dh for a small taxi, 150dh for a big taxi to the Palmeraie. Expect to pay around 100dh in a *petit taxi* (p179 **Taxis**) for up to three passengers to anywhere in the Medina (15-20 mins) or Guéliz (30 mins); to the Palmeraie expect 150-200dh. Prices go up by 50 per cent from 8pm to 6am. Most will accept payment in US dollars, euros or pounds. There is also a half-hourly airport shuttle bus (no.19) to Jemaa El Fna (about 20 mins), which stops at most of the major hotels in Guéliz and Hivernage. Tickets cost 30dh and the service runs 6.15am-9.30pm daily from the airport.

By rail

Trains are operated by the national railway company **ONCF** (0890 20 30 40, www.oncf.ma). The impressive new train station is on the western edge of Guéliz, on avenue Hassan II. Marrakech is the southernmost terminus of two lines, both of which pass through Casablanca and Rabat; some trains then continue north to Tangier, others north-east to Oujda on the Algerian border via Meknes and Fès. There is a taxi rank outside the station; make sure to get a *petit taxi* (not the big Mercedes *grand taxi*). The fare into central Guéliz should be no more than 10dh on the meter (15-20dh to the Medina) but, unless you hail a taxi that is passing by, you will have to pay extra for those that have been waiting at the rank.

Alternatively, buses nos.3 and 8 pass by the station on avenue Hassan II, en route to Jemaa El Fna (4dh).

By bus

The *gare routière* is just beyond the Medina walls at Bab Doukkala. Most long-distance buses stop here, including those operated by national carrier **CTM** (0522 54 10 10, www.ctm.ma). Both the central Medina and Guéliz are walkable from the station; a *petit taxi* will cost 10dh, or catch a local bus for place de Foucauld (Jemaa El Fna). The main CTM terminus and ticket office is in Guéliz, near the Thêâtre Royal, on rue Abou Bakr Seddiq.

Supratours (0890 20 30 40, www.oncf.ma) is another quality long-distance bus service run by the ONCF train operators. Its terminus and ticket office are next to the main train station on avenue Hassan II. The Supratours bus timetable is shown on its website along with the train information.

Public transport

Marrakech has a city bus network radiating from the Medina out to the suburbs. Other than along avenue Mohammed V, no buses operate within the confines of the city walls, where streets are prohibitively narrow.

Few local bus services are of much use to visitors, however. The possible exceptions are those services that run between the Medina and Guéliz, which is a fairly long walk, but it's much less hassle (and still relatively inexpensive) to take a taxi.

Buses

ALSA buses (0524 33 52 70, www.alsa.ma) are regular city buses with no air-conditioning. They charge a flat fee of 4dh payable to the driver. Beware: the drivers never have any change.

All the following buses leave from the main terminus on place de Foucault, 100m west of Jemaa El Fna.

Local bus routes

No.1 to Guéliz along avenue Mohammed V.
No.2 to Bab Doukkala for the *gare routière*.
No.3 to Douar Laskar via avenue Mohammed V, avenue Hassan II and the train station.
No.4 to Daoudiate (a northern city suburb) via avenue Mohammed V.
No.8 to Douar Laskar via avenue Mohammed V, avenue Moulay Hassan and the train station.
No.10 to boulevard de Safi via Bab Doukkala and the *gare routière*.
No.11 to the Menara Gardens and passing by the airport.
No.14 to the train station.
No.19 to the airport terminal.

Taxis

Taxis are plentiful and easy to find, whatever the time of day or night. They are also cheap enough that it makes little sense bothering with buses. The standard ride is known as a **petit taxi** and is usually a little khaki-coloured four-door Dacia Logan or Peugeot 205. By law, they can carry a maximum of three passengers. Drivers are reluctant to use the meter. Asking for them to switch it on sometimes works, otherwise it's just a question of knowing the right fare. From Jemaa El Fna to Guéliz costs around 10dh; from Jemaa El Fna to the Palmeraie 60dh-100dh, depending on distance. Expect to pay about 50 per cent more after about 8pm.

You can flag a taxi if it is passing. If there are already passengers aboard, you first tell the driver your destination and he will let you know if he is headed in that direction. The first passenger in is the first to be dropped off. If the taxi is empty, then you just hop in and command your destination. The driver may then pick up other passengers along the way. He should re-set the meter for each new passenger.

Grand taxis are Mercedes cars that can squeeze in six people and are normally more expensive. They loiter outside hotels and the railway station. Avoid them, unless you are a group of four or more, or are travelling long distance: some *grand taxis* operate like minibuses running fixed routes to outlying suburbs, villages and towns.

Taxi Vert (0524 40 94 94) is an excellent new dial-a-cab system. You can order a *petit taxi* by phone and be guaranteed a pick-up at any location at any time. The cost is the metered rate plus an extra 15-20dh and tip.

ESSENTIALS

Trams

At the time of writing a new urban development plan is in progress and roadworks are under way to install a tram system in Marrakech. It will link the train station, bus station, suburban areas, football stadium and the industrial zone of Sidi Ghanem.

Driving

A car can be useful for venturing out of the city, especially for trips out of town, but unless you are a resident a car is of limited use within Marrakech itself. For short-term visitors, taxis are cheap and plentiful and easily hired by the day for around 400dh in and around the city; ask your hotel for help in finding a reputable driver.

Vehicles drive on the right in Morocco. The old French rule of giving priority to traffic from the right is observed at roundabouts and junctions: in other words cars coming on to a roundabout have priority over those already on it. Speed limits are 40km/h (25mph) in urban areas, 100km/h (62mph) on main roads, 120km/h (74mph) on autoroutes. There are on-the-spot fines for speeding and other traffic offences. It is compulsory to wear seatbelts front and back.

Be very wary when driving at night as cyclists and moped riders often have no lights. Neither do sheep, goats and pedestrians, and street lighting can be poor. In the case of an accident, report to the nearest *gendarmerie* to obtain a written report, otherwise insurance will be invalid.

Car hire

To hire a car in Morocco, you must be over 21, have a full current driving licence and carry a passport or national identity card. Rental isn't cheap; daily rates with a local agency start at about 300dh for a small, basic no-frills car with unlimited mileage. At the international companies like Avis, Budget or Hertz, expect to pay about 25 per cent more. All these companies have agents in the arrivals hall at Marrakech airport.

The drawback with many of the local hire firms is the back-up service – cars may be old and may not be very well maintained. Breakdown support is lacking and replacement vehicles are not always forthcoming.

Be aware that payments made in Morocco by credit card often incur an additional five per cent fee. This is one of several reasons why it works out cheaper to arrange your car rental in advance.

The major companies allow you to rent a car in one city and return it in another. Rental cars in Morocco are delivered empty of petrol and returned empty. Almost all agencies will deliver cars to your hotel and arrange pick-up at no extra charge.

If you are heading south over the mountains, note that you are responsible for any damage if you take a car off-road or along unsuitable tracks. Four-wheel drives are available from most hire companies and start at around 1,200dh per day.

Avis
Aéroport Marrakech Menara (0524 43 31 69, www.avis.com). **Open** 8am-11pm daily.
Hertz
154 avenue Mohammed V, Guéliz (0524 43 99 84, www.hertz. com). **Open** 8.30am-12.30pm, 2.30-6.30pm Mon-Sat.
Aéroport Marrakech Menara (0524 44 72 39). **Open** 8am-11pm daily.

Sixt

*9 rue El-Mansour Eddahbi, Guéliz
(0524 43 31 84, www.sixt.com).*
Open 8.30am-12.30pm, 2.30-6.30pm
Mon-Fri; 8.30am-12.30pm Sat.

Parking

Wherever there's space to park
vehicles you'll find a *gardien de
voitures*. They're licensed by the
local authority to look after parked
vehicles and should be tipped about
10dh (the local rate is 4dh during the
day, 10dh at night, but as a visitor
you're not going to get away with
paying that). Street-side parking is
easy enough in the Ville Nouvelle
but troublesome in the Medina:
there is a car park behind the
Koutoubia Mosque and gardens
(off avenue Mohammed V) and at
the bottom of rue Fatima Zahra
across from the Koutoubia. Some
areas now have ticket machines
for pay-and-display parking.
The hourly rate is 2dh and you
will be clamped if you overstay
or park illegally. If you get clamped,
a notice will be left on your
windscreen with a number for
you to phone. One quick call and
a man will appear to release you
at a cost of 40dh.

Repairs & services

The garage below should be able to
help get you back on the road.

Auto Speedy

*6 avenue Abdelkrim Elkhatta, route
de Casablanca – next to Marjane
supermarket (05 24 30 59 58).*

Cycling

Bicycles, mopeds and motorbikes
are hugely popular modes of
local transport – despite the
inconvenience of widespread
potholes, choking bus fumes and

the perils of having to share the road
with the average lunatic Marrakchi
motorist. If you fancy taking to the
streets on two wheels, try one of the
places listed below for bike rentals.

Note that most rental places do not
offer any kind of lock so if you want
to leave the bike or scooter anywhere
it'll have to be with a *gardien de
voitures* (see left **Parking**). Wearing
a helmet on a scooter or motorbike is
compulsory and you risk getting
fined or having the bike confiscated
without one.

Argan Sports

*Rue Fatima Al Fihria, near
Agdal gardens (0524 40 02 07,
www.argansports.com).*
Bicycle rental – city bikes, mountain
bikes and road-bikes from 250dh per
day, with 12 hours' notice required.

Marrakech Roues

*3 rue Bani Marine, Imm Roux,
Medina (mobile0663 06 18 92,
www.marrakech-roues.com).*
Motorbikes, scooters and bicycles for
hire, with insurance, helmet and lock
included in the price.

Walking

Walking is the only way to get
around the Medina, which is
where most visitors spend the
bulk of their time. It's a compact
area, perfect for exploring on foot.
Many of the streets and alleys are
too narrow for anything bigger
than a motorcycle or donkey
cart anyway.

Be sure to pack a pair of
comfortable, flat-soled shoes
because the streets in the Medina
are rarely paved and full of ruts
and potholes. Visitors coming
any time from November to April
should bring cheap and/or
waterproof footwear because
the slightest bit of rain turns
the whole of the Medina into
a mudbath.

ESSENTIALS

Resources A-Z

Accident & emergency

Police 19 or 112 from a mobile.
Fire 15.
Ambulance 15 or 0524 40 40 40.

Lost/stolen credit cards

All lines of the companies listed below have English-speaking staff and are open 24hrs daily.
American Express +44 1273 696 933 (UK)
Barclaycard +44 1604 230 230 (UK)
MasterCard +1 636 722 7111 (reverse charge call to USA)
Visa 00 211 0011, await second dial tone and enter 866-654-0163 (USA-based call centre for all Visa card holders)

Customs

The following allowances apply for bringing duty-free goods into Morocco: 250g of tobacco, 200 cigarettes or 25 cigars and 1 litre of spirits.

Moroccan dirhams are not legal tender outside the country. There is no limit to how much foreign currency you can bring in, but you are limited to changing back a maximum of 50 per cent of the amount you changed into dirhams. Keep all transaction receipts in case of questioning on departure.

Iif you have significant amounts of camera or electrical gear, you may have it written into your passport. Anything that can't be presented on leaving will be assumed to have been 'sold' and liable to a heavy duty tax. If the property has been stolen, you need police documentation to prove it. Any items you bring in that are deemed to be 'new' (less than six months old) will be taxed, so keep proof of purchase date.

Disabled

Marrakech is tough on anyone with a mobility problem. Roads and pavements are uneven and pitted, and frequently rutted. Routes through the Medina are narrow and crowded and it's necessary to be nimble. Aside from the bigger hotels (La Mamounia and the Sofitel all lay claim to disabled facilities), few buildings make concessions.

Drugs

Morocco is the world's largest cannabis producer and most of it is exported. Although discreet use is usually tolerated, Moroccan law maintains stiff penalties for sale or consumption.

Electricity

Morocco operates on 220V AC. Plugs are of the European two-pin variety. Adapters are available for about 50dh. Visitors from the USA will need to bring a transformer if they intend to use appliances from home.

Embassies & consulates

British Embassy
28 avenue SAR Sidi Mohammed, Souissi, Rabat (0537 63 33 33, www. gov.uk/government/world/organisations/ british-embassy-rabat). **Open** 8.30am-12.30pm, 1.30-4pm Mon-Thur; 8.30am-12.30pm Fri.

British Honorary Consulate Marrakech

47 avenue Mohammed V, Guéliz (0524 42 08 46). **Open** 8.30am-12.30pm Mon-Thur; 8.30-11.30am Fri.

Canadian Embassy

13 rue Jaafar Es Sadiq, Agdal, Rabat (0537 68 74 00, www.canada international.gc.ca). Also handles Australian consular affairs.

French Consulate

Rue Camille Cabana, Hivernage, Marrakech (0524 38 82 00, 24hr emergency hotline 0661 34 42 89, www.consulfrance-ma.org). **Open** 8.30-11.30am Mon-Fri.

United States Embassy

2 avenue de Mohamed El Fassi, Rabat (0537 76 22 65, www.morocco. usembassy.gov). **Open** 8am-5.30pm Mon-Fri.

Health

Morocco has no reciprocal health care agreements with other countries, so taking out your own medical insurance is essential. No vaccinations are required for Marrakech. Bring anti-diarrhoea capsules, such as Imodium, and avoid tap water: bottled water is inexpensive and available at all restaurants and cafés.

Should you become ill, be warned: the Moroccan healthcare system is ropey. While good doctors can be found and pharmacies are well stocked and knowledgeably staffed, for anyone afflicted with serious illness, the best route to take is the one straight to the airport.

Dentists

Dental care in Marrakech is of a reasonable standard. It may be hard to get an appointment with the best practitioners.

Docteur Houriya Eljai Oubaaz

2nd floor, apartment 3, Residence Caroline, Avenue Mohammed VI & Route de Targa (near Lycée Victor Hugo), Guéliz (0524 42 24 37). **Office** 9am-noon, 3.30-6pm Mon-Fri. No credit cards. Female dentist who speaks good English and is popular with expats.

Doctors

Docteur Samir Bellmezouar

1st floor, Immeuble Benkirane, 6 rue Fatima Zohra Rmila (opposite Hammam Al Bacha), Medina (0524 38 33 56, mobile 0661 24 32 27 emergency). **Office** 10.30am-12.30pm, 4.30-6.30pm Mon-Fri. No credit cards. No English, but does make house calls.

Doctor Frederic Reitzer

4th floor, Immeuble Moulay Youssef, rue de la Liberté (above Café Zohra), Guéliz (0524 43 95 62, mobile 0661 17 38 03 emergency). **Office** 9.30am-noon, 3.30-7pm Mon-Fri; 10am-noon Sat. No credit cards. Speaks English.

Hospitals

There are two private clinics in Marrakech, frequented by the expat community and wealthier Moroccans. Avoid public hospitals, where conditions are shocking.

International Clinic

Route de M'Hamid, Bab Ighli (0524 36 95 95, www.clinique-internationale-marrakech.com).

Polyclinique du Sud

rue Yougoslavie, Guéliz (0524 44 79 99). **Open** 24hr emergency service.

Pharmacies

Pharmacies are clearly marked with a green cross and/or green crescent. There's at least one in every neighbourhood. The drugs

ESSENTIALS

may have strange names, but staff can usually translate. When closed, each pharmacy should display a list of alternative pharmacies open after hours. Also see www.syndicat-pharmaciens-marrakech.com.

Internet

Computers are expensive in Morocco, but smartphones, tablets, 3G and free Wi-Fi zones have changed the face of daily life. The few remaining internet cafés are the domain of gadget-free tourists, college students and those needing to print out documents. Most hotels and cafés offer free Wi-Fi.

Cyber Hassna *Rue Beni Marine, Medina (no phone).* **Open** 10am-11pm Mon-Thur, Sat, Sun. **Rates** 10dh/hr.
Cyber Efet *183 avenue Mohammed V, Hivernage (no phone).* **Open** 8.30am-8.30pm daily. **Rates** 10dh/hr.

Money

The local currency is the Moroccan dirham, abbreviated dh (in this book) and sometimes MDH, or MAD. There are 100 centimes to a dirham. Coins come in denominations of 5, 10, 20 and 50 centimes (all useless) and 1, 2, 5 and 10dh. Hoard small change: it's useful for tips and taxis. Banknotes come in denominations of 20 (being phased out), 25, 50, 100 and 200dh.

Excess dirhams can be exchanged for euros or dollars (pounds sterling are often not available) at a bank. You may be asked to show the exchange receipts from when you converted your hard currency into dirhams.

At the time of writing, £1 = 13dh.

ATMs

Cashpoints (*guichets automatiques*), are common in most Moroccan towns and cities, and it's perfectly possible to travel on plastic. Most banks set a daily withdrawal limit of 2,000dh (currently around £154) per card, per day on ATM withdrawals – so it's always wise to carry at least a couple of days' 'survival money' in cash.

Look for machines bearing the Cirrus, Link and Maestro symbols (if they carry just a Visa symbol, they will only accept locally issued Visa cards). ATMs are concentrated along rue Bab Agnaou in the Medina and around place Abdel-Moumen in Guéliz. Beware of Monday mornings when machines are often empty.

Credit cards

MasterCard and Visa are accepted at larger shops, restaurants, nightclubs and hotels in the city centre; American Express less so. Paying by credit card may incur an extra five per cent charge. Credit card fraud is a problem in Marrakech, so keep all receipts to check against your statement.

Opening hours

The working week is Monday to Friday, with a half-day on Saturday. Many places close in the afternoon for a siesta. Note that hours vary during Ramadan, when businesses open and close later.

Banks 8.30am-3.45pm Mon-Fri.
Museums & tourist sights 8am-6pm daily.
Pharmacies 9am-6-7pm Mon-Fri (and sometimes Sat am or pm).
Shops 9am-1pm, 3-7pm Mon-Sat.

Photography

Photography is not permitted of the following: government buildings, royal palaces, mosques, airports, checkpoints, and military and police personnel. In Marrakech, the locals can be quite aggressive towards snap-happy tourists who take their picture without asking. Women and elderly folk in rural areas especially do not like to be photographed.

Police

Crime against visitors is rare and physical violence almost unheard of, but do watch your pockets and bags, particularly around Jemaa El Fna. If you are robbed, go to the office of the **Brigade Touristique** (Tourist Police; 0524 38 46 01) on the north side of Jemaa El Fna. These plain-clothed officers watch out for the safety and security of tourists. They patrol the Medina undercover and will be quickly on the scene if you have a problem.

Note, if you are the victim of crime outside Marrakech, then you must make a report to the local police wherever the incident occurred – do not wait until your return to the city.

Post

Stamps are sold at a dedicated *timbres* counter, but can also be bought at a tabac or at the reception desks of big hotels. Parcels should be taken unwrapped for examination. Mail delivery is painfully slow. Post offices provide an express mail service (EMS), also known as *poste rapide*. For really urgent mail, use an international courier.

PTT Centrale

Place du 16 Novembre (opposite McDonald's), Guéliz. **Open** 8am-8pm Mon-Fri; 8.30am-6pm Sat.
Rue Moulay Ismail, between Jemaa El Fna & Koutoubia Mosque. **Open** 8am-8pm Mon-Fri; 8.30am-6pm Sat.

Smoking

Morocco is firmly in thrall to nicotine. Few cafés and restaurants recognise the concept of a clean-air environment. Foreign cigarette

brands cost 40dh (about £3) for 20, while the best of the domestic product goes for even less.

Telephones

Phoning abroad from a public phone in Marrakech is no problem. Use the cardphones that are dotted around town (cards are bought from post offices, tabacs or news vendors) or one of the numerous *téléboutiques*.

To call abroad, dial 00, then the country code followed by the telephone number. When calling within Morocco, you need to dial the area code (0524 in Marrakech) even if you are calling from the same area. Mobiles begin with the prefix 06; landlines begin with 05.

Information 160
International assistance 130

Mobile phones

Three main mobile service providers offer a pay-as-you-go option: the national operator Maroc-Télécom, Méditel and Inwi. Most European networks have arrangements with one of the first two, so that visitors can use their mobiles in Morocco (note: it's expensive). Alternatively, buy a pre-paid SIM card (around 20dh) and then top-up at booths or shops around town.

Inwi

Marrakech train station, Avenue Hassan II, Guéliz (0529 80 01 98, www.inwi.ma). Also has purple kiosks on most major intersections in Guéliz.

Maroc-Télécom

Avenue Mohammed V (opposite McDonald's), Guéliz (0524 43 44 53, www.iam.ma).

Méditel

279 avenue Mohammed V, Guéliz (mobile 0664 82 58 25, www.meditel.ma).

ESSENTIALS

Time

Morocco follows Greenwich Mean Time (GMT) all year round (it's on the same time as Britain and Ireland) and in recent times has synchronised with Europe to follow the same daylight savings winter and summer time changes.

Tipping

Tipping is expected in cafés and restaurants (round up the bill or add 10-15 per cent), by guides and porters, and by anyone else that renders you any sort of small service. Five or ten dirhams is sufficient. Tip taxi drivers around 10 per cent if they have been honest enough to use their meter, otherwise do not bother.

Toilets

Public toilets are a rarity – use the facilities when in bars, hotels and restaurants. They're usually decent enough. It's a good idea to carry tissues as toilet paper is not always available. At cafés, the toilet attendant expects a few dirhams as a tip; it's bad form not to oblige.

Tourist information

ONMT

place Abdel-Moumen, Guéliz (0524 43 61 31, www.visitmorocco.com). **Open** 8.30am-noon, 2.30-6.30pm Mon-Fri; 9am-noon, 3-6pm Sat.
The Marrakech branch of the Office National Marocain du Tourisme.

Visas & immigration

No visas are required for nationals of Australia, Britain, Canada, Ireland, New Zealand, the US and most EU countries. If in doubt, check with your local Moroccan embassy.

Travellers can stay in Morocco for three months from the time of entry.

Long-term extensions mean applying for the official residence permit or *carte de séjour* – a tedious and bureaucratic procedure involving trips back and forth to the Bureau des Etrangers at the Préfecture de Police. You need to prove you have sufficient funds and a regular income deposited into a Moroccan account, provide bank statements, proof of address in Morocco, obtain a police security check from your home country, a medical certificate and more.

For a simpler option, leave the country for a few days and re-enter, gaining a new three-month stamp.

Bureau des Etrangers

Préfecture de Police, route de Fès, Daoudiate – behind the Wilaya de Marrakech administration building (0524 33 03 63). **Open** 9.30am-3pm Mon-Thur; 9.30-11.30am Fri.

When to go

March to May is the perfect time to visit, but beware of price hikes at Easter. Summers can be oppressive, with daytime temperatures around 35°C (95°F), rising to 40°C (104°F). Things cool off in September. Daily winter temperatures are 15-20°C (59-68°F), but evenings can be chilly (stay in a hotel with heating). December and January can be overcast and rainy. Hotel rates soar over Christmas.

Women

Although Morocco is a Muslim country, the dress code for women is not strict, and no one expects to find foreigners covered from head to toe). But to avoid unwanted attention, leave the mini skirts, shorts and spaghetti-strapped tops at home. Avoid direct eye contact and don't smile at men. Ignore come-ons or obnoxious comments.

Vocabulary

In French, as in other Latin languages, the second person singular (you) has two forms. Phrases here are given in the more polite *vous* form. The *tu* form is used with family, friends, children and pets. Courtesies such as *monsieur*, *madame* and *mademoiselle* are used more often than their English equivalents.

General expressions

good morning/hello bonjour
good evening bonsoir
goodbye au revoir
hi (familiar) salut
OK d'accord; **yes** oui; **no** non
How are you? Comment allez vous?/vous allez bien?
How's it going? Comment ça va?/ça va? (familiar)
Sir/Mr monsieur (M)
Madam/Mrs madame (Mme)
Miss mademoiselle (Mlle)
please s'il vous plaît
thank you merci
thank you very much merci beaucoup
sorry pardon
excuse me excusez-moi
Do you speak English? Parlez-vous anglais?
I don't speak French Je ne parle pas français
I don't understand Je ne comprends pas
Speak more slowly, please Parlez plus lentement, s'il vous plaît
how much?/how many? combien?
Have you got change? Avez-vous de la monnaie?
I would like… Je voudrais…
it is c'est; **it isn't** ce n'est pas
good bon (m)/bonne (f)
bad mauvais (m)/mauvaise (f)
small petit (m)/petite (f)

big grand (m)/grande (f)
beautiful beau (m)/belle (f);
well bien
badly mal
expensive cher
cheap pas cher
a bit un peu
a lot beaucoup;
very très
with avec; **without** sans;
and et; **or** ou; **because** parce que
who? qui?; **when?** quand?; **which?** quel?; **where?** où?; **why?** pourquoi?;
how? comment?
at what time/when? à quelle heure?
forbidden interdit/défendu
out of order hors service/en panne
daily tous les jours

Getting around

When is the next train for…? C'est quand le prochain train pour…?
ticket un billet
station la gare;
platform le quai
bus/coach station gare routière
entrance entrée; **exit** sortie
left gauche; **right** droite;
interchange correspondence
straight on tout droit; **far** loin;
near pas loin/près d'ici
street la rue; **street map** le plan;
road map la carte
bank la banque;
is there a bank near here? est-ce qu'il y a une banque près d'ici?
post office La Poste
a stamp un timbre

Sightseeing

museum un musée
church une église
exhibition une exposition;
ticket (for museum) un billet;
(for theatre, concert) une place
open ouvert

closed fermé
free gratuit;
reduced price un tarif réduit

Accommodation

Do you have a room (for this evening/for two people)?
Avez-vous une chambre (pour ce soir/pour deux personnes)?
room une chambre
bed un lit; **double bed** un grand lit;
(a room with) twin beds (une chambre) à deux lits
with bath(room)/shower avec (salle de) bain/douche
breakfast le petit déjeuner
included compris
lift un ascenseur
air-conditioned climatisé

At the café or restaurant

I'd like to book a table (for three/at 8pm) Je voudrais réserver une table (pour trois personnes/à vingt heures)
lunch le déjeuner; **dinner** le dîner
coffee (espresso) un café; **white coffee** un café au lait/café crème;
tea le thé **wine** le vin; **beer** la bière
mineral water eau minérale;
fizzy gazeuse; **still** plate
the bill l'addition

Behind the wheel

no parking stationnement interdit/ stationnement gênant;
speed limit 40 rappel 40
petrol essence

Numbers

0 zéro; 1 un (m), une (f); 2 deux; 3 trois; 4 quatre; 5 cinq; 6 six; 7 sept; 8 huit; 9 neuf; 10 dix; 11 onze; 12 douze; 13 treize; 14 quatorze; 15 quinze; 16 seize; 17 dix-sept; 18 dix-huit; 19 dix-neuf; 20 vingt; 21 vingt-et-un; 22 vingt-deux; 30 trente; 40 quarante; 50

cinquante; 60 soixante; 70 soixante-dix; 80 quatre-vingts; 90 quatre-vingt-dix; 100 cent; 1,000 mille; 1,000,000 un million.

Days, months & seasons

Monday lundi; **Tuesday** mardi;
Wednesday mercredi; **Thursday** jeudi; **Friday** vendredi; **Saturday** samedi; **Sunday** dimanche.
Spring printemps; **summer** été;
autumn automne.

Moroccan Arabic

In urban areas you can get by in French, which is spoken by all educated Moroccans. However, a little effort with Arabic goes a long way. Moroccan Arabic is a dialect and is not the same as the Arabic spoken elsewhere in North Africa and the Middle East, although there are some words and phrases in common. Transliteration from Arabic script into English is a highly inexact science and a wide variety of spellings are possible.

Arabic pronunciation

Arabic has sounds that non-speakers have trouble in pronouncing.
gh - like the French 'r', slightly rolled
kh - like the 'ch' in loch

Emergencies

leave me alone esmahli la
help! tekni!
help me, please awenni afak
call the police ayyet el bolice
thief sheffar
I'm lost tweddert

General expressions

good evening masr el kheir
good morning/hello sabah el kheir/salaam aleikum
goodbye masalaama

please min fadlak (to a male);
min fadlik (to a female)
yes aywa/anam; **no** la
How are you? labas/kifhalak
(to a male)/kifhalik (to a female)
thank you shukran
no thanks la shukran
sorry/excuse me esmahli
Do you speak English?
Itkelim Ingleezi?
I don't speak Arabic
Metkelimsh Arabi
I don't understand Mafayimtish
who? shkun?; **why?** lash?; **which?**
ashmen?; **where?** feyn?
today el-youm
tomorrow ghedda;
yesterday imbara
tips baksheesh
let's go yalla
passport basseport

Shopping

how much?/how many? bekam?
Do you have…? Wahesh
andakum…?
Have you got change? Maak sarf?
credit card kart kredi
good mleah; **bad** mish imleah
small seghir; **big** kebir
that's expensive ghali bezzaf
enough kafi

Getting around

Where is…? Feyn keyn…?
Where is the hotel? Feyn keyn
el-otel?
airport el-mattar
station el-mahatta
bus/coach station mahattit
d'el-ottobisat
ticket office maktab el-werka;
ticket werka
train station el-gar
bus stop plasa d'el-ottobisat
museum el mathaf
embassy el-sifara
pharmacy farmasyan
bank el-banka
post office el-busta

stamp etnaber
restaurant el-mattam
mosque jamaa
left yassar; **right** yemeen
stop here haten hinayer
here hina; **there** hinak

Accommodation

Do you have a room? Andak beit?
key srout
room beit
shower doush
toilet vaysay
breakfast iftar

At the café or restaurant

table for… tabla dyal…
I'm a vegetarian makanakulsh
el-lahm
I don't eat… makanakulsh…
meat el lahm
chicken dzhazh
fish el-hut
bread el-khobz
coffee qahwa; **tea** atay
beer birra; **wine** shshrab
mineral water sidi ali
the bill, please lahsab afak

Numbers

0 sifer; **1** wahid; **2** itnehn; **3** telata;
4 arbaa; **5** khamsa; **6** setta; **7** seba;
8 tamanya; **9** tesa; **10** ashra; **11**
hadasha; **12** itnasha; **13** teltash; **14**
arbatash; **15** khamstash; **16** settash;
17 sebatash; **18** tamantash; **19**
tesatash; **20** eshreen; **21** wahid
w'eshreen; **22** itnehn w'eshreen; **30**
telateen; **40** arba'een; **50** khamseen;
60 setteen; **70** seba'een; **80** tamaneen;
90 tesa'een; **100** mea; **1,000** alef.

Days & months

Monday el-itnehn; **Tuesday**
el-teleta; **Wednesday** el-arbaar;
Thursday el-khemis; **Friday**
el-jomaa; **Saturday** el-sebt;
Sunday el-ahad.

ESSENTIALS

Index

ESSENTIALS

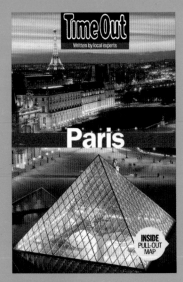

Time Out
Written by local experts

Paris

INSIDE
PULL-OUT
MAP

Written by
local experts,
rated 'Top
Guidebook
Brand'
by Which?

Travel
beyond